ID
90B161

PROPERTY OF INTEL CORPORATION
LIBRARY & INFO SERVICES   SC9

MISSION
LEARNING RE

66003627

D0442097

DATE DUE

3 1215 00091 4322

A Gift to the

LIBRARY

of

MISSION COLLEGE

Donated by

INTEL Corporation

PROPERTY OF INTEL CORPORATION
LIBRARY & INFO SERVICES SC9

QUANTITATIVE METHODS FOR QUALITY AND PRODUCTIVITY IMPROVEMENT

PROPERTY OF INTEL CORPORATION
LIBRARY & INFO SERVICES SC⁹

QUANTITATIVE METHODS FOR QUALITY AND PRODUCTIVITY IMPROVEMENT

Marilyn K. Hart
Robert F. Hart

TS
156
.H348
1989

QUANTITATIVE METHODS FOR QUALITY AND PRODUCTIVITY IMPROVEMENT

Marilyn K. Hart
Robert F. Hart

Library of Congress Cataloging-in-Publication Data

Hart, Marilyn K., date.
    Quantitative methods for quality and productivity
improvement / Marilyn K. Hart, Robert F. Hart.
        p. cm.
    Bibliography: p.
    Includes index.
    ISBN 0873890566
    1. Quality control — Statistical methods. 2. Production
management — Quality control. 3 Quality control — Charts,
diagrams, etc. I. Hart, Robert F., date. II. Title.
    TS156.H348 1989
    658.5'62—dc19

Copyright ©1989 by ASQC Quality Press
All rights reserved. No part of this book may be reproduced
in any form or by any means, electronic, mechanical,
photocopying, recording, or otherwise, without the prior
permission of the publisher.

10987654321

ISBN 0-87389-056-6

Acquisitions Editor: Jeanine L. Lau
Production Editor: Tammy Griffin
Cover design by Artistic License. Set in Century Schoolbook by
    DanTon Typographers. Printed and bound by Edwards Brothers.

Printed in the United States of America

ASQC Quality Press, American Society for Quality Control
310 West Wisconsin Avenue, Milwaukee, Wisconsin 53203

Table of Contents

Preface

This book was written to fulfill four objectives:

1. To show that all organizations need to have "continuous improvement" in their quality and productivity through statistical process control methods, and that the proper management philosophy is needed for these improvements to take place.

2. To be a primer in the use of the statistical process control methods of Drs. Shewhart and Deming. These methods include the usual $\overline{X}$ and R chart plus special approaches for special cases such as short runs.

3. To show the limitations of these methods and some idea of the vast preponderance of occasions when other, less difficult methods would be used for process control.

4. To teach Shewhart's methods of control statistics for data analysis using "rational subgroups" as opposed to subgrouping data only in time order. (These methods have largely lain fallow since Shewhart's original work.)

We wish to thank all of the people with whom we have worked in the past decade in hundreds of seminars and many more hundreds of days of working toward quality and productivity improvement within their organizations. These people, our friends, have graciously allowed us to share their experiences with the reader and have provided their material to be used as case studies.

We offer particular thanks to Thomas Lewis (Mercury Marine), Richard Stanula (Moll Tool and Plastics), Hal Vickerman, John Clifton (Falk Corporation), Larry Short (Ross Gear Division of TRW), Vince Barry, Stanley Straus (Miller Electric), and Dr. W. Edwards Deming for their support and encouragement. We have learned from each of them.

Our thanks to George Koller for his programming. Much of the analysis and some of the figures have been made on his StatScan® software in Milwaukee. And thanks to Adam, Wendy, and Dawn for their help with the figures.

Part I. Introduction to Quality

In the light of world competition, quality has become a key issue in the manufacturing of products and in service organizations. Simple but powerful graphical and statistical tools are needed to monitor the product (both goods and services) as it is being produced to ensure good quality throughout the organization, not only in production. The needs of the consumer and the quality of design are at least as important as the quality of conformance. But the tools are not enough. The proper management philosophy is needed to lay the groundwork for these tools to be effective.

Chapter 1 Quality

Background

A change is taking place in the way we evaluate quality. Instead of evaluating excellence simply on the basis of conformance to specifications, we are looking beyond specifications to evaluate how little variability we achieve when measured about the target value and continuously striving to decrease this variability about the target value to make more uniform product. Ironically, this is an all-American idea, born here in 1926, exported to Japan in 1950, and only now coming home to roost. Our current acceptance of this philosophy is born of dire necessity — the loss of our markets to foreign competitors.

In 1926, Dr. W. A. Shewhart introduced the concept of using statistical methods to study the quality of manufactured product. Building on his methods, Dr. W. Edwards Deming has carried the *statistical control of quality* and the management philosophy needed for these methods to be effective to the far corners of the world. The teachings of Deming, starting in 1950, have been a primary input to the success the Japanese have had in the world markets. Dr. J. M. Juran, another eminent quality control consultant, has also brought the message of total quality control to attention around the world.

We have belatedly come to realize that the message of Shewhart and Deming is not only "nice," but it is necessary to economic survival. Our fundamental objective must be to shrink the limits of variability about our target value constantly and forever to make more uniform product.

In the United States, the vast majority of jobs are in nonmanufacturing applications, which occur in both manufacturing companies and service industries. The need for quality and uniformity

1

in these areas is at least as great as that needed in manufacturing.

Statistical Quality Control

In order to ensure high levels of quality, elementary statistical techniques have been developed to "control" or monitor the quality. These techniques and the actions of implementing them are referred to as *statistical quality control*.

Statistical quality control has traditionally been divided into two categories: acceptance sampling and statistical process control. Acceptance sampling is an attempt to judge the quality of lots that have been made from samples from those lots. Based on the quality of a sample, the lot is either accepted and used as is, or rejected. If the lot is rejected, it is either inspected 100 percent to remove the defective units or it is simply sent back to the supplier. Acceptance sampling is really a futile attempt to achieve quality. The defective pieces are still made, hopefully found (although not always), and sorted out. Acceptance sampling does not demand that attempts be made to improve the quality of the process and eliminate the manufacture of the defectives. Acceptance sampling tolerates what Deming (1982) calls: "You burn the toast; I'll scrape it." It is better that we do not burn the toast.

Process control is the use of techniques to monitor the process as the product is being made to ensure that defectives are not being made to begin with — that we don't burn the toast. Process control may be divided into two types: "classical" process control and statistical process control.

"Classical" process control takes action on the process when a piece of product is found to be outside of the specification limits. Statistical process control first determines statistically the variation of the process (if it were stable) and then takes action on the process when it strays outside of these bounds. The "classical" process control methods are appropriate for the "trivial many" features which are causing no problem, perhaps 98 percent of the quality features being considered. We will concentrate on the "significant few," where the classical control methods have not been successful. Since we rely on the process data or process "statistics" for our action limits, Shewhart (1931) has called this *statistical process control*.

Statistical Process Control

Statistical process control (SPC) uses simple but powerful graphical tools to monitor the process to improve quality by decreasing product variability. This narrowing of the limits of variability does not stop when the product meets specifications, but continues thereafter for continuous improvement to make more uniform product.

The statistics used in SPC are simple techniques, requiring only addition, subtraction, multiplication, and division. Problems requiring more sophisticated techniques are rare. The vast majority of times it is the simple techniques that are used to solve a problem.

Relationship Between Quality, Productivity, and Competitive Position

There is a misconception in the minds of many people that quality and productivity are conflicting goals — spend your efforts improving quality and productivity will suffer **or** speed up productivity and quality will suffer. In reality, quality and productivity are directly related, i.e., improve quality and increased productivity will follow. Why? If pieces are made right to begin with, less rework will result, mating parts will fit together with less effort, etc. And with better quality and increased productivity, costs go down and an improved competitive position in the world market follows.

A Brief History of SPC

Statistical process control was introduced by Shewhart at Bell Telephone Laboratories in the 1920s. His book, *The Economic Control of Quality of Manufactured Product*, was published in 1931.

Perhaps the most basic contribution of Shewhart was the recognition that anything beyond a trivial interpretation of data implies a forecast.* Our objective of improving quality is aimed toward the future, not the past. During the past 50 years, this recognition has slowly grown, as indicated by the phrase "defect prevention, not defect detection."

After observing that the business of quality was indeed the business of forecasting, Shewhart noted that we had no mathematical tools with which to accomplish this prediction. The science of classical or distribution statistics taught in our colleges of business and engineering was not invented for the purpose of forecasting,

---

*Used by permission of *Quality*. "Quality Control: Changing Mathematical Tools." (Special Anniversary Issue, 1987): 96-100.

but was universally being used for that purpose with disastrous results. Shewhart filled the void in our statistical theory by inventing "control statistics" for the purpose of giving us criteria to tell us when we could predict, and how these predictions should be made. The differences between control statistics and classical statistics are summarized below (Shewhart 1943).

Classical statistical theory starts with the assumption that a statistical universe (i.e., a *stable* process) exists and that a single large sample is sufficient, the ordering within the sample being ignored. On the other hand, Shewhart's statistical control theory starts with the assumption that a statistical universe does *not* exist (i.e., the process is *not* stable). The role of control statistics is to first see if the process is stable, and hence, predictable. If it is not stable, simple statistical and graphical tools can be used to find sources of instability and eliminate them, if possible, or at least take them into account. Once the process is stable, it is possible to experiment efficiently, knowing that the effects of perturbing the process will be detectable and not lost in the noise of chaos.

The methods of Shewhart's control statistics were introduced to Japan by Deming in the early 1950s, but were not widely used (except in quality control departments) in this country until the late 1970s when the economics of necessity (survival) belatedly brought on Deming's third wave of the industrial revolution.

Chapter 2 Role of Statistical Process Control in an Organization

A major change in the approach to quality over the past 50 years has been a change in philosophy, recognizing that quality improvement must not be restricted to the factory floor. Quality improvement requires totally immersing *all* departments (particularly consumer research and product design engineering) in the theory and practice of control statistics. This results in the "total" control of quality.

Quality is not only important in the manufacturing of product, but is also important in the nonmanufacturing aspects of a manufacturing concern as well as in the service industries. For instance, quality tools can also help improve areas of a manufacturing concern such as safety, inventory, customer complaints, receivables, etc. Many service industries, such as banks, are also finding these tools vital to stay alive in their competitive atmosphere.

Chapter 3 Management's Role in Quality

Management Philosophy Needed

The use of statistical methods is necessary, but this alone is not enough. The right management climate must be present or the statistical activity will be just an idle exercise in arithmetic. Deming's 14 points for management (Deming 1986) define the responsibilities of top management. The points emphasize the intention to stay in business, education and training, use of statistical methods, continual improvement, driving out fear, working only with quality suppliers, removing barriers to pride in workmanship, breaking down barriers between departments, and getting everyone involved to accomplish this transformation. The complete list of these 14 points for management is shown in Table 1.1.

1. Create constancy of purpose toward improvement of product and service, with the aim to become competitive and to stay in business, and to provide jobs.

2. Adopt the new philosophy. We are in a new economic age. Western management must awaken to the challenge, must learn their responsibilities, and take on leadership for change.

3. Cease dependence on inspection to achieve quality. Eliminate the need for inspection on a mass basis by building quality into the product in the first place.

4. End the practice of awarding business on the basis of price tag. Instead, minimize total cost. Move toward a single supplier for any one item, on a long-term relationship of loyalty and trust.

5. Improve constantly and forever the system of production and service, to improve quality and productivity, and thus constantly decrease costs.

6. Institute training on the job.

7. Institute leadership. The aim of supervision should be to help people and machines and gadgets to do a better job. Supervision of management is in need of overhaul, as well as supervision of production worker.

8. Drive out fear, so that everyone may work effectively for the company.

9. Break down barriers between departments. People in research, design, sales, and production must work as a team, to foresee problems of production and in use that may be encountered with the product or service.

10. Eliminate slogans, exhortation, and targets for the work force asking for zero defects and new levels of productivity. Such exhortations only create adversarial relationships, as the bulk of the causes of low quality and low productivity belong to the system and thus lie beyond the power of the work force.

11a. Eliminate work standards (quotas) on the factory floor. Substitute leadership.

11b. Eliminate management by objective. Eliminate management by numbers, numerical goals. Substitute leadership.

12a. Remove barriers that rob the hourly worker of his right to pride of workmanship. The responsibility of supervisors must be changed from sheer numbers to quality.

12b. Remove barriers that rob people in management and in engineering of their right to pride of workmanship. This means, *inter alia*, abolishment of the annual or merit rating and of management by objective.

13. Institute a vigorous program of education and self-improvement.

14. Put everybody in the company to work to accomplish the transformation. The transformation is everybody's job.

(Source: W. Edwards Deming. *Out of the Crisis*. Cambridge: MIT, 1986, pp. 23-24.)

Table 1.1 Deming's 14 Points

Deming's 14 points constitute a theory of management whose application will transform management. Their application gives fertile ground for quality and productivity improvement. Deming also speaks of "deadly diseases" that stand in the way of this transformation (Deming 1986).

In particular, he admonishes management that uses only visible figures. The company using only visible figures "will in time have neither company nor figures" (Deming 1986, p. 121). The most important numbers may be unknown or unknowable, such as the multiplying effect of a happy customer or an unhappy customer.

Roadblocks

Two major roadblocks to quality are encountered by many companies. One is the lack of top management's participation.

> It is not enough that top management commit themselves for life to quality and productivity. They must know what it is that they are committed to — i.e., what they must do. These obligations cannot be delegated (Deming 1981, p. 15).

If management is not truly participative, a typical scenario shows production finding an assignable cause by using a control chart, but not being able to remove the assignable cause due to management's lack of participative action.

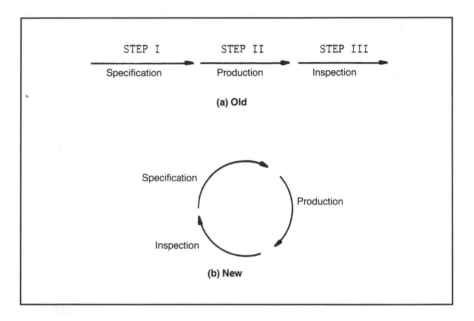

Figure 1.1 Shewhart's Concept

The second major roadblock is the existence of barriers between departments. Quality is not just the responsibility of production, but is a joint effort. Shewhart (1939) pointed out that the old method of putting a product in the marketplace was simply to "specify," "produce," and "inspect" as indicated in Figure 1.1a. With the advent of statistical methods, things are no longer so simple. As shown in Figure 1.1b, there is a closed loop where each of the three areas require statistical knowledge from each of the others. Deming and Juran elaborated on Shewhart's concept, building in the notion of continuous improvement as one goes repetitively through the Shewhart cycle. Figure 1.2 shows four steps in the cycle — following Deming we show the consumer research as a distinct part of the loop (separating it from the "in-house" inspection). The economic lesson we have learned in the world marketplace in recent years is that survival will demand the use of statistical methods in each of these four areas to improve product and service continuously and forever.

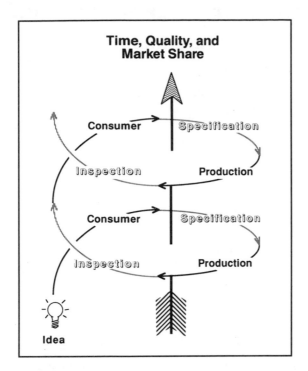

Figure 1.2 Quality: Spiral of Progress (Built on the Ideas of Deming and Juran)

Chapter 4   Handling Data

Terminology

For an initial judgment of the quality of a product, we check to see if its dimensions are "correct." What defines "correct"? Typically, a design engineer determines tolerance limits within the dimension must fall. These limits are referred to as *specification limits*, or *specifications*. Dimensional specifications may be given in the form of $2.000 \begin{smallmatrix} +.010 \\ -.000 \end{smallmatrix}$ which could be written [2.000, 2.010] i.e., 2.000 being the lower specification limit (LS) and 2.010 being the upper specification limit (US). A symmetrical specification limit might be written 3.000 ± .0015, or [2.985, 3.015]. The values 2.000 and 3.000 are used as the "name" of the dimension, hence they are called the *nominal* dimension ("nominal" meaning "name"). The ideal value for the dimension is referred to as the *aim point* or *target value*. The target value may or may not be the nominal.

Perhaps the simplest proof that *nominal* does not mean *target value* is in the one-sided tolerance cited previously, $2.000 \begin{smallmatrix} +.010 \\ -.000 \end{smallmatrix}$. Clearly aiming at the nominal value of 2.000 would be foolish, for no margin would be left for variability below the target value.

The practice of specifying the target value for a dimension has been greatly neglected in this country, resulting in much confusion. Without guidance, different operators tend to aim for different target values resulting in much variability in the process, thus yielding poor quality, increased costs, etc. It is imperative that design engineers realize the importance of specifying a target value for a dimension and communicating it to all involved. In fact, it has been recognized that the real ongoing goal of quality is the reduction of variation about the target value, which will be discussed later in Part V.

PROBLEM

1.1 For each of the following specifications, give the upper specification limit, the lower specification limit, and the nominal value:

a. $6.00 \pm .05$

b. $2.700 \begin{array}{l} + .006 \\ - .000 \end{array}$

c. $10.275 \pm .008$

d. $2.370 \begin{array}{l} + .005 \\ - .003 \end{array}$

Coding Data

When pieces are measured, the readings typically result in many digits. Carrying a lot of digits is time-consuming and cumbersome. To avoid carrying so many digits, data are often *coded*. The following procedure should be followed to code data.

Procedure for Coding Data

Step 1 A base value is chosen that can easily be subtracted from all the readings. Sometimes a target value is used. (In the coded form, the *coded zero* equals this base value.)

Step 2 The base value is subtracted from all the readings.

Step 3 These remainders are then divided by the unit of measure. (In the coded form, 1.00000 equals this *coded unit*.)

Example 1.1

The inside diameter of a journal is a quality characteristic of interest. Ten consecutive journals are measured and the results in codes are (read across):

2.513	2.512	2.511	2.515	2.510
2.518	2.512	2.511	2.513	2.517

Procedure

Step 1 A number that can be easily subtracted is 2.510. This will be chosen as the base value or *coded zero.*

Step 2 The number 2.510 is subtracted from all the readings yielding:

0.003	0.002	0.001	0.005	0.000
0.008	0.002	0.001	0.003	0.007

Step 3 These remainders are then divided by 0.001, the value of the *coded unit*, resulting in coded data of:

Coded Zero = 2.510″   Coded Unit = .001″

3	2	1	5	0
8	2	1	3	7

Example 1.2

The target value of an outside diameter of a shaft is given at 1.375 inches. Five shafts are measured and the results are (in inches):

1.377	1.375	1.372	1.374	1.378

Procedure

Step 1 Since a target value of 1.375 is specified, 1.375 will be chosen as the base value of *coded zero.*

Step 2 The number 1.375 is subtracted from all the readings yielding:

$$1.377 - 1.375 = 0.002$$
$$1.375 - 1.375 = 0.000$$
$$1.372 - 1.375 = -0.003 \quad \text{(The negative denotes that}$$
the reading was *below* the target value.)

$$1.374 - 1.375 = -0.001$$
$$1.378 - 1.375 = 0.003$$

Step 3 These remainders are then divided by 0.001, the *coded unit,* yielding coded data of:

Coded Zero = 1.375"   Coded Unit = .001"

2	0	-3	-1	3

PROBLEMS

1.2 Code the following data into thousandths of an inch over 21.250″.

    21.251   21.259   21.254   21.262

1.3 Code the following data into hundredths of an inch over 8.00″.

    8.02   8.00   7.95   8.01

1.4 Code the following data into tenths of an inch over 6.5″.

    6.6   6.5   6.3   6.8

1.5 Code the data from Problem 1.4 into tenths of an inch over 6″.

1.6 Code the data from Example 1.1 with a coded zero = 2.5″ and a coded unit = 0.001″.

1.7 Coded data are 3, −1, 0, −2 with the coded unit = 0.001″ and the coded zero = 3.6″. Find the uncoded values.

1.8 Coded data are 2, 0, 5, −3 with the coded unit = 0.0001″ and the coded zero = 4.2″. Find the uncoded values.

Part II. Fundamentals

Statistical process control uses simple but powerful tools. The techniques rely heavily on graphs and elementary statistics. The objective in the use of these methods is process *improvement*, to find and solve problems and to reduce variation.

Chapter 5   The Basic Tools*

Where to Start?

When the management of a company is first starting to use SPC, it is best for them to start small, broadening their base as improvement is attained. Otherwise they become spread too thin and nothing gets accomplished. So where should they start?

A company should pick a quality problem related to their customer's biggest complaint, for that should be the company's greatest concern. If there are no major complaints, a problem related to one of the largest amounts of scrap and/or rework should be chosen. Simple but powerful graphical and statistical tools should be then used to solve problems and to improve the process.

Tally Sheet

Once a problem area has been identified, such as a high rate of errors on purchase orders, a tally sheet should be introduced to monitor errors. The tally sheet is used to tally the various types of errors in real time as they occur.

Figure 2.1 shows a tally sheet for the daily number of errors on purchase orders for an entire week. As seen from Figure 2.1, the errors on the purchase orders fall into several categories, primarily in the form of incorrect price. Incorrect information on items also appears to be a major source of error. This information will be pointed out by the Pareto chart, discussed in the following section.

A second use of the tally sheet will be seen in Part VII where we use one or more tally sheets to regularly feed into a *percent defective summary chart*.

---

*Used by permission of American Production and Inventory Control Society. Adapted from "Tools for Quality." APICS Conference Proceedings, Atlanta, pp. 121-124.

Procedure for Making a Basic Tally Sheet

Step 1 For the problem area, list the types of errors (or defects, defectives, etc.) that can occur along the left margin. A "miscellaneous" category is usually included but should seldom account for more than a small percentage of the occurrences.

Step 2 List intervals of time along the top margin. These may be one-hour intervals, one-day intervals, one-shift intervals, etc.

Step 3 Make a grid to accommodate these margin categories.

Step 4 As an error is found make a "tick" mark in the appropriate box.

Step 5 At the end of each time interval compute the total number of errors and record the errors and the number of items inspected for that interval at the bottom of the column.

Step 6 After some period of time, compute the totals across for each type of error and record them at the right side of the tally sheet.

Purpose: To tally the various types of errors in real time as they occur to identify the errors that are the largest source of the problems.

INSPECTION OF PURCHASE ORDERS

Date: 9/22 - 9/26/86   Dept.: C

type of error \ day	M	T	W	Th	F	Totals
Missing information on customer			I		II	3
Missing information on item				I		1
Missing quantity				II	I	3
Missing price						0
Incorrect information on customer					II	2
Incorrect information on item	I		I	II	III	7
Incorrect quantity		I			I	2
Incorrect price	II	II	II	IIII	THL I	16
Total errors	3	3	4	9	15	34
Total orders inspected	152	147	161	157	156	773

Figure 2.1 Tally Sheet of Errors in Purchase Orders

Pareto Chart

Arranging these errors in order, from the error with the highest frequency to the error with the lowest frequency, and displaying this as a *bar graph* with the type of defect along the horizontal axis and frequency of occurrence along the vertical axis, gives a resultant graph that is often referred to as a Pareto chart. (A Pareto chart could also be made by *dollar amounts*, etc., instead of frequency.)

Procedure for Making a Basic Pareto Chart

Step 1 Arrange the errors (or defects, defectives, etc.) in order of decreasing frequency, from the error with the highest frequency to the error with the lowest frequency.

Step 2 List the errors in the above order along the horizontal axis.

Step 3 Label the vertical axis "Frequency" and a scale for the frequency.

Step 4 For each error listed along the horizontal axis, draw a bar the height of the frequency of that error. The bars from each error should be wide enough to touch (i.e., where the bar from the first error listed ends, the bar from the next error should begin).

Purpose: To summarize and graphically display the errors in order of decreasing frequency giving a way to prioritize efforts to eliminate these errors.

Using this procedure for the data given in Figure 2.1, the errors in order of decreasing frequency are listed as follows:

Types of Error	Frequency
Incorrect Price	16
Incorrect Information on Item	7
Missing Information on Customer	3
Missing Quantity	3
Incorrect Quantity	2
Incorrect Information on Customer	2
Missing Information on Item	1
Missing Price	0

Figure 2.2 shows a Pareto chart displaying the data given in Figure 2.1. The tally sheet and the Pareto charts are both saying that incorrect prices are the most prevalent error occurring on the purchase orders. Problems with incorrect information on the items also occur quite regularly: missing quantity, information on customer, information on item or price, and incorrect quantity or information on customer occurring occasionally. Any efforts to lower the error rate on the purchase orders should concentrate first on the big problems.

The Pareto chart displays the principle of the significant few and the trivial many. It is typically a few types of errors, defects, items, etc., that are causing most of the problems. The Pareto chart is a way of prioritizing efforts to eliminate problems.

Sometimes the Pareto chart is displayed as a "cumulative" chart. This chart will tell what fraction or percentage of the errors are caused by a cumulative number of sources.

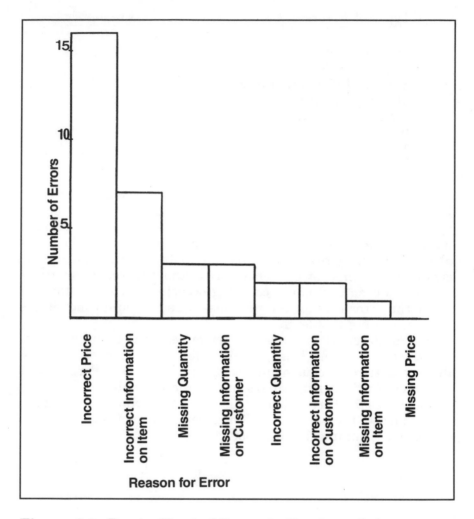

Figure 2.2 Pareto Chart of Errors in Purchase Orders

Procedure for Making a Cumulative Pareto Chart

Step 1 Arrange the errors (or defects, defectives, etc.) in order of decreasing frequency, from the error with the highest frequency to the error with the lowest frequency. Total the frequencies.

Step 2 Accumulate the frequency of the errors from the high end with a running subtotal. That is, for the most frequently occurring error, the cumulative frequency is simply its frequency. The cumulative frequency of the second most frequently occurring error is the sum of the frequency of the first error plus the second. For the third most frequent error, add the frequencies from errors one, two, and three, etc. Note that the cumulative frequency of the least frequently occurring error is simply the sum of all the frequencies of the errors, the total number of errors made (N).

Step 3 Divide each cumulative frequency by N. Express the result either as a decimal or as a percentage. This is the cumulative relative frequency.

Step 4 Label the horizontal axis with the errors in the order arrived at in Step 1.

Step 5 Label the vertical axis "Cumulative Relative Frequency" and a scale from 0 to 1.00 (or 0 percent to 100 percent).

Step 6 For each error along the horizontal axis, mark a point at the cumulative relative frequency.

Step 7 Mark a point at the intersection of the two axes, i.e., zero errors made 0 percent of the errors.

Step 8 Connect the points.

Purpose: To summarize and graphically display the errors in order of frequency telling what fraction (or percentage) of the errors are caused by a cumulative number of sources.

Following this procedure, the list of errors and order of decreasing frequency is repeated, with the frequencies totaled and accumulated.

Type of Error	Frequency	Cumulative Frequency	Composition
Incorrect Price	16	16	
Incorrect Information on Item	7	23	(16 + 7)
Missing Information on Customer	3	26	(16 + 7 + 3)
Missing Quantity	3	29	(16 + 7 + 3 + 3)
Incorrect Quantity	2	31	(... + 2)
Incorrect Quantity	2	33	(... + 2)
Missing Information on Item	1	34	(... + 1)
Missing Price	0	34	(... + 0)
Total	34		

These cumulative frequencies are then divided by 34 (the total of all the frequencies) giving the cumulative relative frequency, and expressed here as a percentage.

Type of Error	Cumulative Relative Frequency
Incorrect Price	47.1%
Incorrect Information on Item	67.6%
Missing Information on Customer	76.5%
Missing Quantity	85.3%
Incorrect Quantity	91.2%
Incorrect Quantity	97.1%
Missing Information	100.0%
Missing Price	100.0%

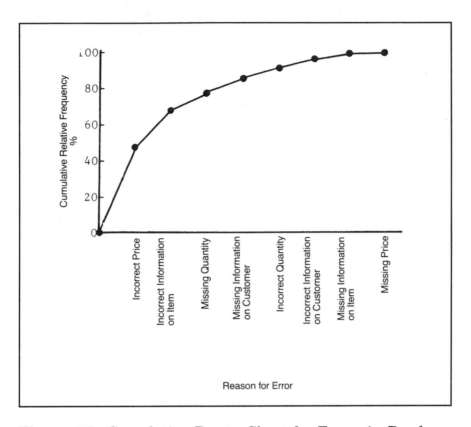

Figure 2.3 Cumulative Pareto Chart for Errors in Purchase Orders

The resulting graph is illustrated in Figure 2.3 as a cumulative Pareto chart. Note the information given by this chart. For instance, the two most frequently occurring errors (incorrect price and incorrect information on the item) comprise 67.6 percent of all the errors — the significant few.

PROBLEMS

2.1 From the following tally sheet of defective formed steel bars, make a Pareto chart.

% DEFECTIVE 100% VISUAL INSPECTION

DATE: Project No. _____

PART NO.	RUN NO.	CUSTOMER	DEPT.	LINE	SHIFT	OPERATOR/INSPECTOR SUPERVISOR		

HOURS	7-8	8-9	9-10	10-11	11-12	12-1	1-2	2-3	3-4	Total Defects
TYPE OF DEFECT	I									
HOLES OFF LOCATION										1
MISSING HOLES	III						I	I		5
DISTORTED HOLES								I		1
BURRED HOLES										
CRACKS						I	I	I		3
LAMINATED STEEL										
SEAMY STEEL										
DIE SCORE										
PILOT PULL	I				I	II	III	I		8
SHORT STOCK					I		I			2
BENT BARS	IIIII				II	IIIII	IIII	IIIIII		21
MISC.										
Total Defective	11				3	8	7	8		
Total Run	105			41	141	171	89	154		

Comments: _____

2.2 From the following tally sheet of injuries by department, make a Pareto chart.

Week

Department	1	2	3	4	5	Total Injuries
Assembly	1					1
Machining		1	1		1	3
Stamping	11	11	111	11	1	10
Test			1			1
Welding	111	1111	111	111	~~1111~~	18
Total Injuries	6	7	8	5	7	33

2.3 For the data in Problem 2.1, make a cumulative Pareto chart.

2.4 For the data in Problem 2.2, make a cumulative Pareto chart.

Flowchart and Cause-and-Effect Diagram

A process may be viewed as a transformation or a black box that transforms a set of inputs into a set of outputs.

In order to improve the process it is desirable to be able to portray graphically how that process "works." One may consider two types of "flows" through the process:

1. The flow of the product (goods or services) through the process from start to finish. This is called a *flowchart*.
2. The flow from causes (inputs) to effects (outputs) through the process for any particular effect one wants to study. The effect of interest is often poor quality and/or poor productivity. The diagram used to study the flows of causes and effects through a process is called a *cause-and-effect diagram*.

Procedure for Making a Simple Flowchart

Step 1 Study the process from start to finish, step by step.

Step 2 Sketch these steps as they "flow," including loops back to previous steps, decision points where the process might split into two paths, etc.

Purpose: To illustrate the sequence and relationships of the steps of the process logically to help define the relationship between these steps.

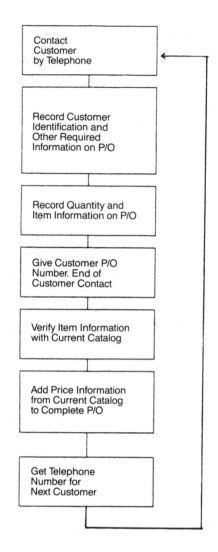

Figure 2.4 Flowchart for Writing a Purchase Order

Figure 2.4 shows a sample flowchart for writing a purchase order (P/O). Note that it looks at all the steps involved from start to finish, from getting the customer's phone number to completing the P/O.

Procedure for Making a Simple Cause-and-Effect Diagram

Step 1 Study the process to identify the various sources of inputs into the process. For example, check out inputs of people, material, machine, methods, environment, and measurement system.

Step 2 Study each source of input to find the various components of that input.

Step 3 Refine your list.

Step 4 Graph the relationship of these inputs to the output. A long horizontal line going to the right represents the output. Main diagonal lines leading into this horizontal line represent the various sources of inputs. Other diagonal lines leading into the main diagonal lines and into other lines show the components of each source of input.

Purpose: To display the relationship between the inputs and the outputs of a process graphically to help identify the sources of the problems (the opportunities to improve).

A cause-and-effect diagram, sometimes called a fishbone chart (because of the way it looks) or Ishikawa diagram (because of its founder's name), is a graphical portrayal of the interrelationships between the various inputs into the process and the problem being studied which might be poor quality or low productivity. Figure 2.5 shows a cause-and-effect diagram for the P/O problem already considered in Figures 2.1 and 2.2. Figure 2.5 shows the interrelationship of the various inputs from the customer, the clerk, the catalog, and the inspector to the errors occurring in P/Os. From this cause-and-effect diagram, possible sources of the problems causing the errors can be identified and then monitored until the contributing sources are found. In this case, it was discovered from the cause-and-effect diagram that the two largest items on the Pareto chart, incorrect price and incorrect information, were both inputs from the catalog. Upon investigation, it was found that some of the orders taken had used the previous year's catalog. Removal of the outdated catalog and distribution of the current catalog solved the problem.

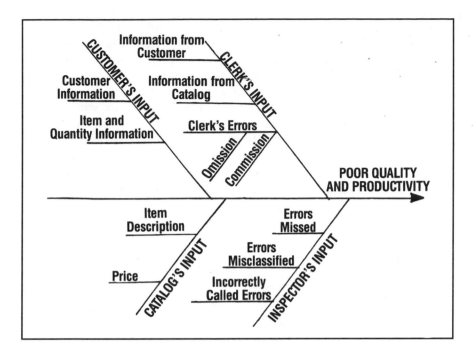

Figure 2.5 Cause-and-Effect Diagram for Purchase Orders

PROBLEMS

2.5 The accounts receivable department of a company is having problems with late payments. Draw a cause-and-effect diagram showing the inputs that may be possible sources contributing to the problem.

2.6 A plastic injection molding company is having problems with cracks in the formed plastic part. Draw a cause-and-effect diagram showing the inputs that may be possible sources contributing to the problem.

Scatter Diagram

The scatter diagram is a plot of one variable versus another to see if there is any relationship between the two. It is sometimes referred to as a *cross plot*. For example, Figure 2.6 looks at the relationship between the number of items on the order and the number of errors. If the scatter diagram had looked similar to Figure 2.6a, we would have noticed that the number of errors tends to increase with an increasing number of items on the order. We might then have concluded that the errors were primarily on items. Thus, the more items, the more errors. If instead the scatter diagram would have looked similar to Figure 2.6b, we would have noticed that the number of errors tends to remain constant, regardless of the number of items on the order. We might then have concluded that the errors were unrelated to the number of items. In this case, the errors might be related, for example, to the customer since there is only one customer per order.

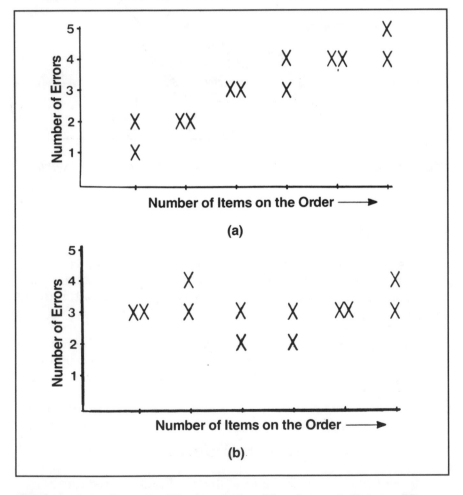

Figure 2.6 Scatter Diagram for Number of Errors Versus Number of Items on the Order

Procedure for Making a Scatter Diagram

Step 1 Decide which two variables whose relationship you wish to explore.

Step 2 For each piece inspected, record the value for each of the two variables.

Step 3 Label the horizontal axis with one variable and the vertical axis with the other, both with appropriate scales.

Step 4 For each piece inspected, make a mark on the graph at the appropriate coordinate for the value of the two variables.

Purpose: To plot one variable versus another to see if there is any relationship between the two.

PROBLEMS

2.7 The following scatter diagram plots the relationship between quality and productivity on the output from several machines that were doing the job. Comment.

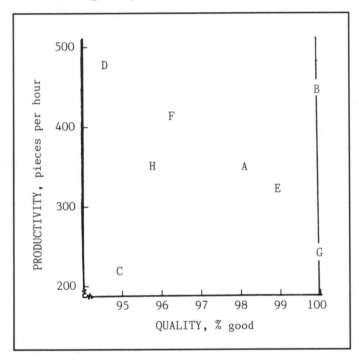

2.8 To discover what machine speed yielded the greatest number of pieces before the tool wore enough to warrant a change, different speeds were experimented with, yielding the following results. Comment.

Speed (Pieces/Minute)	Number of Pieces Made
20	150
25	172
30	196
35	198
40	185
45	160
50	120

Run Chart*

A *run chart* is a graphical representation of data in order of time. Once a dimension or some other characteristic of a process is identified as critical or as a potential source of a problem, a run chart is kept on it to study the behavior of that characteristic over time. Using the run chart, we look for evidence of nonrandomness either in the form of nonrandom patterns or as obviously excessive points.

Procedure for Making a Run Chart

Step 1 Time is displayed along the horizontal axis, the dimension or other characteristic being studied is plotted along the vertical axis. The characteristic of interest may, for example, be a count of the number of occurrences of a defect, a fraction defective, or a measurement of interest.

Step 2 One hundred percent inspection is used. As each piece or group of pieces is inspected, it is marked on the graph.

Step 3 The points are connected to help the eye identify any pattern.

Example 2.1

Suppose the length of a connecting rod has been a dimension of interest. In attempts to obtain information about the nature of the process, 40 consecutive machined connecting rods are measured, keeping the readings in time order. The data were coded as thousandths of an inch over 8″. The results are as follows (read across):

9	9	10	10	14	6	11	13
9	10	9	7	10	11	8	10
13	9	10	12	7	8	10	11
9	11	12	11	8	9	9	8
8	10	7	10	10	10	7	8

*Used by permission of *Quality*. Adapted from "Use of the Run Chart." Quality (March 1987): 87-88.

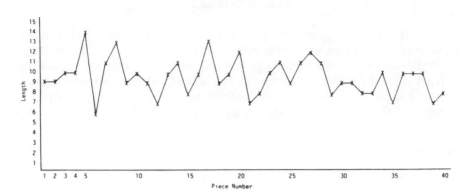

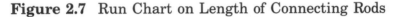

Figure 2.7 Run Chart on Length of Connecting Rods

The run chart for these observations is illustrated in Figure 2.7. Note that this run chart might have been prepared directly from observations made using a dial indicator, as these observations were being made. It would not even be necessary to record the observed readings in a digital or tabular form.

> Purpose: The run chart is used to look for evidence of non-randomness: trends or cyclical patterns (Figure 2.8a) or obviously excessive points (Figure 2.8b).

The run chart in Figure 2.7 appears to be free from nonrandom patterns or obviously excessive points (i.e., the data appear to be random).

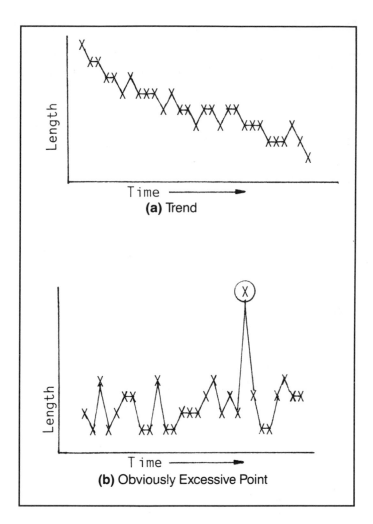

Figure 2.8 Run Charts Exhibiting Nonrandom Pattern

Classroom Exercise

Collect data in the classroom; for example, the number of working TV sets (or radios, etc.) in each household, and pretend they are coded data taken in order of production.

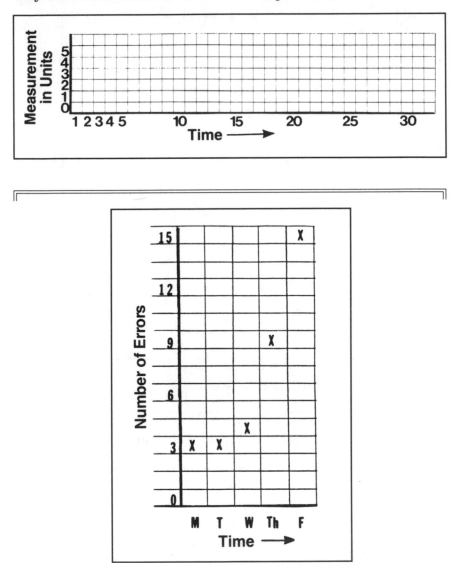

Figure 2.9 Run Chart of Errors on Purchase Orders

Example 2.2

The run chart in Figure 2.9 looks at the total number of errors on P/Os per day as shown in Figure 2.1. We can look at the total number of errors rather than the percent in error because the number of P/Os was relatively constant per day. It can be noted that the number of errors increased on Thursday with another large increase on Friday. Unless there were some additional complications, such as more complex orders on Thursday and Friday, we might conclude that it is a worker-related problem — starting the weekend early. More weekly data would have to be analyzed before any firm conclusions could be drawn and corrective action taken.

Example 2.3

This example on the run chart comes from a manufacturer of engines. The dimension being monitored here is the exhaust valve stem diameter after finish grind. The spikes and the cyclical pattern in the run chart (Figure 2.10) completely identified a serious quality problem that had existed in this operation for several years. As a first step in studying the excessive variability in finish stem diameter, an inspector was asked to make a run chart, using 100 percent inspection for one hour. The alert inspector recognized that the notes he would put on the chart were at least as important as the data points. The annotation on the chart

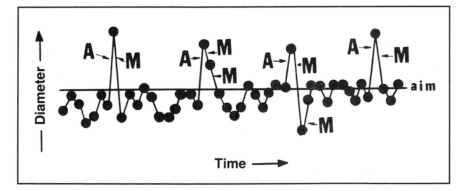

Figure 2.10 Run Chart of Stem Diameters of Exhaust Valve

pointed to the fact that it was after an automatic compensation (denoted by an "A" on the chart) on every twelfth piece that the product measurement deviated most from target. The operator even had problems using the manual adjustment (denoted by an "M" on the chart), for the chart showed that it would take him one and sometimes two tries to bring the product back to target. From the chart it was apparent that the operator needed to be trained in the use of the automatic compensator and in the use of the manual adjustments. Unfortunately, to everyone's dismay, no one in the whole plant knew how to make the proper adjustments and the supplier of the machinery had to be called in to train the operators and tool engineers. As Deming says, we all need to "work smarter, not harder."

Example 2.4*

In the manufacture of crankshafts for internal combustion engines, the final operation was lapping the main bearing journals. Subsequent inspection showed an excessive number of defective crankshafts due to variation in the main bearing diameter after lapping or failure to "clean up" during the lapping process. Indications were that the problem may have been due to excessive variability in journal diameter after the preceding operation, finish grinding. Figure 2.11 displays a run chart of the diameters of the finish ground bearing journal on consecutively manufactured crankshafts before lapping. After inspection, it can be seen that the three different shifts appear to be using a different target value. Inquiring into the reasons for this, the finish grind operator from each shift was questioned: "Where are you trying to hold the process and why?" The operator from the first shift answered that he had at one time performed the lapping operation. It had been his experience that holding the finish ground diameter at the low end made for less material removal and hence greater productivity in lapping. He therefore held the ground diameter at the low end. The operator from the second shift had never been told where to hold the process. Given no further information, he targeted for the specification midpoint. The operator from the third shift was concerned about leaving enough material so the lapping operation would "clean up" without going undersize. Consequently, the third

*Used by permission of *Quality*. Adapted from "What Target?" *Quality* (August 1985): 34.

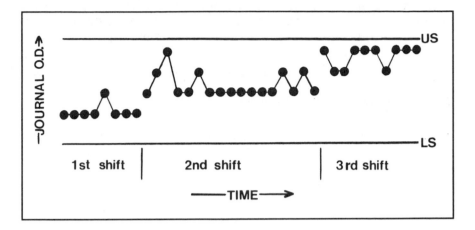

Figure 2.11 Run Chart on the Diameters of a Ground Bearing Journal on Crankshafts Before Lapping

shift operator held the finish ground diameter on the high side.

Engineering had not defined a target. The result: no communication, confusion, and poor quality. It is important for engineering, or manufacturing, to intelligently decide on a target value for a quality characteristic and make that value known.

(Note: This example is *not* a unique experience. Such confusion arises everywhere.)

Note that in its strictest sense, a run chart applied to measurement data shows the results for individual pieces with 100 percent inspection over time. This is necessary, at least for a short time, to identify the basic nature of the process. The broader definition of the run chart allows for the plot of any characteristic of interest over time (percent defective, averages of readings, etc.), not necessarily with 100 percent inspection.

The run chart makes a handy problem-solving tool that aids the operator in monitoring the process. A run chart is essential in learning about the nature of the process and is vital as a first step in problem solving. Without knowing the basic nature of process variation over time, one may use an inappropriate tool in analyzing the data. For instance, a control chart (a more sophisticated tool to be discussed later) or histogram may hide tool wear if frequent tool changes and adjustments are made between subgroups of observations, and the cyclic nature of the process of Figure 2.10

might never have been discovered if a run chart had not been used. A run chart (with 100 percent inspection where feasible) should always precede the use of control charts on averages.

PROBLEMS

2.9 The following data show the wall thickness at a random location on each of 40 consecutively manufactured thick-walled tubes. The data are coded in thousandths of an inch above 0.500 inch (read across). Make a run chart.

28	25	15	20	31	16	13	21
21	15	24	23	16	18	18	24
23	13	14	23	17	13	19	22
22	21	25	25	20	25	28	11
19	15	28	19	18	14	20	16

2.10 The following coded data give the lengths of consecutively manufactured connecting rods. Make a run chart. What appears to be happening (read across)?

First shift:	35	40	27	30	30	34	26	31
Second shift:	24	23	20	15	23	17	16	21
	15	13	28	18	16	22	24	16
Third shift:	8	20	9	5	11	16	5	9
	13	16						

Histogram

The histogram is a graph with the measurement or value of interest typically along the horizontal axis and the frequency of occurrence of that dimension along the vertical axis. The bars are of equal width and usually touch, i.e., where one bar ends, the next one begins.

Procedure for Making a Histogram

Step 1 Make a tally of all the readings.

Step 2 Label the horizontal axis with the dimension or characteristic of interest and an appropriate scale of values. Label the vertical axis "Frequency" and an appropriate scale.

Step 3 For each value, make a bar that is the width of the measurement interval and the height of the frequency of that value. Note that the bars usually touch, i.e., where one bar (value) ends, the next bar (value) begins. The exception is when the value has a frequency of zero and no bar exists.

Purpose: To gain information into the nature and the distribution of the data.

Example 2.5

To make a histogram from the data from Example 2.1, we first make a tally of all the readings. Note that a reading is denoted by the letter X. Here we have used coded data.

X	TALLY
6	1
7	1111
8	̶1̶1̶1̶1̶ 1
9	̶1̶1̶1̶1̶ 111
10	̶1̶1̶1̶1̶ ̶1̶1̶1̶1̶ 1
11	̶1̶1̶1̶1̶
12	11
13	11
14	1

By counting up the tallies, we make a *frequency table*, which is a table displaying each reading (X) along with its frequency (denoted by f).

Frequency Table

X	f
6	1
7	4
8	6
9	8
10	11
11	5
12	2
13	2
14	1

The results from the frequency table can be graphed in a histogram as seen in Figure 2.12. The bars "touching" reflects the fact that we are graphing measurement data. This type of data

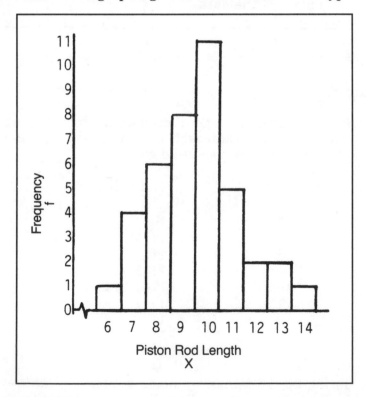

Figure 2.12 Histogram of Connecting Rod Lengths (Coded Data)

is *always* rounded. For instance, a measurement of 6 really fell between 5.5 and 6.5 (thousandths) and has been rounded to 6. A value of 7 represents 6.5 to 7.5, etc. Note that the initial tally of these data made, in effect, a histogram that would be adequate for most purposes.

Classroom Exercise

Make a histogram for the data collected earlier to make the run chart.

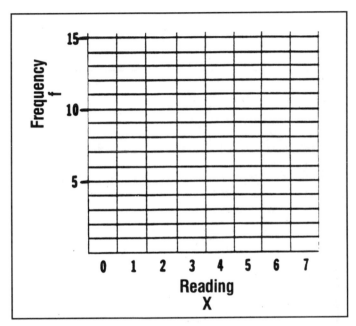

Histograms give useful information about the "shape" of the distribution. They can also be a useful problem solving tool, as seen by the following example.

Example 2.6

The distance from the center of the shaft to the end of the arm, as shown in Figure 2.13, is a dimension of interest.

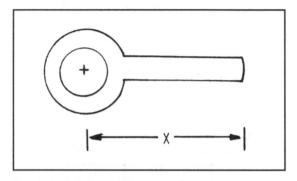

Figure 2.13 Dimension of Interest

A histogram of the data is shown in Figure 2.14.

Note the lack of data just below the lower specification limit (LS). This could have happened by chance, but that possibility seems highly unlikely. What appears to be more likely is that the

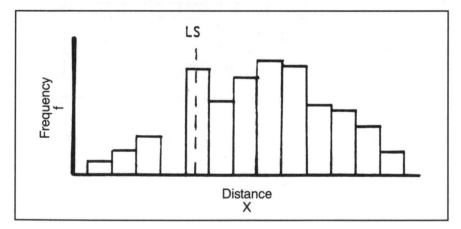

Figure 2.14 Histogram of Distances from Center of Shaft to End of Arm

operator, knowing that product under the LS is undesirable, recorded those readings that were just barely out of specification as being within specification limits. This falsification of the data is very common and has been referred to as *flinching* (i.e., flinching away from unwanted results) by Juran and Deming. Deming suggests that flinching is the result of fear — the operator afraid of getting into trouble for making product outside of specification, fear of the quality of the measurement instrument, fear of his ability to use the measurement system. Recall Deming's eighth point: "Drive out fear, so that everyone may work effectively for the company." The observations that are shown to be out of specification are there because they were so far below the LS that the inspector was unwilling to "move them up" into the acceptable range.

A histogram, as useful as it is, can be misleading. For example, the histogram of the inside diameter of a bearing in Figure 2.15 appears to have nothing unusual about it. It is not perfectly symmetric, but results seldom are. One might get the impression that the spread of the distribution could be approximated from the histogram, until he or she looked at the run chart. The run chart (Figure 2.16) of the data that made up this histogram shows that the process has a strong trend over time; it is not *stable*. Note

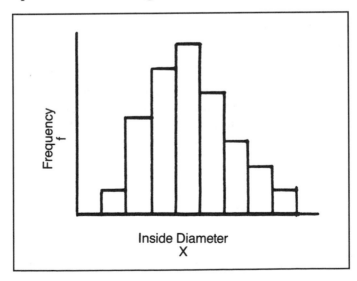

Figure 2.15 Histogram of the Inside Diameter of Bearings

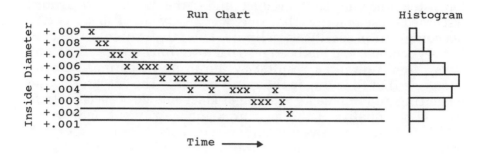

Figure 2.16 Run Chart and Histogram of the Inside Diameters of Bearings

that the histogram has no meaning whatsoever unless the process is *stable over time.*

Note one primary shortcoming of the histogram: It loses the order of production. If there is a time trend (such as from tool wear), or some other nonrandom pattern, the histogram will bury this information.

For these reasons, a histogram alone *cannot* be used to define process capability (the average and spread of the process) as has sometimes been done. In the preceding example, the process is not stable, so defining its distribution, either digitally or graphically, has no meaning.

CAUTION: A histogram is only a valid "picture" of a process if that process is stable over time.

It should be noted that there is no substitute for the histogram as seen by Figure 2.14 and the following examples. However, the interpretation of what one sees is affected dramatically by the number of cells into which the data are divided if the data are grouped. (Six to 14 cells will generally suffice.) *The Probability Plot*, in Chapter 15, does not have this sensitivity to the user's decision regarding plotting.

PROBLEMS

2.11 Discuss the following histogram.

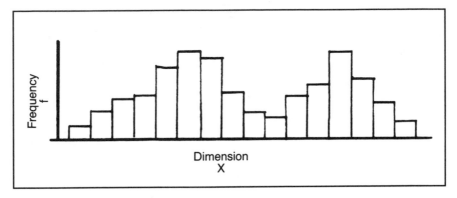

2.12 Discuss the following histogram.

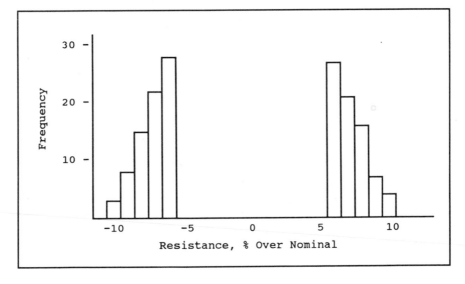

2.13 Make a histogram for the connecting rod data given in Problem 2.10.

2.14 Make a histogram for the following wiring harness data. Use one unit as the cell width. What peculiarity of the data is discovered?

Subgroup Number	Date	Time	Readings 1	2	3	4	5
1	05-04-87	10:00	30	30	30	28	28
2		11:15	30	26	26	24	26
3	05-05-87	8:15	32	34	34	30	36
4	05-06-87	1:00	30	24	31	25	30
5		3:15	21	24	22	23	22
6	05-07-87	7:10	26	32	22	22	23
7		8:40	23	24	24	24	28
8		10:00	23	18	23	24	22
9		11:30	24	31	28	25	24
10		1:45	27	25	25	23	26
11		2:30	18	22	18	24	18
12		3:30	24	16	22	26	20
13	05-08-87	11:15	24	26	30	30	30
14		12:30	25	28	25	26	25
15		12:45	22	22	26	20	24
16	05-11-87	7:30	22	28	24	22	24
17		8:15	26	20	26	26	26
18		8:30	27	19	24	22	22
19		9:00	36	36	28	30	28
20		9:30	26	26	28	24	24
21		10:00	28	26	24	28	28
22		10:45	30	26	26	26	30
23	05-12-87	12:30	26	22	28	24	30
24		1:30	30	24	28	26	24
25		2:30	24	24	26	24	28

Chapter 6 Introduction to Descriptive Statistics

Subgroups from the Process

When we measure a few pieces from a process, the data constitute a *sample* of the process. In statistical process control work, a sample is referred to as a *subgroup* because it is a grouping of the data from the process. We may later "subgroup" the same data in several different ways.

We typically sample from the process because the process is producing so many parts that it is economically infeasible to measure them all. Also, measurements on sample pieces often tend to be more accurate because when measuring only a few pieces, there is less chance of operator fatigue.

The idea behind sampling is to estimate what the process is doing by measuring only pieces that have been selected in a predetermined scheme which has been carefully planned.

Types of Data

The purpose of descriptive statistics is to summarize and describe the data. Generally, data are categorized into two types: variables and attribute.

Variables data involve measurement, such as length, weight, or time. These quantities exist on a continuous scale, or on a scale that could be divided into an infinite number of increments. However, given physical limitations, the measurement scale is only divided into a finite number of increments. Thus, variables data is always rounded to some increment. We often assume that the distribution of variables data has the familiar *bell-shaped* curve which means that it is *near-normal.*

The other category of data of interest to us is *attribute* or *count-type* data. The more common classification of attribute data relates simply to whether each piece of product is either "good" or "bad," and we speak of the number of defective (nonconforming), or the proportion, fraction, or percent defective. Also in the category of attribute or count-type data are the number of defects (noncon-formities) per unit, where one unit of production may be considered to have multiple defects rather than just being evaluated as "good' or "bad."

PROBLEM

2.15 Classify the following into attribute or variables data:

    a. Weight of a ball bearing
    b. Length of a connecting rod
    c. Number of blemishes in the paint finish of a fender
    d. Inside diameter of a bearing
    e. Percent of defective steering wheels
    f. Number of surface imperfections in a windshield
    g. Number of surface blemishes in a coil of steel

Measures of Central Tendency

A set of data is most simply described by a measure of central tendency. There are several different measures of central tendency. Two of primary interest to us are:

1. Mean (Average)

    Definition: The *arithmetic* average.

    Symbol: $\overline{X}$ or X bar (read as X bar).

    Procedure: Step i Add all the readings.
                   Step ii Divide by the number of readings.

    Formula: $\overline{X} = \dfrac{\Sigma X}{n}$

    Notes:
- X is the symbol for a reading.
- Σ is the symbol used to indicate summation. It means *add them up*. Σ is the capital Greek letter sigma.
- n is the number of readings.

    Comments:
- $\overline{X}$ is the most commonly used measure of central tendency. Usually when one says "average," he or she is referring to the mean (X bar).
- $\overline{X}$ is mathematically the strongest measure of central tendency. It uses all the data.

2. Median

Definition: The *middle* reading.

Symbol: $\tilde{X}$(read X tilde)

Procedure: Step i Arrange all readings in order from the smallest to the largest.

Step ii If the number of readings is odd, select the reading in the middle. (If the number of readings is even, we would calculate the mean of the *middle two*, but in fact we will only use the median of subgroups of size 3 or possibly of size 5.)

Comments: • Very easy to compute.
• Sometimes used because it is less affected than the mean by extreme values.
• Rarely used when the number of subgroups is even.

There is another measure of central tendency that is sometimes used, but which will be of little interest to us.

3. *Mode*

Definition: The reading with the highest frequency.

Symbol: None that are generally accepted.

Procedure: Step i Make a frequency table.
Step ii Select the reading with the highest frequency.

Comments: The only use we will have for the mode is in the adjective "bimodal" referring to a distribution that has two modes (looks like it has two "humps"), as in Problem 2.11.

Example 2.7

Data: 3, 5, 2, 8, 2   n = number of pieces of data = 5

Calculations:

mean = X bar

$$\overline{X} = \frac{\Sigma X}{n} = \frac{20}{5} = 4$$

median = X tilde

$$\widetilde{X} = 3$$

Example 2.8

Data: 5, 8, 3, 14   n = 4

$$\overline{X} = \frac{\Sigma X}{n} = \frac{30}{4} = 7.5$$

Note that when there is an even number of pieces, there is no "middle" number. In these cases, it is customary not to use the median.

PROBLEMS

2.16 Compute the mean and median of the following data:

9, 7, 11, 1, 3, 7, 4

2.17 Compute the mean and median for each of the following sets of data:

a. 3, 6, 3
b. 4, 3, 3, 6, 8
c. 9, 11, 6
d. 39, 36, 37, 42, 37
e. 0.83, 0.79, 0.64, 1.23, 0.98
f. $-6, -8, -4$
g. $-3, 2, 1, -8, -2$

Example 2.9

One company has three manufacturing lines (A, B, C) which make the same product. In order to compare the lines, seven pieces are taken from each line and measured. After "ordering" the data (putting it in order from the smallest to largest) we obtain the following results:

A	B	C
15	14	1
15	15	2
15	15	15
15	15	15
15	15	15
15	15	28
15	16	29

Compute the mean of data from each of the three lines. Note that for each set, the mean is 15. How well does the average describe the data? The number 15 describes the data from line A very well. The number 15 describes the data from line B "pretty well." The number 15 does *not* describe the data from line C well at all. The point is that one number is not enough to describe data. It takes two numbers to describe data: one to describe the central tendency, the other to describe the spread or dispersion.

Measures of Dispersion

The most common measure of spread is the range. The range is simply the highest reading minus lowest reading. The symbol for the range is R.

Continuing with the previous example, the range for the data from each of these three lines is as follows.

Line A: R = highest − lowest = 15 − 15 = 0
Line B: R = 16 − 14 = 2
Line C: R = 29 − 1 = 28

Reflect on what was said about the average of 15 describing the data: It described A very well, B "pretty well," and C poorly. This is the same story as implied by the three ranges above. Now suppose it is found that line D also manufactures the same part. Seven pieces are measured from line D. The measurements are given in the following table along with the previous data.

Example 2.9 (cont.)

A	B	C	D
15	14	1	1
15	15	2	1
15	15	15	1
15	15	15	15
15	15	15	29
15	15	28	29
15	16	29	29

The mean of these data from line D is also 15. The range is still 28, the same as from C. The data from line D, however, reflects a process which has more spread than process C. This fact is not reflected in the range. The range is not the best measure of the spread because it only uses two readings, the high and the low. A better method of measuring variability is needed.

Standard Deviation

A measure of spread that is better than the range is the standard deviation, which uses all of the data. The estimate of the population standard deviation from a sample is symbolized by s, and is calculated using the formula:

$$s = \sqrt{\frac{\Sigma\,(X - \overline{X})^2}{n - 1}}$$

This is a mathematical formula that is handy for statisticians to use, and many theorems and tables have been developed using the measure of spread.

Procedure for Calculating Standard Deviation

We must first have calculated $\overline{X}$, then:

Step 1 Calculate: $X - \overline{X}$
    (deviation of each reading from $\overline{X}$, i.e., subtract)

Step 2 Square these numbers: $(X - \overline{X})^2$

Step 3 Add up these squares: $\Sigma\,(X - \overline{X})^2$

Step 4 Divide by n − 1: $\dfrac{\Sigma\,(X - \overline{X})^2}{n - 1}$
    This is called the sample *variance*. It is the unbiased estimation of the population variance.

Step 5 Take the square root: $\sqrt{\dfrac{\Sigma\,(X - \overline{X})^2}{n - 1}}$

    This is called the sample *standard deviation,* s.

Example 2.10

Calculating the range for the data in Example 2.7,
Data: 3, 5, 2, 8, 2   n = 5
  High = 8
  Low   = 2
  Range = R = high − low
        = 8 − 2
        = 6

Recall that $\overline{X} = 4$. Calculating the standard deviation (the data here are ordered from low to high; this was an optional step).

	Step 1	Step 2
	$X - 4$	
X	$X - \overline{X}$	$(X - \overline{X})^2$
2	-2	4
2	-2	4
3	-1	1
5	1	1
8	4	16
20		26

Step 3   Step 4   Step 5

$$s = \sqrt{\frac{\Sigma (X - \overline{X})^2}{n - 1}} = \sqrt{\frac{26}{4}} = \sqrt{6.5} = 2.55$$

Note: Arranging the subgroup in order makes it easier to find the range, but it is not necessary for the computation of standard deviation.

Recall that the purpose of sampling is to get estimates of the population or process, particularly estimates of the process mean and standard deviation. These estimates are only meaningful if the process is stable. Techniques for determining the stability of the process will be given in Parts III and IV. The symbols for the mean and standard deviation of the process and sample are given in Table 2.1.

	Mean	Standard Deviation
Population or process	μ (mu)	σ (sigma)
Sample	$\overline{X}$	s

Table 2.1 Symbols for Mean and Standard Deviation

How the process values (μ and σ) are estimated by the sample values ($\overline{X}$ and s) will be discussed in Part V.

PROBLEMS

2.18 Calculate the range and standard deviation for the data in Example 2.8.

Data: 5, 8, 3, 14

2.19 Calculate the range and standard deviation for the following data:

9, 7, 4, 11, 1, 3, 7

2.20 Calculate the standard deviation for each of the following sets of data:

a. 3, 6, 3
b. 4, 3, 3, 6, 8
c. 9, 11, 6
d. 39, 36, 37, 42, 37
e. 0.83, 0.79, 0.64, 1.23, 0.98
f. −6, −8, −4
g. −3, 2, 1, −8, −2

The Normal Distribution

If the histogram of all the data appears to be symmetric and can be smoothed over with a bell-shaped curve, as illustrated in Figure 2.17, it may be said to have approximately a normal distribution.

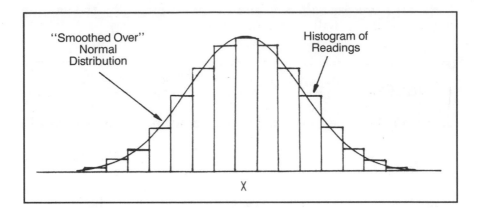

Figure 2.17 Normal Distribution

Many, and perhaps most, processes yield data roughly following the normal distribution. The normal distribution is easy to work with because much research has been done on it. In particular, if the true mean and standard deviation of the process, symbolized by the Greek letters μ and σ ($\overline{X}$ and s are for the sample), are given, the complete distribution of all the data is known. Approximately 68 percent of the readings are within 1 standard deviation above or below the mean, 95 percent within 2 standard deviations, and 99.7 percent within 3 standard deviations as illustrated in Figure 2.18.

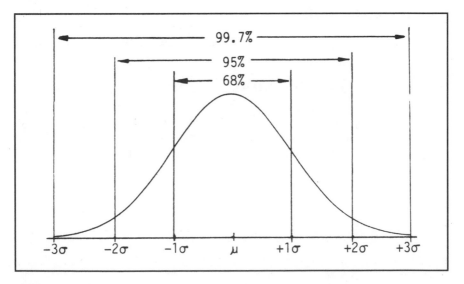

Figure 2.18 Percentages of the Normal Distribution

Example 2.11

If the distribution of the lengths of rods is approximately normally distributed with a mean of 20″ and a standard deviation of .01″:
- Approximately 68 percent will be within .01″ of 20″ (between 19.99″ and 20.01″)
- Approximately 95 percent will be within .02″ of 20″ (between 19.98″ and 20.02″)
- Approximately 99.7 percent will be within .03″ of 20″ (between 19.97″ and 20.03″)

Caution: These percentages are true only if the process producing these rods is really stable over time (which we will learn to identify in Parts III to V) and the process really is approximately normally distributed.

Since distributions are never exactly normal, the percentages are never exact. The percentages are mentioned here only to give general approximations and to note that it is assumed that almost all normally distributed data fall within plus or minus 3 standard deviations of the mean.

Since data from some processes are not even close to a normal distribution, much of the work in quality control works with the averages of samples. One reason for this is that the averages of samples tend to be normally distributed regardless of the shape of the distribution from which the samples were drawn. This tendency is described by the Central Limit Theorem.

Central Limit Theorem

The philosophy behind the Central Limit Theorem provides the basis for most of the work in future chapters. In quality control work we will only be working with very large (potentially infinite) populations. Associated with the Central Limit Theorem are three important points:

1. The average of the means of many samples $(\overline{\overline{X}})$ will approximate the average of the population or the process (μ), i.e., $\overline{\overline{X}} \doteq \mu$ ($\doteq$ means approximates).

2. The sample means from the process have less variability than the individuals. The standard deviation of the averages $(\sigma_{\overline{x}})$ is equal to the standard deviation of the individuals (σ) divided by the square root of the subgroup size, i.e.,

$$\sigma_{\overline{x}} = \frac{\sigma}{\sqrt{n}} .$$

3. The averages of subgroups tend toward normality even though the original distribution of individual readings was not normally distributed, as illustrated by the following example.

Example 2.12

Twenty-five subgroups of size n = 3 were taken and displayed in a *run chart*, three readings at a time, as illustrated in Figure 2.19a. Note from the histogram at the right (Figure 2.19b) that

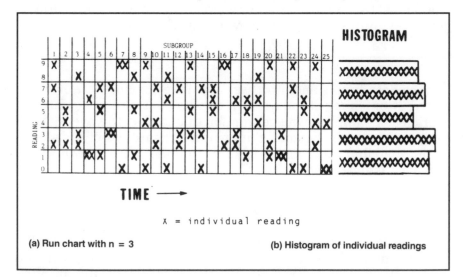

(a) Run chart with n = 3

(b) Histogram of individual readings

Figure 2.19 Run Chart and Histogram of Individual Readings, Nonnormal Data

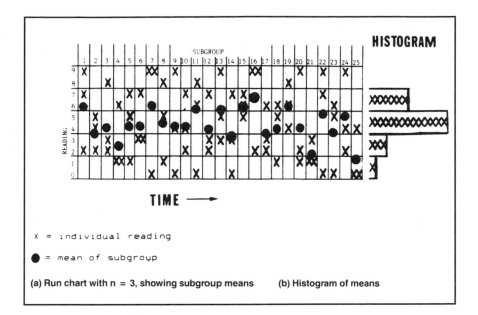

Figure 2.20 Run Chart and Histogram of Subgroup Means

the data are not normally distributed. The mean of each subgroup is shown in Figure 2.20a and the histogram of these means is shown in 2.20b. Note that the histogram of means at the right of the run chart, Figure 2.20b, appears to be more nearly normally distributed than the histogram in Figure 2.19b.

The Central Limit Theorem tells us that almost all means of subgroups should naturally fall within 3 standard deviations (of the means) from the overall process mean. This fact is important for the control charts that will be covered in the next few chapters.

Part III.
The Control Chart in General

There is variation in everything. The control chart is a graphical tool used to separate variation that appears to be natural to the system from the variation that appears to be unnatural to the system (the variation that is greater than we should reasonably expect by chance). The control chart helps us to identify the causes of the excessive variation so that we may take corrective action; the result is a more uniform product.

Chapter 7 The Nature of Variation

Variation in a Process

There is sometimes the misconception that if we have "constant" inputs of people, material, machines, methods, environment, and measurement system, the output will always be constant, i.e., a given quality characteristic will always be measured as the same value, X, as illustrated in Figure 3.1. In reality, there is natural

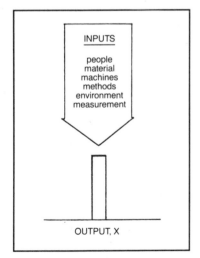

Figure 3.1 Misconception of Output

variation in everything, in all the inputs, in all the outputs. The result is a distribution of the measured values of the quality characteristic, as illustrated in Figure 3.2. Try as you might to

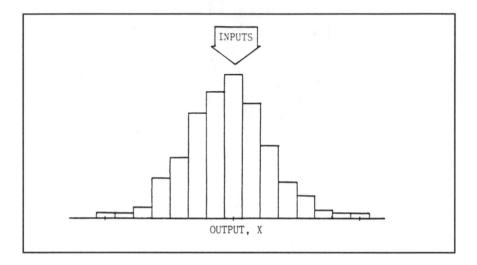

Figure 3.2 Reality: Variation of Output

make all the inputs perfectly identical in the hopes of getting identical outputs, you can't eliminate all variation. Pioneering work was done by Shewhart, who did his work in the 1920s to 1940s to identify the nature of variation: How much of it is "natural" to the system and how much of it is not?

Historical Background

Shewhart noted that some variation appeared to be due to chance. The sum total of the variation due to chance is relatively small, no major part of which can be traced to a single cause. This chance variation behaves in a random manner.

Some of the variation in a quality characteristic is produced by factors other than chance causes. Shewhart called these factors *assignable causes* and observed that "assignable causes of variation may be found and eliminated" (Shewhart 1931, p. 14).

Juran (1945, pp. 109-110) points out that the difference between assignable and chance causes is not clear-cut:

> Instead of using the word "assignable," we might well have used the term "dominant" causes of variation, for the practical distinction between an assignable and a nonassignable cause is also one of order of magnitude...big enough to make itself noticeable...There

is...no clean-cut separation between assignable and nonassignable causes of variation. The practical difference is whether the variation in question shows the process out of control, as evidenced by the control chart. Thus the attainment of control is in a sense the identification of the dominant variables and the shrinking down of the effect of such variables to such a level that the variable no longer has a dominant effect.

A point outside the control limits is an indication of the presence of an assignable cause. The assignable cause may have existed before it manifested itself dramatically enough to be detected by the control chart. Hence, it might have contributed some additional variation to the process when the control limits were first calculated and the process was considered to be in the state of statistical control. When the assignable cause did manifest itself enough to finally be detected, its elimination may therefore reduce the variability of the process. Causes of variability that were once considered chance causes might thereafter be detected as assignable causes.

Deming (1956) called assignable causes "special" causes because often they may be specific to a certain worker, a certain machine, etc. These special causes can easily be identified by the use of a control chart. Deming took Shewhart's suggestion (eliminating assignable causes of variation to leave the remaining variability to chance) one step further. Deming proposed that the remaining variability after assignable causes have been-removed is due to "common causes" of variability that should be investigated further and should not be left to chance.

"Common causes" of variability are common to a whole group of workers, machines, etc.; they belong to the system; they are faults of the system (Deming 1956). Examples are machines not suited to the process, inadequate training and supervision, incoming material not suited to the process, poor design, etc. (Deming 1982). Some faults of the system may be isolated by judgment, by experiment, or by examination of records of operations and materials suspected of being offenders (Deming 1975).

PROBLEMS

3.1 a. Another name for assignable causes is _____
   _____ as given by Deming.
   b. Deming has called chance causes by the name _____
   causes because they should not all be left to _____.

3.2 Identify the following as a special or common cause.
   a. a broken tool
   b. a poor operator
   c. poor training for all operators
   d. one batch of poor incoming material
   e. poor gauging

3.3 a. Variation that appears to be natural to the system is due
   to _____ causes.
   b. Variation that is not typical of the process is due to
   _____ causes.

Chapter 8 The Philosophy of the Control Chart

Shewhart invented the control chart to separate the assignable causes from the chance causes. The control limits define the extent of the predictable variation due to chance or common causes. The points that fall outside the control limits are large, unpredictable variation due to assignable causes. When the assignable causes are eliminated so that all the points fall within the control limits on a control chart and no nonrandom patterns appear to be present, we say that the process is stable and is in a *state of statistical control* or in a *state of control*. Shewhart (1931, p. 6) defined control by saying:

> A phenomenon will be said to be controlled when through the use of past experience, we can predict, at least within limits, how the phenomenon may be expected to vary in the future. Here it is understood that prediction within limits means that we can state, at least approximately, the probability that the observed phenomenon will fall within the given limits.

The British Standard BS 600 written by Pearson (1935, p. 38) has used the term "statistically uniform" to describe this state of stability:

> . . . to avoid the confusion which has been found to occur when using the words "statistical control" between the concept of statistical uniformity and the pragmatic interpretation of the phrase as the act, for example, of a process manager.

An example of a control chart on percent defective is given in Figure 3.3. A subgroup size of 100 has been taken each day and the daily percent defective plotted. The centerline of 5 percent means that the process appears to be running around 5 percent defective. Due to natural variation, daily subgroups will be a little under or a little over 5 percent defective. How much is "a little"; i.e., by how much can we expect the daily percent defective to vary from 5 percent due to pure chance? The control limits tell us how much. (Computations will be presented in Part VII.) From Figure 3.3, we see the control limits are 0 and 11.5 percent. This implies that if the process really is producing 5 percent defectives under conditions of statistical uniformity, we could expect from our

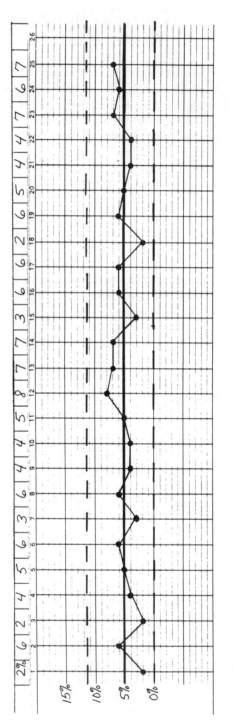

Figure 3.3 Control Chart on Percent Defective

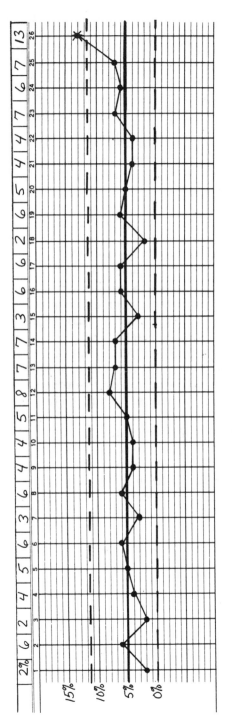

Figure 3.4 Point Out of Control on a Control Chart

samples of size 100 to get between 0 and 11.5 percent defective. Note that all the samples have percents defective falling within these limits. We say that the process is in a state of control or is statistically uniform. That means that the process is stable, producing 5 percent defectives on the average. Day-by-day variation from this 5 percent defective is only natural variation. All the variation appears to be due to common causes affecting the whole process.

On day 26, a subgroup of size 100 is taken and found to have 13 defectives yielding a percent defective of 13 percent. Note that this falls outside of the control limits as shown in Figure 3.4, which implies that this was not natural random variation but due to an assignable (special) cause of variation. That means that something (the assignable cause) must have happened to change the process and increase the percent defective. Deming (1982, p. 112) warns us that "a statistical chart detects the existence of a cause of variation that lies outside the system. It does not find the cause." It would be our job to go to the process and investigate the process in an attempt to identify the assignable cause. Perhaps a tool broke, or perhaps we got a batch of poor incoming material. Once the assignable cause is found, action must be taken to correct the process, i.e., remove the assignable cause — repair the tool, send the poor incoming material back to the supplier, etc. If you do not intend to take corrective action on the process when it is needed, don't bother to collect the data. As Juran (1945, pp. 120-121) warns:

> The control chart technique is admirably suited to executive review. This executive review carries with it the responsibility to see to it that corrective action is taken where such action is indicated. In the absence of corrective action, the control chart technique deteriorates into a sterile paper work procedure!

PROBLEMS

3.4 A point falls outside the control limits. It is due to a(n) _____ cause.

3.5 The points that fall inside the control limits are due to _____ causes.

Chapter 9 Managerial and Other Service Figures

Control chart techniques are useful for quality improvement in both manufacturing and service organizations. They can be even more important in management. Figure 3.5 is an example of a typical management report for productivity.

April 1987			
Part Number	Scheduled	Actual Production	Deviation, Number of Pieces
214	500	500	0
236	300	291	−9
315	350	345	−15
354	325	310	−15
358	400	387	−13
419	675	652	−23
424	600	600	0
426	550	520	−30
519	400	352	−48
534	350	340	−10
561	420	383	−37
571	415	430	+15

Figure 3.5 Productivity Figures for the Month of April 1987

With which products should management be concerned and take corrective action? What type of corrective action should be taken? Take, for instance, the deviation of −48 for part number 519. Is that high compared to the others or is it just "running with the pack"? Is that high for that part, or does it always do that poorly? Management needs a tool to study its managerial figures to understand the variability of these numbers, from part to part and for a given part over time. A control chart (to be discussed in Part V), such as in Figures 3.6 and 3.7, will help management decide what variation is part of the system and what is not. This will guide their actions in planning and aid their efforts toward improvement. For instance, in Figure 3.6 the deviation of −48 for part number 519 appears to be part of the system in April when productivity deviations for all parts averaged -15.4. Any desire for improvement would require a change in the system, affecting all parts. Figure 3.7 indicates that a deviation of -48 is not out of control for part number 519; it had been running at an average of -12.75.

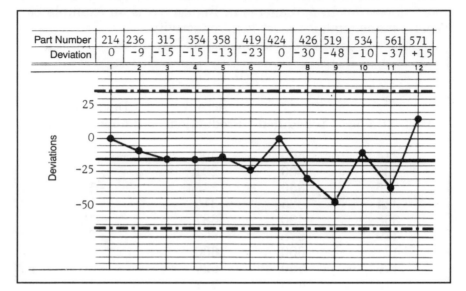

Figure 3.6 Control Chart for Productivity Deviations for April 1987

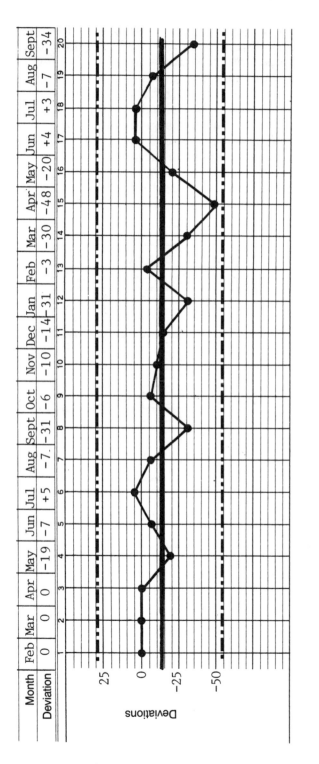

Month	Feb	Mar	Apr	May	Jun	Jul	Aug	Sept	Oct	Nov	Dec	Jan	Feb	Mar	Apr	May	Jun	Jul	Aug	Sept
Deviation	0	0	0	-19	-7	+5	-7	-31	-6	-10	-14	-31	-3	-30	-48	-20	+4	+3	-7	-34

Figure 3.7 Control Chart for Productivity Deviations, Part Number 519, from February 1986 to September 1987

In Figure 3.8, the control limits established for part number 519 during the period from February 1986 to September 1987 (Figure 3.7) are projected into the future to see if the deviations of part number 519 continue their usual behavior. In the period from October 1987 to January 1988 they had. However, in February 1988 the deviation of −64 yielded a point outside of the control limits. This is an unusually large deviation and not part of the usual system. It appears a special cause influenced the deviation for that month — perhaps a lengthy machine breakdown, a shortage of material, or whatever. Only investigation will reveal the special cause and will reveal what action might be taken to avoid such setbacks in the future.

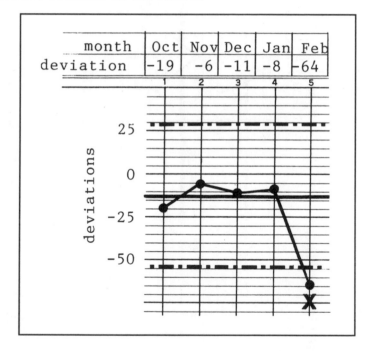

Figure 3.8 Control Chart for Productivity Deviations, Part Number 519, from October 1987 to February 1988, Using Established Limits

Attendance
Safety (lost time)
Downtime
Profit sharing
Schedule requirements
Inventory
Earned hours
Performance
Warranty
Customer complaints
Quality loss
Work force
Dealer surveys
Customer surveys
Product tests
Manufacturing capacities (capabilities)
Cash flow
Payables
Receivables
Operating costs
Supplier performance
Sales
Design reviews (tests)
Audit results
Work-in-process
Budget performance
Utilization of office equipment

Table 3.1 Service and Other Nonmanufacturing Applications (Our thanks to Mr. Thomas Lewis for this list.)

Table 3.1 is a partial list of managerial and other nonmanufacturing situations where a control chart could be useful to monitor variation and guide actions to reduce that variation.

Part IV.
The Control Chart for Variables Data

Recall that Shewhart invented the control chart in attempts to isolate the assignable causes so the remaining variability will be due only to chance (common) causes. The usual Shewhart control charts for variables data work with subgroup averages (mean and median) and measures of subgroup dispersion (range or standard deviation).

The control chart can be used on past data to see if the process was in control over time or it can be used in "real time" on an ongoing process. The control chart may also be used for data which has been formed into *rational* subgroups other than time (such as vendor-to-vendor or machine-to-machine).

Chapter 10
The Basic Control Chart Calculations

In order to obtain some initial familiarity with control charts for variables data we will first illustrate the basic control chart calculations for data after all the data have been collected. We will first consider charts for subgroup averages and subgroup variation using time-ordered data. Charts of this type are the ones most commonly seen in industry today. Charts for individuals instead of subgroup averages will be considered later.

These calculations will be shown for three types of charts;
1. The $\overline{X}$ and R chart (mean and range chart) which is the most commonly used chart.
2. The $\widetilde{X}$ and R chart (median and range chart) which is somewhat easier to use, but of lower statistical efficiency.
3. The $\overline{X}$ and s chart (mean and standard deviation chart) which is mathematically the strongest chart.

The $\overline{X}$ and R Chart

In order to study time-ordered data, a control chart works with many small subgroups over time rather than only a few large subgroups. The subgroup size (denoted by n) is typically 3, 4, or 5. In most applications, the pieces of product comprising a subgroup should be consecutive pieces in order of production to keep the subgroup composed of similar pieces (as similar as possible). These subgroups are then as *homogeneous* as possible. This property of homogeneity is the basic requirement for a subgroup.

How often the subgroups should be taken is arbitrary and usually determined by experience. Suppose for the initial subgroups we had used a subgroup size n = 3 every hour. If the process appears to be running into trouble, we may wish to subgroup more often, say every half hour or every 15 minutes. If the process appears to be running smoothly, we may wish to subgroup less often, say once every two hours or once every four hours.

For small subgroups of time-ordered data, the number of subgroups (denoted by k) should be at least 25 (following Shewhart). To get started, you may wish to set up temporary limits after as few as 10 subgroups. *Some of the examples worked here have fewer subgroups, but that is only to keep the arithmetic short.* A general rule of thumb is that either k or n must be at least 25. This implies at least k = 25 subgroups for ongoing process control where n must be kept small to meet the principal requirement for subgroups, *homogeneity*.

The terminology is summarized in Table 4.1.

Term	Definition
subgroup	A "sample" of a number of homogeneous pieces — for data over time a subgroup is usually a small number of consecutive pieces
k	Total number of subgroups
n	Number of pieces in each subgroup
X	Measurement on one individual piece
$\overline{X}$	Subgroup mean
R	Subgroup range
$\overline{\overline{X}}$	Mean of all the subgroup means
$\overline{R}$	Mean of all the subgroup ranges
UCL	Upper control limit
LCL	Lower control limit

Table 4.1 Terminology for $\overline{X}$ and R Charts

The steps for constructing an $\overline{X}$ and R chart for time-ordered data are listed here and illustrated in Example 4.1.

Procedure for Constructing $\overline{X}$ and R Charts for Time-Ordered Data

Step 1 At least 25 subgroups of readings are taken.

Step 2 From each subgroup, calculate $\overline{X}$ and R.

Step 3 Find the center line for each chart, the mean of all the $\overline{X}$ values to obtain $\overline{\overline{X}}$, and the mean of all the R values to obtain $\overline{R}$.

Step 4 Calculate the control limits for the charts. (Note these are 3-sigma limits, a concept to be discussed later.)

For the $\overline{X}$ chart:
$$\text{UCL } (\overline{X}) = \overline{\overline{X}} + [A_2\overline{R}]$$
$$\text{LCL } (\overline{X}) = \overline{\overline{X}} - [A_2\overline{R}]$$

For the R chart:
$$\text{UCL } (R) = D_4\overline{R}$$
$$\text{LCL } (R) = D_3\overline{R}$$

Note: For most circumstances, LCL (R) = 0, which is true when the subgroup size, n, is not larger than 6. Values of A_2, D_3, and D_4 are found in Appendix A for a given value of n.

Step 5 Plot the center lines and control limits. Put appropriate scales on the chart for the $\overline{X}$ values (called an $\overline{X}$ chart) and on the chart for the R values (called an R chart). Collectively the pair of charts is called an $\overline{X}$ and R chart. Draw lines to denote the center lines, $\overline{\overline{X}}$ and $\overline{R}$. Also draw lines to denote the upper control limits (UCLs) and the lower control limits (LCLs). Label these lines with the appropriate values to make reading the chart easier.

Step 6 Plot the $\overline{X}$ and R values from each subgroup. The $\overline{X}$ values and R values are usually connected by lines to make the visual display of the data more clear. All points out of control (outside the control limits) should be clearly marked to point them out immediately to the viewer.

Example 4.1

Lengths of a piston rod have been recorded as coded data in thousandths of an inch in excess of 8 inches with subgroups of size n = 3. The number of subgroups for this small example is k = 4. The data are given in Table 4.2

		Time			
		8:00 am	9:00	10:00	11:00
Reading	1	39	29	37	30
	2	31	34	22	30
	3	28	44	37	30

Table 4.2 Data for an $\overline{X}$ and R Chart

Using the steps previously mentioned, we will make an $\overline{X}$ and R chart for ongoing process control using the data in Table 4.2.

Step 1 At least 25 subgroups of readings should be taken. From the data in Table 4.2, we have:
k = 4 subgroups
n = 3

Note: This example contains too few subgroups. This is done solely to ease the arithmetic calculations for learning purposes.

Step 2 From each subgroup, calculate $\overline{X}$ and R.

		Time			
		8:00 am	9:00	10:00	11:00
Reading	1	39	29	37	30
	2	31	34	22	30
	3	28	44	37	30
$\overline{X}$		32.7	35.7	32	30
R		11	15	15	0

Step 3 Find the center lines for each chart, the mean of all the $\overline{X}$ values to obtain $\overline{\overline{X}}$, and the mean of all the R values to obtain $\overline{R}$.

$$\overline{\overline{X}} = \frac{\Sigma \overline{X}}{k} = \frac{32.7 + 35.7 + 32 + 30}{4} = \frac{130.4}{4} = 32.6$$

$$\overline{R} = \frac{\Sigma R}{k} = \frac{11 + 15 + 15 + 0}{4} = \frac{41}{4} = 10.25$$

Step 4 Calculate the control limits for the charts. A_2 and D_4 are found in Appendix A for a given value of n.
For $n = 3$, $A_2 = 1.02$, $D_4 = 2.58$

For the $\overline{X}$ chart:

$$
\begin{aligned}
\text{UCL } (\overline{X}) = \overline{\overline{X}} + [A_2\overline{R}] &= 32.6 + [(1.02)\,(10.25)] \\
&= 32.6 + 10.5 \\
&= 43.1 \\
\text{LCL } (\overline{X}) = \overline{\overline{X}} - [A_2\overline{R}] &= 32.6 - 10.5 \\
&= 22.1
\end{aligned}
$$

For the R chart:

$$
\begin{aligned}
\text{UCL } (R) = D_4\overline{R} \quad &= (2.58)\,(10.25) \\
&= 26.4 \\
\text{LCL } (R) = 0 \quad &\text{(since the subgroup size } n = 3 \text{ is} \\
&\text{not larger than 6)}
\end{aligned}
$$

Step 5 Plot the center lines and control limits. Put appropriate scales on the chart for the $\overline{X}$ values (called an $\overline{X}$ chart) and on the chart for the R values (called an R chart). Collectively the pair of charts is called an $\overline{X}$ and R chart. Draw lines to denote the center lines, $\overline{\overline{X}}$ and $\overline{R}$ and also to denote the UCLs and LCLs. Label these lines with the appropriate values to ease reading of the chart (Figure 4.1).

Step 6 Plot the points. Plot the $\overline{X}$ and R from each subgroup. The $\overline{X}$ values and R values are usually connected by lines to help the visual display of the data. All points out of control (outside the control limits) should be clearly marked to point them out immediately to the viewer.

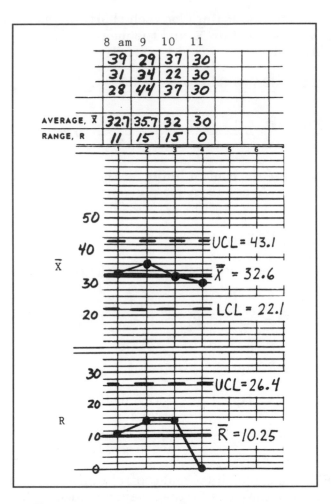

Figure 4.1 $\overline{X}$ and R Chart for Subgroups of Three Consecutive Pieces Taken Each Hour

The $\overline{X}$ control chart takes advantage of the Central Limit Theorem as discussed in Part II. For ongoing process control, many subgroups are taken, and the $\overline{X}$ and R values are computed for each subgroup. Then:

1. $\overline{\overline{X}}$ = mean of the $\overline{X}$ values = best estimate for the process mean.

2. The $\overline{X}$ values will be approximately normally distributed. Hence almost all of them will fall within 3 standard deviations of the mean from $\overline{\overline{X}}$. The UCL will be 3 standard deviations of the means above $\overline{\overline{X}}$; the LCL will be 3 standard deviations of the mean below $\overline{\overline{X}}$. These limits are then referred to as 3-sigma limits or 3σ limits.

The R values from subgroups of constant size taken from a normal distribution are *not* normally distributed, but instead are severely skewed (not symmetrically distributed). Following Shewhart, we use 3-sigma limits on the ranges anyway, with excellent results.

It is noted here, and will be discussed in detail later, that the estimates of sigma used for the 3-sigma limits on *all* control charts are estimated from only the within-subgroup variability (R is this case).

As noted earlier, the purpose of the control chart is to discover evidence of lack of statistical control (uniformity). This evidence may come from points outside of the control limits or from *nonrandom patterns* (which will be discussed in more detail in Chapter 13). Technically, the R chart should be investigated first for evidence of lack of control. If the variability within a subgroup cannot be held in control, there is really no way we can say that variability between subgroups can be held in control.

In Example 4.1 all the points fell within the control limits and no nonrandom patterns appear to be present. In a real case we would be working with k = 25 subgroups. The results from the small amount of data in this example are, at best, inconclusive.

Given no evidence of lack of statistical uniformity (control) there are three possible conclusions we may draw:

1. There is not yet enough data to display the real lack of statistical uniformity.
2. The data have not been properly subgrouped to display the real lack of statistical uniformity (more about this later).
3. The process is in a state of statistical uniformity (control).

For our first look at a process, only the first two conclusions are usually correct. Processes that are just beginning to be monitored are almost never in control. They must be worked on, and detrimental assignable causes identified and eliminated one-by-one. If they appear to be in control at the first look, it is sometimes because we have too little data, but much more often because we fail to consider alternate methods of subgrouping the data, as will be seen in Chapter 11.

For expediency here, let us *act* as if we thought the process was truly in a state of statistical uniformity, that is, the process is in a *state of statistical control* or simply is *in control*. That implies that only common causes of variation are in effect. If a point fell out of either the $\overline{X}$ or R chart, we would say it was *out of control* and look for the assignable cause that affected the process.

Note also that the reading of 44 does not fall within the control limits. It will usually be the case that individual values fall outside of the $\overline{X}$ control limits, even when the process is in statistical control. The limits for $\overline{X}$ only describe the variability of the $\overline{X}$ values. Individuals have *more* spread than averages, so we expect individuals to fall outside the control limits. We will calculate the estimate of the spread of the individual values in Part V.

The difference between the relatively small natural variation of the $\overline{X}$ values and the relatively large natural variation of the X values causes a *tremendous* amount of confusion among the users of control charts. Control charts for individuals discussed in Part V will avoid this confusion.

PROBLEMS

4.1 Given the following data, make an $\overline{X}$ and R chart. Subgroups are four consecutive pieces taken each half hour.
Is there any evidence of lack of statistical conformity?
Caution: Note that this is only an exercise for practicing procedures. In a real case, much more data should be used. As a rule of thumb, either k or n should be at least 25 whenever this is possible.

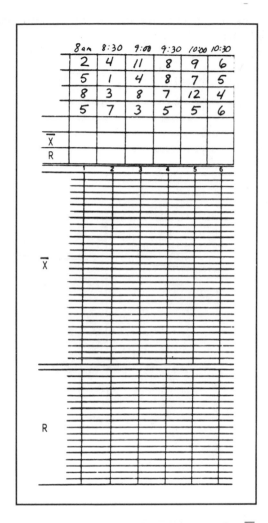

	8 am	8:30	9:00	9:30	10:00	10:30
	2	4	11	8	9	6
	5	1	4	8	7	5
	8	3	8	7	12	4
	5	7	3	5	5	6
$\overline{X}$						
R						

4.2 Using the following eight subgroups, make $\overline{X}$ and R charts. Caution: k should be 25 subgroups or more for a real case.

Time	8:00 am	9:00	10:00	11:00	12:00	1:00	2:00	3:00 pm
	10	9	7	8	4	8	7	3
	8	7	3	9	6	9	2	6
	6	8	15	11	5	8	7	8

Is there any evidence of lack of control? Designate any points out of the control limits.

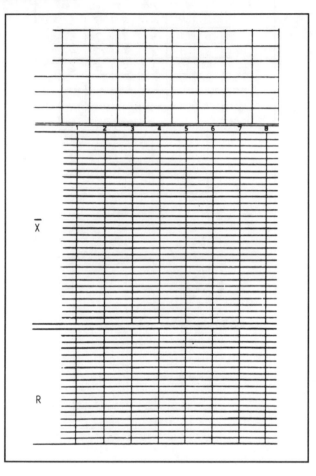

4.3 For the following data, make an $\overline{X}$ and R chart. Is there any evidence of lack of control?
Caution: k should be 25 subgroups or more for a real case.

Time	9:00 am	10:00	11:20	12:15	1:10 pm
	2	0	0	6	1
	−8	2	−1	0	12
	−12	2	8	10	3
	−6	1	4	−4	10

4.4 For the following data, make an $\overline{X}$ and R chart. Is there any evidence of lack of control?
Caution: k should be 25 subgroups or more for a real case.

Time	9:15 am	10:10	11:00	12:30	1:15 pm
	−5	−4	−5	11	−2
	−6	12	3	9	1
	−1	−2	−6	11	7
	−3	−3	4	17	4

4.5 For the following data, make an $\overline{X}$ and R chart. Is there any evidence of lack of control?

Subgroup Number			Readings		
1	27	20	19	18	23
2	9	24	17	28	16
3	14	18	26	28	23
4	31	19	25	24	23
5	20	17	20	16	23
6	21	22	18	13	12
7	22	24	21	19	18
8	27	29	26	20	23
9	21	20	17	18	17
10	17	20	20	23	24
11	24	21	14	18	24
12	23	19	18	21	19
13	27	23	16	18	22
14	26	30	15	27	23
15	23	18	30	16	25
16	22	19	21	18	18
17	20	17	26	20	8
18	21	26	32	15	21
19	15	29	9	24	15
20	17	30	26	20	17
21	16	25	20	15	19
22	27	25	19	17	21
23	23	20	28	27	15
24	18	20	21	16	15
25	20	19	19	22	13

4.6 For the following data, make an $\overline{X}$ and R chart. Is there any evidence of lack of control?

Date	Time	Subgroup Number	Readings			
Mon	8:00	1	19	11	18	13
	9:00	2	15	15	19	15
	10:00	3	16	15	15	16
	11:00	4	6	9	12	16
	12:00	5	12	12	16	14
	1:00	6	19	21	13	11
	2:00	7	12	12	14	16
	3:00	8	20	12	13	17
	4:00	9	11	15	17	17
	5:00	10	18	10	11	14
Tues						
	8:00	11	17	15	16	20
	9:00	12	19	12	15	16
	10:00	13	25	13	19	6
	11:00	14	16	15	10	11
	12:00	15	22	7	19	10
	1:00	16	16	9	14	9
	2:00	17	13	10	14	16
	3:00	18	9	13	16	14
	4:00	19	16	11	11	22
	5:00	20	17	13	11	17
Wed						
	8:00	21	19	11	14	11
	9:00	22	13	11	16	22
	10:00	23	14	11	16	15
	11:00	24	16	15	19	17
	12:00	25	11	16	16	12

The $\tilde{X}$ and R (Median and Range) Chart*

The $\tilde{X}$ and R chart is popular because it is easy to use. The terminology for the $\tilde{X}$ and R chart is the same as for the $\overline{X}$ and R chart (Table 4.1) with two exceptions:

$\tilde{X}$ subgroup median is used instead of $\overline{X}$

$\overline{\tilde{X}}$ mean of all subgroup medians is used instead of $\overline{\overline{X}}$

The steps for construction are similar to those for making an $\overline{X}$ and R chart, with a few exceptions (these are indicated).

The requirement of at least 25 subgroups for ongoing process control is even more important with the median chart than with the $\overline{X}$ chart because $\tilde{X}$ is statistically less efficient.

Example 4.2

Using the same data as in Example 4.1, construct an $\tilde{X}$ and R chart. Recall that we would not use so few subgroups in a real case. This example is only to illustrate the computational procedures.

Step 1 Collect the data (same as before).

Note here: n = 3 = number in each subgroup
k = 4 = number of subgroups

Step 2 From each subgroup, calculate $\boxed{\tilde{X}}$ and R. Subgroups are three consecutive pieces taken each hour.

---

*Used by permission of *Quality*. Adapted from "Simpler Than X-Bar and R." *Quality* (June 1987): 66-67.

		Time			
		8:00 am	9:00	10:00	11:00
Reading	1	39	29	37	30
	2	31	34	22	30
	3	28	44	37	30
$\widetilde{X}$		31	34	37	30
R		11	15	15	0

Note: Sometimes the median is simply circled. When working with subgroups of size n = 3, the uncircled numbers are then the high and low readings. The range is easily calculated as the difference in the two uncircled numbers. These simplified computational procedures are the great advantage of the $\widetilde{X}$ and R chart.

Step 3 Find the center lines: the mean of all the $\boxed{\widetilde{X}}$ values to obtain $\boxed{\overline{\widetilde{X}}}$, and the mean of all the R values to obtain $\overline{R}$.

$$\overline{\widetilde{X}} = \frac{\Sigma \widetilde{X}}{k} = \frac{31 + 34 + 37 + 30}{4} = \frac{132}{4} = 33$$

$$\overline{R} = \frac{\Sigma R}{k} = \frac{11 + 15 + 15 + 0}{4} = \frac{41}{4} = 10.25$$

Step 4 Calculate the 3-sigma control limits for the charts. $\boxed{\widetilde{A}_2}$ and D_4 are found in Appendix A for a given value of n.

Note: D_4 is the same for the $\widetilde{X}$ and R chart as for the $\overline{X}$ and R chart which has the same subgroup size, n.

For n = 3: $\widetilde{A}_2 = 1.19$
$D_4 = 2.58$, as before

For the $\widetilde{X}$ chart:

UCL ($\widetilde{X}$) = $\boxed{\overline{\widetilde{X}}}$ + [$\boxed{\widetilde{A}_2}$ $\overline{R}$] = 33 + [(1.19) (10.25)]
$\phantom{UCL (\widetilde{X}) = \boxed{\overline{\widetilde{X}}} + [\boxed{\widetilde{A}_2} \overline{R}] }$ = 33 + 12.2
$\phantom{UCL (\widetilde{X}) = \boxed{\overline{\widetilde{X}}} + [\boxed{\widetilde{A}_2} \overline{R}] }$ = 45.2
LCL ($\widetilde{X}$) = $\boxed{\overline{\widetilde{X}}}$ − [$\boxed{\widetilde{A}_2}$ $\overline{R}$] = 33 − 12.2
$\phantom{LCL (\widetilde{X}) = \boxed{\overline{\widetilde{X}}} − [\boxed{\widetilde{A}_2} \overline{R}] }$ = 20.8

For the R chart:

$$\text{UCL (R)} = D_4\overline{R}$$

= (2.58) (10.25)
= 26.4, as before

$$\text{LCL (R)} = 0$$

as before (since $D_3 = 0$ for n <7)

Step 5 Plot the center lines and control limits. Put appropriate scales on the chart for the $\overline{X}$ values (called an $\overline{X}$ chart) and on the chart for the R values (called an R chart). Collectively the pair of charts is called an $\overline{X}$ and R chart. Draw lines to denote the center lines, $\widetilde{\overline{X}}$ and $\overline{R}$ and also to denote the control limits. Label these lines with the appropriate values to ease reading of the chart (Figure 4.2)

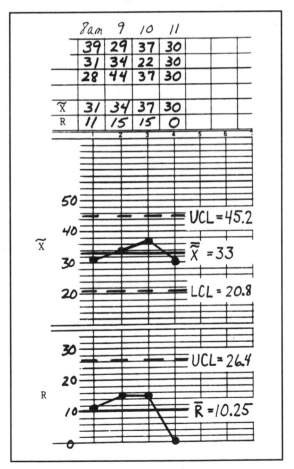

Figure 4.2 $\widetilde{X}$ and R Chart

Step 6 Plot the points. Plot the $\widetilde{X}$ and R from each subgroup. The X values and R values are usually connected by lines to help the visual display of the data. All points out of control (outside the control limits) should be clearly marked to point them out immediately to the viewer (Figure 4.2)

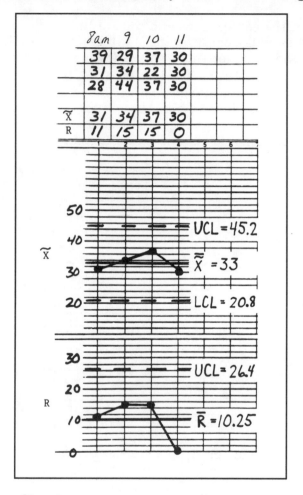

Figure 4.2 $\widetilde{X}$ and R Chart

Note that the process shows no evidence of lack of control, which leaves us with the same three possible conclusions as discussed earlier.

PROBLEMS

4.7 Prepare a median and range chart for the following k = 6 subgroups of n = 3. Plot. Which subgroups, if any, show evidence of lack of control?

Caution: For a real case, k should be at least 25 subgroups.

Time	7:30 am	8:00	8:30	9:00	9:30	10:00
	7	8	11	15	10	7
	9	10	9	12	8	6
	8	8	13	15	6	7

4.8 Given the following data, make an $\tilde{X}$ and R chart. Is there evidence of lack of statistical uniformity?
Caution: For a real case, k should be at least 25 subgroups.

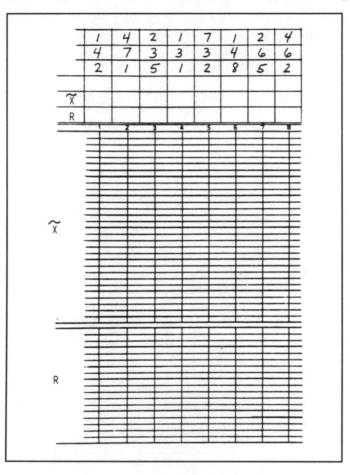

	1	4	2	1	7	1	2	4
	4	7	3	3	3	4	6	6
	2	1	5	1	2	8	5	2

4.9 Given the following data, make an $\tilde{X}$ and R chart. Is there evidence of lack of control?
Caution: For a real case, k should be at least 25 subgroups.

Time	7:00 am	8:00	9:00	10:00	11:00
	17	28	16	14	18
	16	18	22	26	30
	21	16	15	20	19
	15	22	26	21	15
	13	24	22	23	21

94

4.10 Given the following data, make an $\widetilde{X}$ and R chart. Is there evidence of lack of control?

Caution: For a real case, k should be at least 25 subgroups.

Time	8:15 am	9:10	9:55	10:45	12:00 pm
	5	0	−4	2	8
	10	0	1	3	−8
	−3	4	−4	5	−1

4.11 Given the following data, make an $\widetilde{X}$ and R chart. Is there evidence of lack of control?

Subgroup Number	Readings		
1	16	15	13
2	18	15	20
3	17	12	10
4	15	12	16
5	12	16	13
6	16	14	17
7	17	15	14
8	16	14	17
9	17	13	13
10	13	13	11
11	14	17	17
12	15	16	10
13	14	15	15
14	21	13	19
15	13	15	18
16	16	8	7
17	16	12	17
18	13	13	15
19	17	14	17
20	11	11	16
21	20	14	13
22	16	13	13
23	11	16	8
24	10	13	17
25	2	14	28

4.12 Given the following data, make an $\tilde{X}$ and R chart. Is there evidence of lack of control?

Subgroup Number	Readings		
1	23	11	9
2	13	21	23
3	19	18	15
4	12	15	11
5	18	16	17
6	13	8	7
7	17	19	16
8	14	13	22
9	24	21	15
10	18	16	15
11	12	13	12
12	12	15	15
13	18	19	19
14	16	9	13
15	19	18	14
16	13	16	14
17	22	18	11
18	13	17	21
19	25	10	22
20	18	18	13
21	25	11	20
22	17	14	16
23	13	13	15
24	12	21	15
25	3	16	21

For the following problems (4.13 to 4.16), complete the control chart as indicated. Solutions are on page 101.

PART IV. THE CONTROL CHART FOR VARIABLES DATA

VARIABLES CONTROL CHART (X̄ & R)

	CHART NO.
PART NO. A527	4.13

SPECIFICATION LIMITS: 10 – 40 (CODED)
ZERO EQUALS 1.400"

PART NAME (PRODUCT): HARNESS CLAMP (LENGTH)
OPERATION (PROCESS): INJECTION MOLD
OPERATOR: SMITH
MACHINE: A127
GAGE: DIAL CALIPER
UNIT OF MEASURE: .001"

DATE	5-4-87		5-5	5-6-87		5-7-87					5-8-87					5-11-87						5-12-87		
TIME	10:00	11:15	8:15	1:00	3:15	7:10	8:40	10:00	11:30	1:45	2:30	3:30	11:15	12:30	12:45	7:30	8:15	9:00	9:30	10:00	10:45	11:30	1:30	2:30
SAMPLE MEASUREMENTS 1	30	32	30	21	26	23	23	24	27	18	24	25	22	22	22	26	27	36	26	30	30	26	30	24
2	30	34	24	24	32	24	18	31	25	22	16	28	22	28	28	20	19	36	26	26	22	22	24	24
3	30	34	31	22	22	24	23	28	25	18	22	30	26	25	24	24	24	28	28	24	26	28	28	26
4	28	30	25	23	22	24	24	24	23	24	26	26	20	26	24	22	26	30	24	26	26	28	26	24
5	28	26	30	22	23	28	22	24	24	18	20	25	24	20	24	24	22	28	24	28	30	30	24	28
SUM																								
AVERAGE, X̄	29.2	33.2	28	22.4	24.6	24.6	22	26.4	25.2	20	21.6	25.8	22.8	22.8	24.8	24	22.8	31.6	25.6					
RANGE, R	2	6	7	3	6	10	5	6	4	6	10	3	6	6	6	6	8	8	4					
NOTES																								

AVERAGES

RANGES

(Problem 4.13)

97

VARIABLES CONTROL CHART (X̄ & R)

PART NAME (PRODUCT)	OPERATION (PROCESS)	PART NO.	CHART NO.
HARNESS CLAMP (LENGTH)	INJECTION MOLD	A527	4.14

OPERATOR	MACHINE	GAGE	SPECIFICATION LIMITS	UNIT OF MEASURE	ZERO EQUALS
SMITH	A127	DIAL CALIPER	10 – 40 (CODED)	.001"	1.400"

DATE	5-4-87		5-5	5-6-87		5-7-87						5-8-87				5-11-87							5-12-87		
TIME	10:00	11:15	8:15	1:00	3:15	7:10	8:40	10:00	11:30	1:45	2:30	3:30	11:05	11:30	12:45	7:30	8:05	8:30	9:00	9:30	10:00	10:05	11:30	1:30	2:30
1	30	30	32	30	21	26	23	23	24	27	18	24	24	25	22	22	26	27	36	26	29	30	26	30	24
2	30	26	34	24	24	32	18	18	31	25	22	16	28	28	22	28	20	19	36	28	26	26	22	24	24
3	26	24	34	31	22	22	24	23	28	25	18	22	30	25	26	24	26	24	28	24	28	28	24	28	26
4	28	24	30	25	23	22	24	24	25	23	24	26	26	30	20	22	26	22	30	22	24	26	26	24	24
5	28	26	36	30	22	23	28	22	24	26	18	20	30	25	24	24	26	22	28	28	24	28	30	24	28

SUM

AVERAGE, X̄

RANGE, R

NOTES

X̄ (AVERAGES)

(RANGES)

(Problem 4.14)

PART IV. THE CONTROL CHART FOR VARIABLES DATA

VARIABLES CONTROL CHART (X̄ & R)

PART NAME (PRODUCT)	OPERATION (PROCESS)		PART NO.	CHART NO.
HARNESS CLAMP (LENGTH)	INJECTION MOLD		A527	4/5

OPERATOR: SMITH   MACHINE: A127   GAGE: DIAL CALIPER

SPECIFICATION LIMITS: 10 – 40 (CODED)
ZERO EQUALS: 1.400"
UNIT OF MEASURE: .001"

DATE	5-4-87		5-5	5-6-87		5-7-87							5-8-87			5-11-87						5-12-87			
TIME	10:00	11:15	8:15	1:00	3:15	7:10	8:40	10:00	11:30	1:45	2:30	3:30	11:15	12:30	12:45	7:30	8:15	8:30	9:00	9:30	10:00	10:45	11:30	1:30	2:30
1	30	30	32	30	21	26	23	24	27	18	24	25	22	22	26	27	30	30	26	30	24				
2	26	34	24	32	22	18	31	25	16	26	28	22	28	26	19	36	26	22	22	24	24				
3	30	34	31	24	22	23	28	25	22	30	25	26	24	24	28	28	24	26	28	28	26				
4																									
5																									

SUM

AVERAGE, X̄

RANGE, R

NOTES

X̄   AVERAGES

RANGES

(Problem 4.15)

VARIABLES CONTROL CHART (X̄ & R)

PART NAME (PRODUCT)	OPERATION (PROCESS)	PART NO.	CHART NO.
HARNESS CLAMP (LENGTH)	INJECTION MOLD	A527	4.16

OPERATOR	MACHINE	GAGE	UNIT OF MEASURE	SPECIFICATION LIMITS	ZERO EQUALS
SMITH	A127	DIAL CALIPER	.001"	10 - 40 (CODED)	1.400"

DATE	5-4-87		5-5		5-6-87		5-7-87			5-8-87					5-11-87									5-12-87	
TIME	10:00	11:15	8:15	1:00	3:15	7:10	8:40	10:00	11:30	1:45	2:30	3:30	11:15	12:30	12:45	7:30	8:15	8:30	9:00	9:30	10:00	10:45	11:30	1:30	2:30
1	30	32	30	21	26	23	23	24	27	18	24	16	26	28	22	22	26	27	36	28	30	26	30	24	
2	30	26	34	24	24	32	24	18	31	25	22	16	26	28	22	28	26	20	36	26	30	22	24	24	
3																									
4																									
5																									

SAMPLE MEASUREMENTS

ΣΜ / AVERAGE, X̄ / RANGE, R / NOTES

AVERAGES

RANGES

(Problem 4.16)

100

Solutions for Harness Clamp Charts

4.13 $\overline{X}$ & R, n = 5: $\overline{\overline{X}}$ = 25.7
$\overline{R}$ = 5.8

$\overline{X}$: UCL = 29.1   R: UCL = 12.2
LCL = 22.3   LCL = 0

4.14 $\widetilde{X}$ & $\overline{R}$, n = 5: $\overline{\widetilde{X}}$ = 25.5
$\overline{R}$ = 5.8

$\widetilde{X}$: UCL = 29.5   R: UCL = 12.2
LCL = 21.5   LCL = 0

4.15 $\widetilde{X}$ & R, n = 3: $\overline{\widetilde{X}}$ = 25.9
$\overline{R}$ = 4.7

$\widetilde{X}$: UCL = 31.5   R: UCL = 12.1
LCL = 20.3   LCL = 0

4.16 $\overline{X}$ & R, n = 2: $\overline{\overline{X}}$ = 25.7
$\overline{R}$ = 3.56

$\overline{X}$: UCL = 32.4   R: UCL = 11.6
LCL = 19.0   LCL = 0

Note that here for n = 5, the $\overline{X}$ chart and the $\widetilde{X}$ chart each find six points out of control. The mean is statistically more efficient than the median. However, the $\widetilde{X}$ chart is often favored because $\widetilde{X}$ is much easier to calculate, so operators may be more likely to do the job well. It then becomes easier for the operator to post a chart at the operation and find points out of control in real time. This gives a better chance of finding the assignable causes and eliminating them.

The $\overline{X}$ and s
(Mean and Standard Deviation) Chart

The mathematically strongest chart is the $\overline{X}$ and s. The steps for construction are also similar to those for making an $\overline{X}$ and R chart, with the following few exceptions:

$$\text{UCL } (\overline{X}) = \overline{\overline{X}} + A_3 \overline{s}$$
$$\text{LCL } (\overline{X}) = \overline{\overline{X}} - A_3 \overline{s}$$

$$\text{UCL } (s) = B_4 \overline{s}$$
$$\text{LCL } (s) = B_3 \overline{s}$$

The factors A_3, B_3, and B_4 are found in Appendix A for a given value of n. For n larger than 20, the formulas at the bottom of the table are used to compute the factors. Note from Appendix A that for large subgroup sizes, A_3 exists but A_2 and $\tilde{A}_2$ do not, since the range is not a good estimator of spread for large subgroups. Hence, for large subgroups of variable data, you must use $\overline{X}$ and s charts. This is important because it is usually essential to form large *rational subgroups* of data (*not* time-ordered) to accomplish needed process improvements. $\overline{X}$ and s charts are almost never used for time-ordered data because for small subgroups the range is a fairly good measure of spread and avoids the lengthy calculations.

The calculations for the s of each subgroup are easily done with a statistical calculator. By hand they are much more work, as illustrated in Example 4.3.

Example 4.3

Repeating the data from examples 4.1 and 4.2, an $\overline{X}$ and s chart will be made.

		Time			
		8:00 am	9:00	10:00	11:00
Reading	1	39	29	37	30
	2	31	34	22	30
	3	28	44	37	30
$\overline{X}$		32.7	35.7	32	30
s		5.69	7.64	8.66	0

Note here: n = 3 = number in each subgroup
k = 4 = number of subgroups

$$\overline{\overline{X}} = \frac{\Sigma\overline{X}}{k} = \frac{32.7 + 35.7 + 32 + 30}{4} = \frac{130.4}{4} = 32.6$$

$$\overline{s} = \frac{\Sigma s}{k} = \frac{5.69 + 7.64 + 8.66 + 0}{4} = \frac{21.99}{4} = 5.5$$

The calculations of the control limits become:

$$\text{UCL }(\overline{X}) = \overline{\overline{X}} + [A_3\overline{s}] = 32.6 + [(1.95)\,(5.5)]$$
$$= 32.6 + 10.7$$
$$= 43.3$$

$$\text{LCL }(\overline{X}) = \overline{\overline{X}} - [A_3\overline{s}] = 32.6 - 10.7$$
$$= 21.9$$

$$\text{UCL }(s) = B_4\overline{s} \qquad = (2.57)\,(5.5)$$
$$= 14.1$$

$$\text{LCL }(s) = B_3\overline{s} \qquad = 0\,(5.5)$$
$$= 0$$

The chart is illustrated in Figure 4.3.

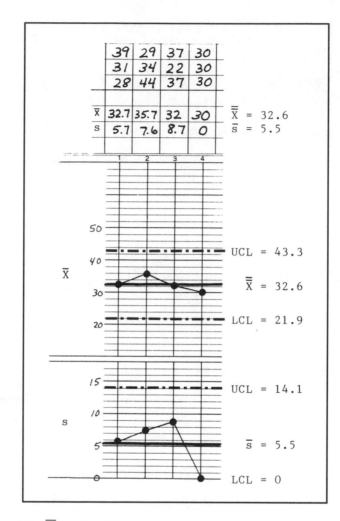

Figure 4.3 $\overline{X}$ and s Chart

PROBLEMS

4.17 For the data in Problem 4.1, make an $\overline{X}$ and s chart.
Caution: For a real case, k should be at least 25 subgroups.

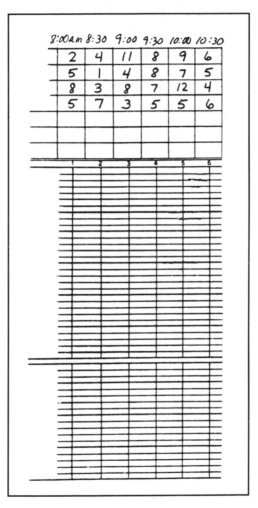

4.18 For the following data, make an $\overline{X}$ and s chart.
   Caution: For a real case, k should be at least 25 subgroups.

Time	8:00 am	9:00	10:00	11:00	12:00 pm
	13	23	26	24	23
	20	13	27	17	17
	15	18	14	32	22

Chapter 11 Subgrouping Data

Note: Subgrouping of data is introduced for convenience here under the study of variables type data. It should be noted that the concepts apply equally well to attribute data.

The most basic concept in science is that of subgrouping elements into homogeneous categories. The ostrich and the orchid are put into separate classifications. If you tried to study the two as a single common group, you would not learn much about either ostriches or orchids. Shewhart pointed out that the success obtained in attempts to improve a process will be directly related to the expert knowledge of how to subgroup the data (i.e., expert knowledge of potential sources of variability in the data).

In a manufacturing process, for example, potentially important sources of variability may be shift-to-shift, inspector-to-inspector, machine-to-machine, operator-to-operator, supplier-to-supplier, heat-to-heat, etc. These potentially important sources of variability are *exactly* the different ways in which subgroups should be formed. Shewhart called these *rational* subgroups, meaning "sensible" ways to subgroup the data. Note that we do not select one subgrouping method or another, but use (in turn) *each* subgrouping method which may be appropriate for the process at hand.

Note that the *sole* requirement for a subgroup is the opinion that the elements within that subgroup will be more alike than all of the elements in general (i.e., you have expert knowledge of the process which leads you to expect that subgroups formed in this way will tend to be homogeneous). Once a particular method of subgrouping has been selected, the question remaining is, "How large should the subgroup's size, n, be? It can easily be shown from the central limit theorem that the answer is "The bigger the better!" Note that we never *want* small subgroups. We want subgroups which are as *large* as possible, subject to the constraint that they must be homogeneous. The reason for using small subgroups for time-ordered data is the need for homogeneity within the subgroup. Since processes can change over time, the only way to get homogeneity over time is with small subgroups. With small subgroups over time, the probability for a change in the process while taking a subgroup will be low.

The discussion of rational subgroups (such as vendor-to-vendor) implies data that have all been collected and are being studied in the past tense.

A control chart of this type is shown in Figure 4.4, an $\overline{X}$ and s chart with n = 500.

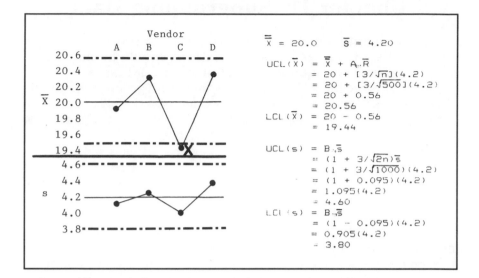

Figure 4.4 X and s Chart of Tensile Strength of Test Specimen by Vendor

We could have used 2-sigma limits in this case following the rule of thumb of using 2-sigma limits wherever the total number of subgroups is 12 or fewer. This will be discussed in Chapter 13.

From Figure 4.4, the s chart tells us that the strengths variability *within* each vendor may well be statistically uniform, but the $\overline{X}$ chart tells us that the average tensile strength of test specimens from Vendor C is so low that it could not reasonably be left to chance. We would then look for an assignable cause. We would also subgroup this same data, or similar data from this same process, in other ways which might be expected to produce homogeneous subgroups. For example: If 10 operators had performed the tests, we might form k = 10 subgroups of size n = 200 to see if there were operator-to-operator differences. If the results had come from five different laboratories, we might look at k = 5 subgroups of size n = 400 to look for an assignable cause due to laboratory-to-laboratory variability.

Shewhart tells us that when we examined data in the *past tense* and have exhausted all reasonable methods of selecting rational subgroups, we should (in desperation or as a default value) look at the individual observations in order of production — in time order of data generation if such a particular time order is present. It was this (perhaps more familiar) use of the control chart that we looked at initially in Chapter 10:

- Variables-type data
- Studied in the past tense
- In order of production
- With $\overline{X}$ and R, $\tilde{X}$ and R, or $\overline{X}$ and s charts

In Chapter 12 we look at the use of control charts on an ongoing basis.

PROBLEMS

4.19 Data on the length of 100 rods were collected from each of three different machines, yielding the following results:

Machine	A	B	C
$\overline{X}$	12.69	12.85	12.89
s	0.21	0.23	0.19

Compare the machines by using an $\overline{X}$ and s chart.

4.20 Data on the length of 200 pins was collected from each of two shifts, with the summarized results listed below. Compare the shifts by using an $\overline{X}$ and s chart.

Shift	1	2
$\overline{X}$	2.52	2.43
s	.14	.11

Chapter 12   Use of the Control Chart

Retrospective versus Ongoing Use of the Control Chart

(No Standard Given versus Standard Given)

There are two uses of the control chart:

1. Retrospective — to find out if the process was in a state of statistical control when the data were gathered (past tense). This was covered in Chapters 10 and 11.

2. Ongoing — to see if the process is staying in control on an ongoing basis (present tense).

We saw that the *retrospective* use of the control chart used the following procedure:

Step 1 Collect the data.
Step 2 Calculate the control limits on the data.
Step 3 Plot the data (from Step 1) against those limits (from Step 2).

The retrospective use of the control chart is used to determine whether or not the process *was* in a state of statistical control at the time the data was gathered, with variations due apparently to pure chance. This use of control charts is often referred to as use of *no standard given*. This terminology is used because the center lines and control limits for these data are calculated from the data; no outside standard is introduced. Most often, processes first being analyzed are not immediately in control. Only action to remove assignable causes can bring the process into control. New control limits are calculated on the recent data. If there is no evidence of lack of statistical uniformity, we will *act* as if we believe the process is in control and the control limits are valid control limits which may be used for the future.

The ongoing use of the control chart typically uses the following procedure:

Step 1 By elimination one by one of assignable causes of variation, bring the process into control over time. Calculate the control limits from these data. (Note this is always a calculation in the past tense, no standard given.)

Step 2 Project these limits out into the future to compare new subgroup data to; the most recently calculated limits are projected out into the future and used as "standard given."

These limits then stay in effect as long as no changes in the process are made and the process still appears to be represented by these limits. If a change in the process is made *or* the process appears to have changed, new limits should again be calculated with no standard given, to be used as standard given for new data in the future.

Example 4.4

Example 4.4 and Figures 4.5 and 4.6 show the use of an $\overline{X}$ and R chart as a two-step charting operation using time-ordered data for ongoing process control.

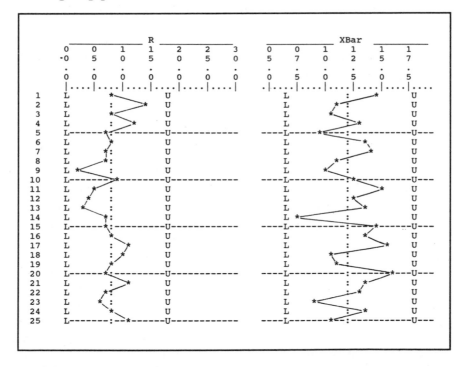

Figure 4.5 Control Chart for the Original Data — No Standard Given

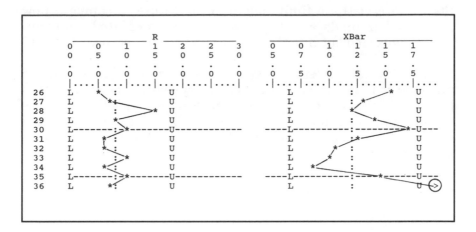

Figure 4.6 Control Chart for the New Data Using Standard Given

1. Find the center lines and control limits on both charts using 25 or more subgroups with no standard given (Figure 4.5). If the charts using these limits show little or no evidence of lack of statistical uniformity, then we may continue. (If the charts show evidence of lack of statistical uniformity, steps must be taken to eliminate the assignable causes or if this is not possible, at least take them into account in the analysis.

2. Using these center lines and limits, as standard given, extend them forward in time to see if the process is still in control (Figure 4.6).

Table 4.3 shows the data for 25 initial subgroups of size n = 4, along with the $\overline{X}$ and R values for each subgroup. In Figure 4.5, the $\overline{\overline{X}}$ and R charts for the initial 25 subgroups with no standard given display no evidence of lack of control so the center lines and limits may be extended into the future. Ten additional subgroups (subgroups 26 to 35) are shown in Table 4.4 and have been plotted in Figure 4.6, using the results from Figure 4.5 as standard given. No evidence of lack of control is seen. As its charting procedure continues, we see that the next subgroup (subgroup 36) falls above the upper control limit on the $\overline{X}$ chart. At this time we should attempt to discover the assignable cause for the point out of control and action should be taken on the process to bring it back into control if this is feasible. If points continued to occur at the next high level, the procedure to find new control limits would be started again.

Subgroup Number		X Values			$\overline{X}$	R
1	16	12	19	11	14.50	8
2	7	8	21	7	10.75	14
3	6	13	8	14	10.25	8
4	14	8	20	10	13.00	12
5	7	11	13	6	9.25	7
6	12	10	14	18	13.50	8
7	12	15	11	18	14.00	7
8	12	8	9	15	11.00	7
9	11	10	9	10	10.00	2
10	11	11	18	9	12.25	9
11	13	18	13	15	14.75	5
12	13	13	10	14	12.50	4
13	12	15	14	12	13.25	3
14	10	7	10	3	7.50	7
15	18	17	12	11	14.50	7
16	11	11	19	13	13.50	8
17	13	17	21	10	15.25	11
18	9	11	6	16	10.50	10
19	12	13	13	5	10.75	8
20	17	11	18	18	16.00	7
21	6	15	17	15	13.25	11
22	13	14	9	16	13.00	7
23	9	12	6	8	8.75	6
24	9	17	15	12	13.25	8
25	5	11	16	10	10.50	11

Table 4.3 Data for Calculation of Control Limits

Subgroup Number		X Values			$\overline{X}$	R
26	16	17	16	12	15.25	5
27	17	10	14	11	13.00	7
28	7	10	22	9	12.00	15
29	18	10	17	11	14.00	8
30	13	17	23	14	16.75	10
31	14	12	15	9	12.50	6
32	13	12	7	10	10.50	6
33	14	15	5	5	9.75	10
34	6	7	12	8	8.25	6
35	16	17	17	7	14.25	10
36	27	21	28	24	25.00	6

Table 4.4 New Data Obtained

Note that once the subgroup size, n, is fixed, the band width between the control limits on *each* chart is determined solely by $\overline{R}$, the average within-subgroup range. When a point on *either* chart falls outside the control limits, we say that there is an assignable cause of variation; the point-to-point (subgroup-to-subgroup) variation is more than might reasonably be explained by the within-subgroup variation.

In evaluating the results of the two charts, we must first examine the R chart. If the R chart is not in control, $\overline{R}$ has no meaning and so the control limits in the $\overline{X}$ chart are not valid. Only after we see no evidence of lack of statistical uniformity on the R chart are we privileged to evaluate the $\overline{X}$ chart. If we find no evidence of lack of control on the $\overline{X}$ chart, we may then use the calculated limits as standard given, extending the center lines and control limits for both charts forward for use in evaluating future observations for ongoing process control.

Note that in Example 4.4 the initial 25 subgroups showed no evidence of lack of control, so we could progress immediately to extending the control limits forward for future use. Unfortunately this is not usually the case. We can usually expect to find evidence of lack of control when we first gather data. Indeed, if we do not, we should be suspicious that we have not subgrouped the data properly.

When lack of control is found in the initial set of subgroups (no standard given), we attempt to find the assignable causes and eliminate them before using our control limits as standard given for the future. If assignable causes can be found for specific indications of lack of control, and if these assignable causes are believed to have had no effect on the other observations, it is possible to simply discard the offending subgroups and recalculate the control limits. However, great restraint should be exercised in throwing out subgroups simply because they are beyond the 3-sigma limits, when no assignable cause can be shown. Although some authorities advocate this practice, it has been the authors' experience that it is not the best practice.

Example 4.5

In Example 4.5, 35 subgroups of size 4 were gathered for time-ordered data in a manufacturing process. The $\overline{X}$ and R values are shown in Table 4.5; and the control chart is displayed in Figure 4.7. It can be seen that the first few R values are out of control, and then they seem to stabilize. This is not at all uncommon. Although called a *learning curve* the phenomenon may be more associated with a *spotlight effect*. The measured data may be unstable until the operator becomes comfortable with the charting activity.

In Figure 4.8, the first five subgroups have been deleted and it is seen that the remaining 30 show no evidence of lack of control. These will then be used as standard given for the data to be gathered in the future. Table 4.6 shows the $\overline{X}$ and R value for 10 additional subgroups. The control chart of Figure 4.9, using results from Figure 4.8 as standard given, continues to show no evidence of lack of statistical uniformity in the process.

Subgroup	$\overline{X}$	R
1	35.75	34
2	44.50	28
3	35.25	25
4	34.25	21
5	39.00	20
6	34.25	13
7	39.25	10
8	36.50	6
9	30.75	4
10	31.50	1
11	33.75	16
12	36.00	14
13	37.00	23
14	33.00	11
15	35.25	6
16	37.25	12
17	36.25	6
18	34.75	3
19	37.25	13
20	34.25	8
21	28.25	17
22	35.50	6
23	31.00	13
24	34.00	7
25	40.00	4
26	35.00	3
27	29.25	9
28	34.75	18
29	34.75	9
30	33.75	18
31	36.00	14
32	30.50	20
33	37.25	10
34	33.00	8
35	35.25	9

Table 4.5 Original Data for Example 4.5

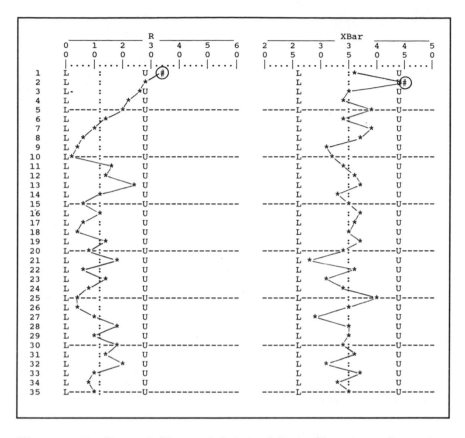

Figure 4.7 Control Chart of Original Data Showing a *Learning Curve*

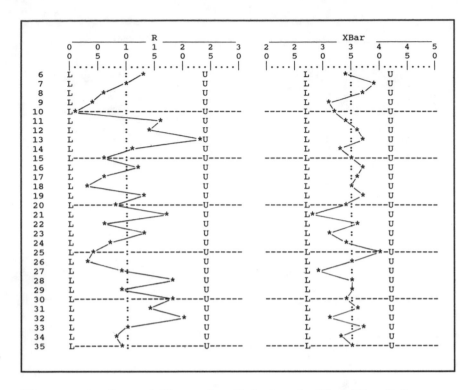

Figure 4.8   Control Chart after Deleting the First Five Subgroups

Subgroup Number	$\overline{X}$	R
36	28.75	12
37	33.75	6
38	41.25	8
39	34.50	5
40	33.75	8
41	33.50	15
42	34.25	12
43	32.25	3
44	33.00	10
45	32.00	20

Table 4.6 $\overline{X}$ and R Values for New Data

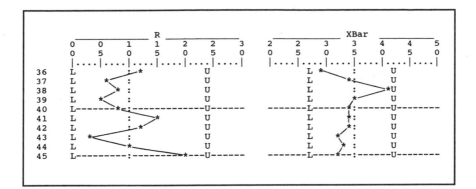

Figure 4.9 Control Chart for Additional Data Using Standard Given

The improvement of a process using a control chart for ongoing control is an iterative procedure: as the process continues, new assignable causes are found and the control limits progressively narrow. This will be illustrated by the following example.

Example 4.6

The control chart in Figure 4.10 is an $\overline{X}$ chart. The R chart which would typically accompany the $\overline{X}$ chart was always in control, and since it was not of interest is not shown here. The example is from a steel forming operation. The dimension being measured is the flange height of a formed U-section.

You will note from Figure 4.10 that the process originally fluctuated wildly. At the circled number 1 the air gauges were adjusted and a straight pilot was replaced in an attempt to stabilize the process. These actions appeared to have little effect. At number 2, a 1/32 inch offset pilot was installed and the air pressure was raised to 30 psi. The process appeared to stabilize somewhat, so after the 42nd subgroup was recorded, the last 20 subgroups were used to set up trial control limits. Note that the process was not yet in control, but these trial limits are projected out into the future to help begin to identify assignable causes. At number 3, a point had just fallen below the lower trial control limit, so an investigation was undertaken. It was discovered that the 1/32 inch offset pilot was cracked below the surface of the die and had been

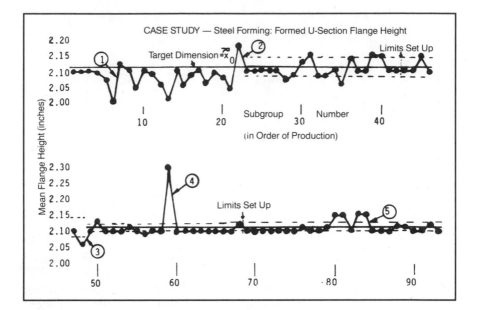

Figure 4.10 Control Chart for Flange Height of a Formed U-Section

contributing to the wild variation in the readings. It was replaced with a 3/64 inch offset pilot. At number 4 a point fell above the upper control limit. An investigation revealed broken bolts which were replaced. After the 68th subgroup was recorded, the process looked stable enough to update control limits. The last 20 subgroups were used, deleting the subgroup with the known assignable cause. At number 5 the process was again giving averages outside the control limits. Investigation revealed the need to regulate the air pressure to 50 psi, and the process returned to its controlled state.

Note how the control limits narrowed with time, reflecting the decrease in the variation of the flange height. Note also how the control limits told the operator when to investigate to find and eliminate assignable causes.

There are other methods of using *standard given*. For instance, sometimes the target value for the quality characteristic is used in place of the value of $\overline{X}$ calculated from the data. The center line on the $\overline{X}$ chart is then symbolized by $\overline{\overline{X}}_0$.

Example 4.7

In Example 4.1, if the target value for the connecting rod is 8.040 inches (40 thousandths of an inch over 8.000 inches), an optional center line for the $\overline{X}$ chart would be $\overline{\overline{X}}_0 = 40$, using the target value as standard given. In this case the control limits would be (using coded data):

$$\text{UCL } (\overline{X}) = \overline{\overline{X}}_0 + A_2\overline{R} = 40 + [(1.02)\,(10.25)]$$
$$= 40 + 10.5$$
$$= 50.5$$

$$\text{LCL } (\overline{X}) = \overline{\overline{X}}_0 - A_2\overline{R} = 40 - 10.5$$
$$= 29.5$$

The use of the target value for $\overline{\overline{X}}_0$ is done in an attempt to force adjustments to bring the process to the target value.

Another use of standard given is to attempt to use limits calculated from one "process" to control another "process." If the attempt is successful (if no evidence of lack of statistical uniformity is found on the second process using the first as "standard given") the two processes may tentatively be considered as one. This concept will be illustrated in Example 4.8.

Example 4.8

The day shift was found to be in control with $\overline{\overline{X}} = 37.1$ and $\overline{R} = 10.0$ using $k = 31$ subgroups of size $n = 3$. The control limits are:

$$\text{UCL } (\overline{X}) = \overline{\overline{X}} + A_2\overline{R} = 37.1 + [(1.02)\,(10.0)]$$
$$= 37.1 + 10.2$$
$$= 47.3$$

$$\text{LCL } (\overline{X}) = \overline{\overline{X}} - A_2\overline{R} = 37.1 - 10.2$$
$$= 26.9$$

$$\text{UCL } (R) = D_4\overline{R} \quad = 2.58\,(10.0)$$
$$= 25.8$$

$$\text{LCL } (R) = D_3\overline{R} \quad = 0$$

The night shift's data were found to be as follows:

		Subgroup			
		1	2	3	4
Reading	1	51	41	48	47
	2	42	52	35	49
	3	43	54	54	44
	$\overline{X}$	45.3	49	45.7	46.7
	R	9	13	19	5

We will first examine the night shift data alone with no standard given. There are not enough subgroups here to do that job satisfactorily. This is meant to be only a short example; in a real situation more data would be used.

Calculations for the control limits for the night shift show:

$$\overline{\overline{X}} = 46.7$$

$$\overline{R} = 11.5$$

$$\text{UCL } (\overline{X}) = \overline{\overline{X}} + [A_2\overline{R}] = 46.7 + [(1.02)(11.5)]$$
$$= 46.7 + 11.7$$
$$= 58.4$$

$$\text{LCL } (\overline{X}) = \overline{\overline{X}} - [A_2\overline{R}] = 46.7 - 11.7$$
$$= 35.0$$

The data from the night shift are plotted against the night shift limits in Figure 4.11. Note that there is no evidence of lack of statistical uniformity, although these results are inconclusive with so little data.

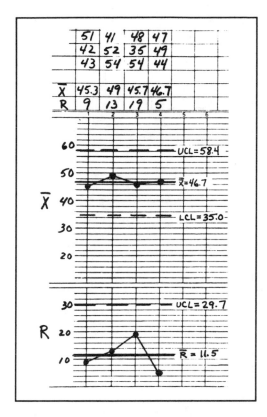

Figure 4.11 Night Shift Data Using No Standard Given

We next look at the night shift data using the day shift results as standard given.

Note that even with this small amount of data, it can be clearly determined that the night shift is out of control on the $\overline{X}$ chart using day shift as standard given (i.e., using the day shift's center lines and control limits) as illustrated in Figure 4.12. The night shift is consistently making pieces with measurements that are greater than those of the day shift.

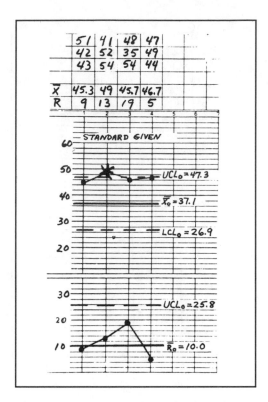

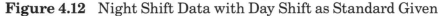

Figure 4.12 Night Shift Data with Day Shift as Standard Given

Two important observations can be made:

1. It is more difficult for a process to be in control with standard given than for it to just be in control (the latter implying no standard given).

2. No inference is drawn here about whether the product of the first shift or that of the second shift is "good or bad." All we know so far is that the reported measurement values could *not* have come from a single process that was common to both shifts. (Perhaps the day shift measurements are in error.)

The results from the control chart must be interpreted with great care. In this example, examination or additional studies would be required to discover the root cause of the reported difference between the two shifts. After removal of this cause, another attempt could be made to treat the day-shift process and the night-shift process as one common process.

Classroom Exercise

Calculate the control limits on the data given on the chart on page 126. Plot the charts. Is the process in control? Project the center lines and the control limits out into the future for use as standard given. Generate new data in class by rolling four dice. Does the process remain in control?

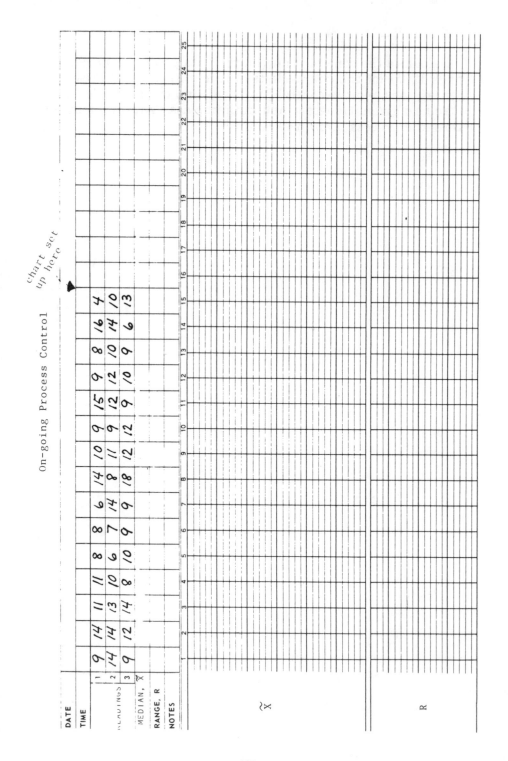

Comparing the
$\overline{X}$ and R, $\tilde{X}$ and R, and $\overline{X}$ and s Charts

The variables control chart was invented for a repetitive manufacturing process making discrete pieces. Consequently, the $\overline{X}$ and R, $\tilde{X}$ and R, and $\overline{X}$ and s charts are used for such a process. Continuous processes, short runs, and other such "different" processes use modifications of such charts and are discussed in Part VIII.

From an historical perspective, Shewhart (1931) invented the control chart for mean and standard deviation. (For calculating the subgroup standard deviation, Shewhart used $\sigma = \sqrt{\Sigma (X - \overline{X})^2/n}$. Modern terminology uses $s = \sqrt{\Sigma (X - \overline{X})^2/(n-1)}$, but the factors for calculating the control limits have been changed accordingly so the charts yield similar results. Since the calculation of standard deviation by hand was so difficult, charts for $\overline{X}$ and R were later developed. Only recently have $\tilde{X}$ and R charts become popular.

From the implementation perspective, the ideal situation is for the operator to maintain his or her own control chart on the process in real time. The operator is the most familiar with the process. If there is a problem with the process, he or she will want to know about it as soon as possible. The operator would be the first to discover when an assignable cause is present. He or she would then, hopefully, be able to take corrective action to eliminate it.

If the operator is keeping the chart, the $\tilde{X}$ and R chart is a likely choice because of its ease of use. Some people opt for the $\overline{X}$ and R chart because it is so popular and the mean is more efficient than the median. (As we will see in Part V, the chart for individuals turns out to be even easier to use and interpret and usually gives even more information on the data since averages often hide information.)

When measurements are difficult or time-consuming, the quality control department may assist the operator by doing the measurements. In that case, or in any other case when analysis may be done using a calculator or computer, an $\overline{X}$ and s chart may be preferred. It is mathematically the strongest chart — the calculations of mean and standard deviation each use *all* the data. With a statistical calculator, s is actually easier to compute than R, since for R one has to pick out the high and low readings manually and then perform a subtraction.

The $\overline{X}$ and s chart is a *necessity* for large subgroups (n > 12) since with large subgroups the range is a poor approximation for standard deviation. Note that n > 12 will almost always be the case when rational subgroups other than time are used and will almost never be the case with time-ordered data.

Regardless which chart is used, remember that the comments on the chart (change in materials, shifts, tools, adjustments, etc.) are at least as important as the readings themselves.

Direct Recording Shop Chart

As mentioned earlier, the $\widetilde{X}$ and R chart is easy to use. The best chart for a process is one tailored to the process so the operator keeping the chart just needs to check off his or her readings and keep notes on this chart that reflect changes in the process or other such comments.

Example 4.9

Suppose control limits for a process are as follows:

UCL $(\widetilde{X})$ = 2.14

LCL $(\widetilde{X})$ = −2.14

UCL (R) = 4.6

LCL (R) = 0

for subgroups of size n = 3. Using these limits projected out into the future, as the readings are taken, they are not recorded with digits, but are instead marked by an X on the pre-prepared chart. The middle number, the median, is circled and compared to the control limits for the medians. The individual readings that are plotted on the chart can be compared to the specification limits which can also be plotted on the chart. (Note that this is *not* true for $\overline{X}$ and R charts. It is only true for this type of $\widetilde{X}$ and R chart since the individuals are plotted and one of the individuals *is* the median.)

To calculate the range of a subgroup, count up from the low reading in the subgroup to the high reading.

The data are as follows and are plotted in Figure 4.13:

		Subgroup					
		1	2	3	4	5	6
Reading	1	2	2	−4	−1	−2	0
	2	−1	2	−1	−1	−5	4
	3	0	0	−2	1	−2	0

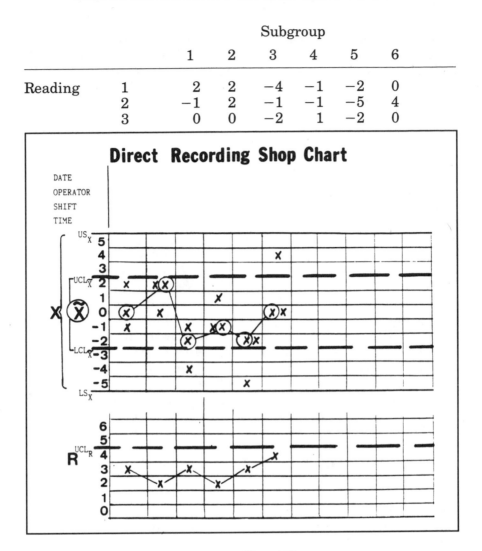

Figure 4.13 Direct Recording Shop Chart

Note that working with negative numbers is easy with an $\tilde{X}$ and R chart. No calculations are needed.

What must be kept straight is that it is the $\tilde{X}$ values (circled) that must fall within the control limits for $\tilde{X}$. The X values may fall outside the control limits for $\tilde{X}$ (individuals have more spread). On this type of chart we can also keep track as to whether the individuals fall within the specification limits since the individual values are also plotted. This is not true for the $\overline{X}$ and R chart.

The $\tilde{X}$ and R chart described above is favored by shop people because of the ease of making the chart. Perhaps the only chart which is better from this point of view is the chart for individuals and ranges of subgroups of size two. Charts for individuals will be discussed in Chapter 17.

What to Chart

A control chart is very demanding. It requires response. If a point falls outside the control limits, someone needs to go to the process, investigate, and act on the assignable cause if at all possible. If the assignable cause is an improvement in the process, an attempt should be made to incorporate this improvement into future practice. If the assignable cause had an undesirable effect, an attempt should be made to eliminate it. Keeping a chart but not taking corrective action when needed degrades the system and causes lack of credibility. It is also a waste of time and effort.

Control charts should only be kept on problem areas (or where required by a customer on a critical quality feature). One's goal in life is *not* to wallpaper the walls with charts. For instance, Bicking and Gryna (1974, p. 23-5) recommend that:

> *Control charts are justified for only a small minority of the quality characteristics.* Furthermore, once they have served their purpose (for problem analysis for breakthrough or control), most should be taken down and the effort shifted to other characteristics needing improvement.

The vast majority of quality features (the trivial many) should be monitored with simple run charts, perhaps adding maintenance limits (see Part VI).

When choosing the quality characteristics to chart, the priorities chosen (in order of importance) are listed as follows:

1. Customer complaints.
2. Quality characteristics that are generating the highest cost of scrap and/or rework.
3. Critical dimensions.
4. Charts the customer wants maintained.

It is best to keep few charts, only those where the resources and commitment are strong.

When first beginning the use of statistical control methods, it is best to start with only one or two problem areas that are meaningful yet do-able. Once the first "home run" is hit, interest in SPC generally spreads and more people become involved. Then more problem solving can be implemented.

PROBLEMS

4.21 For the data in Problem 4.1, calculate control limits using a target value of 6.1 as standard given for $\overline{X}$.

4.22 Using the control limits calculated in Problem 4.1 as standard given from machine A, see if machine B is performing similarly given the following data:

		Subgroup		
		1	2	3
Reading	1	2	11	9
	2	8	3	12
	3	4	8	5
	4	3	5	6

4.23 Recent experience with statistical control has been $\overline{\overline{X}} = 40$ and $\overline{R} = 9$ for subgroups of size 5.
a. Compute control limits for $\overline{X}$ and R charts.
b. Your next two subgroups are:

Subgroup 1	Subgroup 2
26	47
29	39
34	38
32	38
33	55

Using the control limits computed above as standard given, is your process still in control? Plot the graph.

4.24 Case Study: Roller Bearing Failures

Special note to students: The following case study should be considered an essential part of the learning activity. Students are encouraged to study the problem carefully, as they would in the "real world." Afterwards students should complete the assignment in its entirety before reading the solution and discussion. Students should then go back and rework the assignment completely, including the portions displayed in the solution.

The Problem

The rollers of antifriction roller bearings used in a military application have been failing in the field. Failures have been traced to cracks on the outer diameter which occurred during the final grinding operation. Also, high scrap rates occur at inspection after finish grind, due to grinding cracks which were not present after the preceding operation, semifinish grind.

The problem appears to be an excessive amount of variability in diameter from the semifinish grind, which allows too wide a range of stock to be removed during finish grind.

Data

There is only one semifinish grinding machine. Every 12 hours, three successive diameter readings have been taken immediately after semifinish grind. Your 24 lines of data are for 12 consecutive days. The temperature of the rollers is always at ambient when the diameter readings are taken.

Assignment

1. For k = 24 subgroups of n = 3 each, plot median and range charts.
2. Which points, if any, show evidence of lack of control?
3. If there is lack of control, what do you think caused it?
4. Prove it.

ROLLER BEARING DATA

Subgroup	Readings			
1	39	31	28	Roller Bearing Diameters
2	29	34	44	after Semifinish Grind
3	32	34	33	
4	37	45	22	Coded Unit of Measure =
5	36	34	32	.0001″
6	17	23	24	Coded Zero = .6900″
7	25	32	30	
8	50	46	36	
9	33	23	35	
10	23	37	27	
11	29	21	29	
12	50	51	63	
13	37	30	27	
14	34	49	32	
15	30	36	29	
16	41	28	27	
17	25	31	32	
18	40	54	42	
19	32	27	34	
20	40	44	41	
21	30	28	29	
22	52	29	51	
23	40	37	26	
24	24	35	16	

Roller Bearing Data Analysis

PART IV. THE CONTROL CHART FOR VARIABLES DATA

Roller Bearing Data Analysis

Roller Bearing Data Analysis

Roller Bearing Case Study: Solution and Discussion

The problem states that subgroups of observations were taken at 12-hour intervals. This should immediately flag the analyst, warning him or her that the odd numbered subgroups may have been taken by the day shift, and the even numbered subgroups by the night shift. Although such critical information *should* always accompany the data, such is not always the case. Whenever data from potentially different populations are to be plotted on the same chart, it is fundamental that the symbol used for each point clearly identify the population to which that point belongs. In this case, we will flag the second shift with triangles superimposed upon the regular StatScan® median and range chart as shown below.

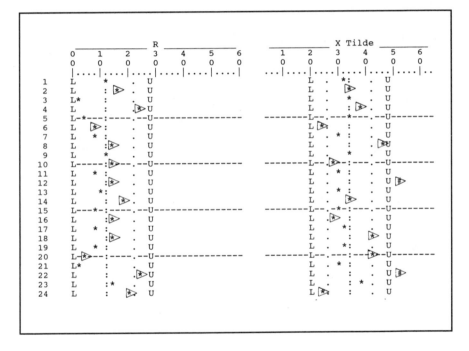

A cursory inspection of the R chart shows that the night shift has higher within-subgroup variability than the day shift. The median chart shows that all of the high points, all of the low points, and all the points out of control were from the second shift. No further analysis is needed. Shift-to-shift variation is clearly an assignable cause. To quote Deming (1951):

Before you sample you must think: Where could there be a source of variability? I suggest you write down the following in your note book, and write it down big: THE CONTROL CHART IS NO SUBSTITUTE FOR THE BRAIN. First of all you must think: Where could there be sources of uncontrolled variability? Then plot the charts so that you discover this variability if it is an uncontrolled one. You must THINK.

Although further statistical analysis is not necessary in detecting shift-to-shift variability as an assignable cause of lack of statistical uniformity, there are further analyses of the data which are of a fundamental nature. These studies should be performed by the student so that he or she may understand the rational steps that are used in problem solving:

1. Make a median and range chart on the 10 subgroups of size 3 that represent the day shift. Is there evidence of lack of statistical uniformity?
2. Do the same for the night shift.
3. Use the shift with the lowest within-subgroup variability as standard given. (Why select this shift? How do we already know that this will be the day shift?) Is the other shift — the night shift — "still" in control? What are these results telling us?
4. As a more general approach to comparing any number of parallel paths, subgroup the data by shift and make an $\overline{X}$ and s chart. (Why are the two shifts parallel paths? How many subgroups will there be? What is the subgroup size?) In practice, we would have used 2-sigma limits on this chart (see Chapter 13). Students should check their own results carefully against the solution following.

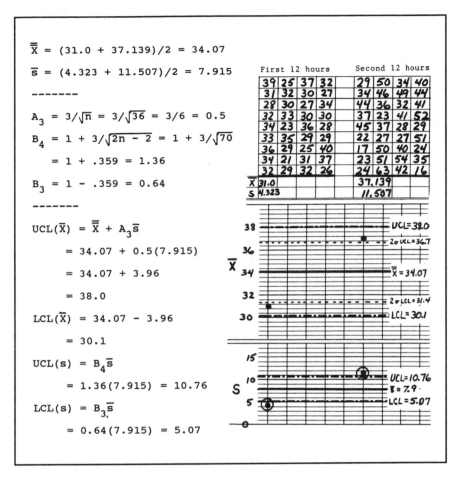

$\bar{\bar{X}} = (31.0 + 37.139)/2 = 34.07$

$\bar{s} = (4.323 + 11.507)/2 = 7.915$

$A_3 = 3/\sqrt{n} = 3/\sqrt{36} = 3/6 = 0.5$

$B_4 = 1 + 3/\sqrt{2n - 2} = 1 + 3/\sqrt{70}$

$\quad = 1 + .359 = 1.36$

$B_3 = 1 - .359 = 0.64$

$UCL(\bar{X}) = \bar{\bar{X}} + A_3\bar{s}$

$\quad = 34.07 + 0.5(7.915)$

$\quad = 34.07 + 3.96$

$\quad = 38.0$

$LCL(\bar{X}) = 34.07 - 3.96$

$\quad = 30.1$

$UCL(s) = B_4\bar{s}$

$\quad = 1.36(7.915) = 10.76$

$LCL(s) = B_3\bar{s}$

$\quad = 0.64(7.915) = 5.07$

First 12 hours / Second 12 hours

39	25	37	32	29	50	34	40
31	32	30	27	34	46	49	44
28	30	27	34	44	36	32	41
32	33	30	30	37	23	41	52
34	23	36	28	45	37	28	29
33	35	29	29	22	27	27	51
36	29	25	40	17	50	40	24
34	21	31	37	23	51	54	35
32	29	32	26	24	63	42	16

X 31.0 — 37.139
s 4.323 — 11.507

4.25 The following data are from four days of production. Each subgroup (SGN) contains data from each of the four days for a specific operator (OP), vendor (V), machine (M), and inspector (I). Is there any evidence of lack of control?

SGN 1	SGN 2	SGN 3	SGN 4	SGN 5
1) 29	1) 21	1) 25	1) 18	1) 33
2) 33	2) 14	2) 23	2) 21	2) 28
3) 24	3) 32	3) 26	3) 17	3) 23
4) 27	4) 15	4) 34	4) 15	4) 17

Subgroup 1) OP=T, V=A, M=W, I=Y
notes: 2) OP=T, V=A, M=W, I=Z
          3) OP=T, V=A, M=X, I=Y
          4) OP=T, V=A, M=X, I=Z
          5) OP=T, V=B, M=W, I=Y

SGN 6	SGN 7	SGN 8	SGN 9	SGN 10
1) 26	1) 28	1) 30	1) 27	1) 27
2) 20	2) 34	2) 19	2) 27	2) 23
3) 23	3) 22	3) 24	3) 29	3) 19
4) 27	4) 26	4) 18	4) 30	4) 24

          6) OP=T, V=B, M=W, I=Z
          7) OP=T, V=B, M=X, I=Y
          8) OP=T, V=B, M=X, I=Z
          9) OP=D, V=A, M=W, I=Y
         10) OP=D, V=A, M=W, I=Z

SGN 11	SGN 12	SGN 13	SGN 14	SGN 15
1) 31	1) 17	1) 34	1) 24	1) 28
2) 23	2) 13	2) 27	2) 19	2) 32
3) 29	3) 17	3) 31	3) 23	3) 31
4) 31	4) 20	4) 23	4) 23	4) 25

         11) OP=D, V=A, M=X, I=Y
         12) OP=D, V=A, M=X, I=Z
         13) OP=D, V=B, M=W, I=Y
         14) OP=D, V=B, M=W, I=Z
         15) OP=D, V=B, M=X, I=Y

SGN 16	SGN 17	SGN 18	SGN 19	SGN 20
1) 17	1) 26	1) 20	1) 37	1) 26
2) 19	2) 40	2) 25	2) 22	2) 24
3) 22	3) 28	3) 19	3) 28	3) 15
4) 16	4) 29	4) 15	4) 21	4) 28

16) OP=D, V=B, M=X, I=Z
17) OP=H, V=A, M=W, I=Y
18) OP=H, V=A, M=W, I=Z
19) OP=H, V=A, M=X, I=Y
20) OP=H, V=A, M=X, I=Z

SGN 21	SGN 22	SGN 23	SGN 24	SGN 25
1) 24	1) 17	1) 25	1) 15	1) 28
2) 35	2) 14	2) 30	2) 16	2) 29
3) 31	3) 19	3) 26	3) 28	3) 26
4) 28	4) 16	4) 30	4) 24	4) 24

21) OP=H, V=B, M=W, i=Y
22) OP=H, V=B, M=W, I=Z
23) OP=H, V=B, M=X, I=Y
24) OP=H, V=B, M=X, I=Z
25) OP=G, V=A, M=W, I=Y

SGN 26	SGN 27	SGN 28	SGN 29	SGN 30
1) 23	1) 25	1) 16	1) 23	1) 29
2) 25	2) 23	2) 22	2) 23	2) 14
3) 17	3) 26	3) 21	3) 35	3) 24
4) 22	4) 23	4) 26	4) 30	4) 14

26) P=G, V=A, M=W, I=Z
27) OP=G, V=A, M=X, I=Y
28) OP=G, V=A, M=X, I=Z
29) OP=G, V=B, M=W, I=Y
30) OP=G, V=B, M=W, I=Z

SGN 31   SGN 32

1)   19   1)   20
2)   27   2)   17
3)   28   3)   23
4)   34   4)   20

                31) OP=G, V=B, M=X, I=Y
                32) OP=G, V=B, M=X, I=Z

4.26 The following data set represents 60 consecutive readings
(reading across) from a process. Analyze it as you see fit.

11	11	10	7	12	21	11	7	7	10
9	16	9	11	9	9	12	15	5	9
7	10	10	15	9	13	12	9	8	17
10	13	9	7	12	19	9	9	11	13
11	16	9	10	8	12	8	19	9	9
11	9	10	14	8	13	11	13	12	18

4.27 The following data set represents 60 consecutive readings
(reading across) from a process. Analyze it as you see fit.

12	15	12	7	8	15	12	8	10	12
8	9	9	8	8	11	7	10	15	10
15	14	13	17	19	19	18	16	12	15
17	18	17	17	16	13	19	13	15	16
14	14	15	17	13	14	20	17	16	19
17	11	19	16	19	16	14	18	19	17

4.28 The following data set represents 60 consecutive readings
(reading across) from a process. Analyze it as you see fit.

8	10	11	10	10	12	13	16	8	12
16	18	18	8	9	8	9	11	11	13
16	19	8	11	15	14	15	18	8	13
12	19	8	12	11	15	16	8	12	13
16	18	8	12	11	11	15	18	8	11
14	14	14	14	17	8	11	14	17	19

4.29 The following 25 subgroups of data are made up of n = 5 readings taken at 8:00 am, 10:00 am, noon, 2:00 pm, and 4:00 pm. Analyze the data.

			Time		
Day	8:00 am	10:00	noon	2:00	4:00 pm
1	40	26	32	31	21
2	32	33	27	34	21
3	35	28	30	28	24
4	39	24	33	31	32
5	30	30	21	22	33
6	37	20	25	24	24
7	39	21	27	34	30
8	34	36	30	24	35
9	44	24	22	24	25
10	33	24	26	29	28
11	33	28	30	30	31
12	36	25	33	35	28
13	34	33	20	30	31
14	39	31	35	26	28
15	42	27	29	29	25
16	36	26	24	25	22
17	40	32	24	30	30
18	31	29	35	23	28
19	46	37	34	22	25
20	39	30	30	32	26
21	33	27	26	28	27
22	39	24	27	24	28
23	32	23	26	31	27
24	32	28	28	23	26
25	33	28	22	23	30

Chapter 13 More on the Control Chart

Criteria for Evidence of Lack of Control

To be in control (i.e., statistically uniform, stable) it is necessary that:
1. There are no points outside the control limits.
2. There are no nonrandom patterns.

In an attempt to help identify nonrandom patterns over time for ongoing process control, criteria for evidence of lack of control have been established. Some criteria are listed below. Some have been taken from Western Electric (1956). Each of these criteria describes a pattern that is unlikely to have happened by pure chance.

Criteria for Evidence of Lack of Statistical Control Over Time (Ongoing)

For Control Charts

1. One point outside of the 3-sigma limit.
2. Two out of 3 successive points above the +2-sigma limit or 2 out of 3 successive points below the −2-sigma limit.
   Note: Some authorities recommend the use of 2 successive points rather than 2 out of 3.
3. Four out of 5 successive points above the +1-sigma limit or 4 out of 5 successive points below the −1-sigma limit.
4. Fifteen successive points within ± 1 sigma.
5. Eight successive points, none within ± 1 sigma.

For Run Charts and Control Charts

6. Eight successive points on one side of the center line.
   Note: This is a *run criterion*. Some authorities recommend seven successive points.
7. Seven successive points constantly ascending or seven successive points constantly descending (regardless of the position of the center line).
8. Number of center line crossings is not within the limits of $k/2 \pm \sqrt{k}$ where k = total number of points.

These criteria are illustrated in Figure 4.14.

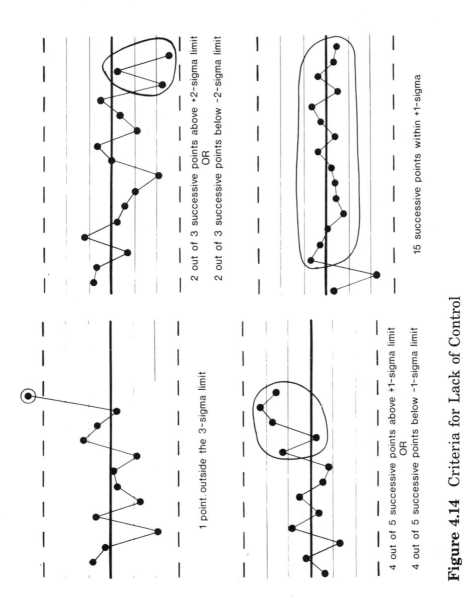

Figure 4.14 Criteria for Lack of Control

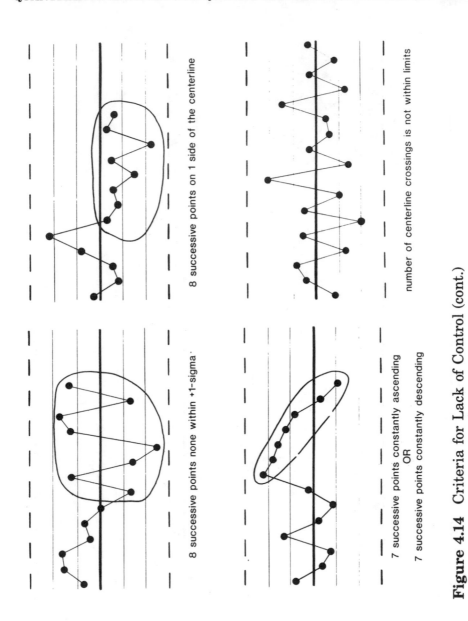

Figure 4.14 Criteria for Lack of Control (cont.)

The criteria listed in 1, 2, 3, and 6 and 7 would typically imply an instability or a change in process. Number 4 would imply *stratification* (to be discussed later). Number 5 would imply that one was sampling from two different processes that are not similar in results. Number 8 would imply that there are too few or too many center line crossings to have happened by pure chance.

Shewhart (1939) pointed out that the criteria used to establish the existence of a state of statistical control must not be applied blindly, but interpreted in every case based on the *intent* of those criteria. These specific criteria (such as no single point outside of the 3-sigma limits) must be considered necessary, but not sufficient. That is to say, not every nonrandom pattern can be recognized in advance and have a rule written for it. Beware of other nonrandom patterns than those stated previously.

For ongoing process control, it must be realized that even events that happen only a few times in 1,000 eventually happen. Furthermore, processes are not as "well-behaved" as mathematical models. Therefore, the American National Standards Institute in ANSI Standard Z1.3 (Deming et al, 1975) have given guidelines for a "high degree of control." In typical manufacturing conditions (which never reach the "ideal" textbook situation) it could be assumed a "high degree of control" exists if:

Zero points were out of control in the last 25 subgroups; no more than 1 point was out of control in the last 35 subgroups; no more than 2 points were out of control in the last 100 subgroups.

PROBLEM

4.30 Given the following control chart with data taken over time, cite all evidence of lack of control.

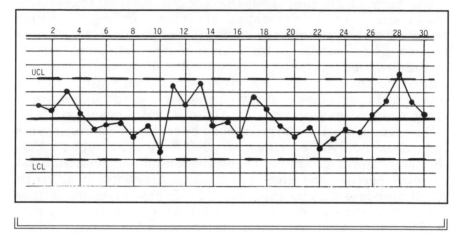

Stratification

The X bar and R chart in Figure 4.15 failed to indicate the cause of variation in quality that was hampering the assembly of main pole to rotor with a 16-inch long rivet, ¾ inch in diameter (Figure 4.16). The rivet was made by upsetting the conical head on full-round bar stock. The cold swaging operation on the head was causing the rivet body to become fat just below the head, so that in some instances, it would hang up on the main pole laminations instead of passing through freely.

Study of the $\bar{X}$ chart shows the points "hugging" the center line too closely, a phenomenon known as "stratification" because too many of the points fall along a narrow central stratum or layer. Overturning the data which make up the chart revealed that the first row came from die number 1, the second row from die number 2, etc. There were a total of four dies involved, with one piece from each die in each subgroup. Checking the data verifies that the smallest of the four pieces in each subgroup seldom occurs in rows 1 or 4. The $\bar{X}$ and s chart in Figure 4.17 verifies this. Each subgroup is *not* homogeneous, which violates the assumption on which the control charts limits are calculated.

What happened in this example of stratification is that the between-die variability was introduced *into* the subgroup. This caused an inflated variability within the subgroups, inflated subgroups ranges, inflated $\bar{R}$, and hence inflated control limits. For this reason, the control chart failed to detect the variations in quality which were present.

The above sample of product from parallel paths being introduced into the subgroup is, perhaps, the most common cause of stratification. It should be noted that the stratification is the symptom; the disease is faulty data collection. Any number of variations in the data recording or in the process behavior might mask the symptom of stratification; the disease would still be present and just harder to detect.

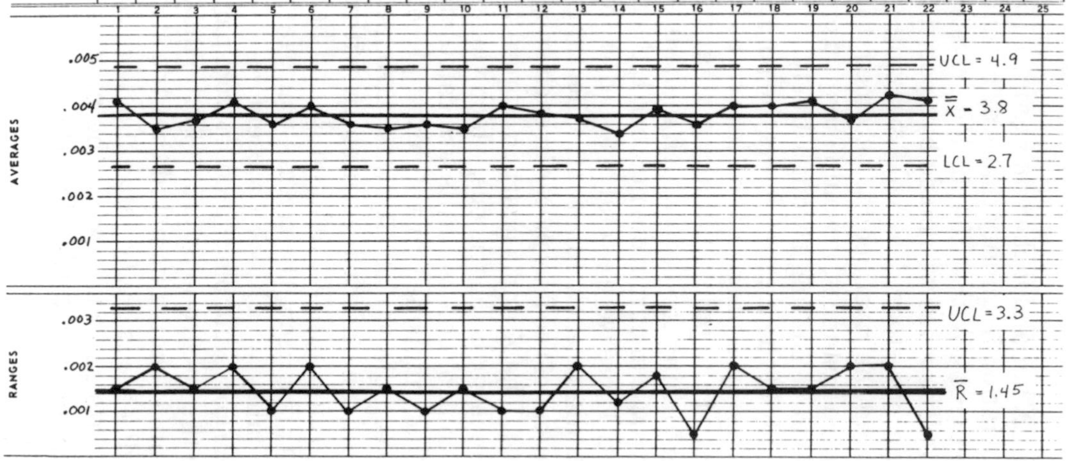

Figure 4.15 $\overline{X}$ and R Chart Showing "Stratification"

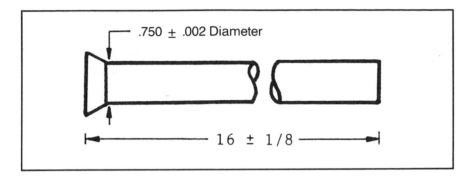

Figure 4.16 Sketch of Product

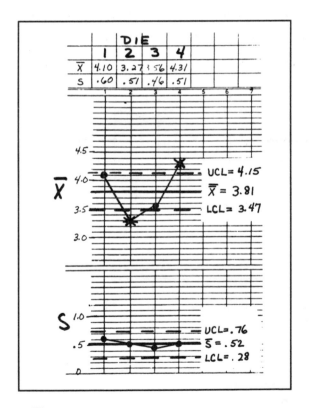

Figure 4.17 X̄ and s Chart Stratification by Die

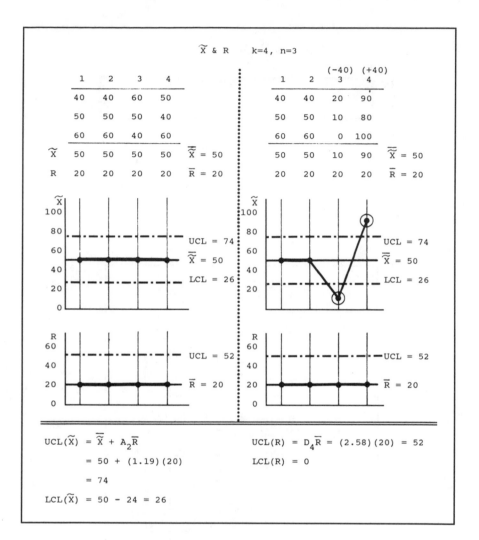

Figure 4.18 "Stratification" and the Calculation of Variability from *Within* Subgroups

Column number 1 of Figure 4.18 shows the second common cause of stratification — data just "penciled in" instead of actually measured. Note that in this limiting case of stratification all of the points fall on the center line on both the charts for median and for range. Note in the second column that the data has been systematically altered and the median chart no longer shows the stratification — but the disease is still present.

Stratification as seen in the first example above is very prevalent.

It is the result of using a control chart to study data in which two-way variation is present; variation in row-to-row as well as variation in column-to-column. Problems of this type must be broken down to one-way variation in order to use ordinary control chart methods, or else more advanced analysis techniques must be used.

The criterion of lack of control that helps detect stratification is "15 successive points within ±1 sigma."

Practical Advantages of a State of Control

The existence of a state of control, denoting the stability of the process, presents the following practical advantages to the manufacturer and the purchaser:
(from ANSI Z1.1 and Deming, *Quality, Productivity, and Competitive Position*, p. 130)

1. With control, there will be a minimum of variation between individual pieces from a process.
2. With control, data from samples of product have the greatest possible reliability for judging the quality of the whole process. Sampling and testing, and therefore the cost of inspection, can be minimized.
3. With control, the process is predictable, and costs and quality are predictable.
4. With control, there is a reliable basis for determining where to set the process target and the specification limits, particularly to optimize mating components. A stable process also provides the groundwork for altering specifications that cannot be met economically.
5. With control demonstrated by suppliers by making their control chart records available, purchasers may dispense with acceptance sampling and yet have a higher degree of assurance in the incoming quality.
6. With control, the fraction defective can be reduced, eliminating scrap and rework, lowering production costs, and increasing productivity.
7. With control, the effects of changes in the system can be measured with greater speed and reliability.
8. With control, the minimum total cost is attained from under-correcting and over-correcting.

Over-Adjustment*

It is well known that a point outside the control limits on a control chart tells the operator when a special cause of variation has occurred. In other words, it tells the operator when to correct or adjust the process. What is not as well known, the control chart also tells the operator when to leave the process alone or there will be the risk of incurring the following losses due to over-correcting:

1. When unnecessary adjustments are made, there are two sources of economic loss: the labor required to make the adjustments and the downtime of the assembly line.
2. Unnecessary adjustments will *increase* the variability of a stable process. An excessive number of adjustments (over-correcting or knob twiddling) can increase the 6-sigma spread of the process by up to 41 percent.

The reason for this is as follows. If the process is originally stable and normally distributed, it has an inherent mean and inherent spread of 6 sigma. Readings will naturally fall within 3 sigma above or below the mean. Any attempt to readjust the level of the process back to "target" after getting a reading less than 3 sigma from the mean will result in moving the whole distribution along with the adjustment, as illustrated in Figure 4.19. This will result in an increased total spread of the data.

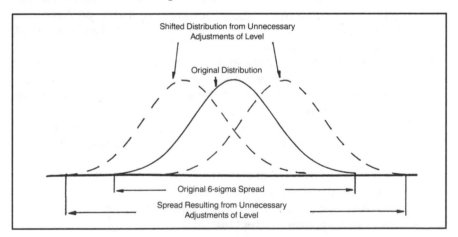

Figure 4.19   Spread of the Data

---

*Used by permission of *Quality*. Adapted from "Overcorrecting." *Quality* (October 1986): 77.

Example 4.10

The following is an example from an electric components manufacturing company. The part was a bracket that needed to be bent to 104° ± 5°. Every time the process made a bend outside of the specifications an adjustment was made in an attempt to bring the process level back to 104°. A histogram of the data from the "over-adjusted" process is illustrated in Figure 4.20. Upon

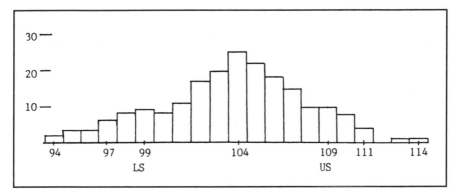

Figure 4.20 Spread of "Over-Adjusted" Process

learning that unnecessary adjustments increase the variability of the process, they decided to let the process run for a while without adjustments. A histogram of the data from the process when it was left alone is shown in Figure 4.21. Note that the

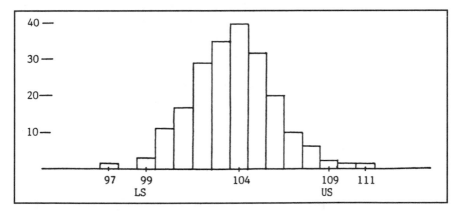

Figure 4.21 Spread of the Process When Left Alone

process is still not meeting specifications, but the spread of the data is much less than when the process is over-adjusted. You cannot "force" a process to have less than its inherent variability. To be able to meet specifications, the company must *improve* the process to decrease the variability, using 100 percent inspection until that is accomplished. Knob twiddling will only make it worse.

Classroom Exercise

In this simulation example, the process has a target value of 50 with specification limits of 50 ± 1. We will use the specification limits as our "action limits." If the process yields a piece outside of these limits, the action we will take is to reset the process to attain the target value. The output dimension of each piece is the sum of the "tool setting" plus the result of a random process. The random process used here is the sum of two dice, which has an expected value of 7.

Since our target value is 50 of which the random process contributes an expected value of 7, what should our control machine setting be? (Answer: 43)

Procedure

Step 1 Roll the 2 dice. Add this random portion to the tool adjustment setting to get the output reading. Plot it.

Step 2 If this output is 49, 50, or 51 (which are all within specification), make no change to the tool adjustment setting. If any other output is obtained, a tool adjustment *change* will be made in the amount (target minus output) in an attempt to force the process to target. For example, if a value of 4 is rolled, the ouput is $43 + 4 = 47$ which is below the lower action limit. A tool adjustment change of $50 - 47 = +3$ will be needed. (The new tool adjustment setting would be $43 + 3 = 46$ per Step 3.) If on the other hand a value of 11 is rolled, the output is $43 + 11 = 54$, which is above the upper action limit. A tool adjustment change of $50 - 54 = -4$ will be needed. (The new tool adjustment setting would be $43 - 4 = 39$.)

Step 3 Calculate the new tool adjustment setting by adding the old adjustment setting and the tool adjustment change. (Watch your signs!)

Step 4 Repeat Steps 1 through 3 nine times until 10 outputs have been generated.

Step 5 To investigate what would have happened if the tool adjustment setting had been left at 43 throughout with no changes, use the same 10 random process components (dice totals) as generated by the dice above. Add these values to the constant tool adjustment setting of 43 in each case to get the 10 output values. Plot these outputs.

Step 6 How do they compare? Which method ("knob twiddling" or "leave-it-alone") appears to have less variability? To verify this with calculations, calculate the standard deviation of each of the two sets of outputs. How do they compare? Calculate the amplification factor due to knob twiddling by dividing the standard deviation of the knob twiddling output by the standard deviation of the leave-it-alone output.

Note: The results from Method I are expected to have more variability than the results from Method II.

METHOD I: READJUST

PIECE #	1	2	3	4	5	6	7	8	9	10
TOOL ADJ. CHANGE										
TOOL ADJ. SETTING	43									
"RANDOM PORTION"										
SUM = OUTPUT										

60
58
56
54
52
50
48
46
44
42
40

UAL----52
LAL----48

METHOD II: LEAVE IT ALONE

	1	2	3	4	5	6	7	8	9	10
TOOL ADJ. SETTING	43	43	43	43	43	43	43	43	43	43
"RANDOM PORTION"										
SUM = OUTPUT										

Why Use Averages?

The typical control chart works with averages rather than individual readings for the following reasons:

1. To take advantage of the Central Limit Theorem. Averages tend toward normality, so their location is known ($\pm$ 3 sigma of the averages). Individual readings could be spread according to a distribution other than the normal distribution, so we wouldn't know their location.

2. Averages are more sensitive to mean shifts. Less total inspection is typically needed to detect a mean shift with the same probability when working with averages than working with individual readings. Mean shifts are typically measured in terms of the number of standard deviations the process mean has shifted up (+) or down (−) as illustrated in Figure 4.22 and in Example 4.11.

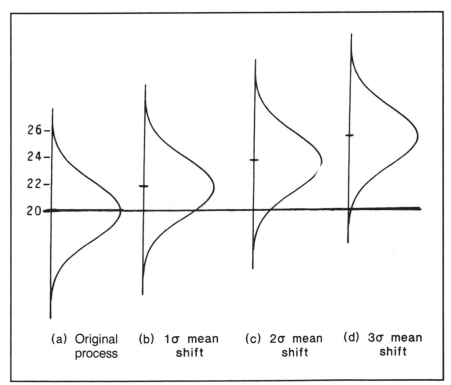

Figure 4.22 Mean Shifts of Process with $\sigma = 2$

3. To provide an estimate of the population standard deviation only using the variation from within the subgroup.

Caution: Using averages has disadvantages as well since they sometimes mask problems. Alternatives will be discussed in Part V.

Example 4.11

To illustrate the idea that averages are more sensitive to mean shifts, consider the following cases:

Case I: Record the data n = 1 piece at a time (i.e., look at individuals).

Case II: Take subgroups of size n = 4 and look at the $\overline{X}$ values.

Summarize:

The following table gives the number of pieces needed to be inspected such that probability of detection of the mean shift is .99

Number of Pieces Needed

Mean shift	Case I: n = 1	Case II: n = 4
1	198	106
2	27	10
3	7	4

That is, only about half as many pieces need to be inspected when using averages to have the same high probability of detection than when using individual readings. (For an example of the arithmetic involved for the above, see Bicking and Gryna 1979.)

Why Use $A_2\overline{R}$?

For an $\overline{X}$ and R chart, the 3-sigma limits for the $\overline{X}$ values are calculated by $A_2\overline{R}$. This is done not because we wish to use an easy approximation for $3\sigma_{\overline{x}}$ but because we wish to approximate $3\sigma_{\overline{x}}$ by the within-subgroup variability. (Recall, we attempted to keep the subgroups as homogeneous as possible.) The value for $3\sigma_{\overline{x}}$ is *never* estimated by $s_{\overline{x}}$ when calculating control limits.

For instance, if the value $3\sigma_{\overline{x}}$ was estimated by:

$$3s_{\overline{x}} = 3 \sqrt{\frac{\Sigma\ (\overline{X} - \overline{\overline{X}})^2}{k - 1}}$$

this would calculate how far the $\overline{X}$ values *are* spread out.

The $\overline{X}$s will almost always fall within the $\pm 3s_{\overline{x}}$ limits, regardless of how much the process wanders, as illustrated in Figure 4.23.

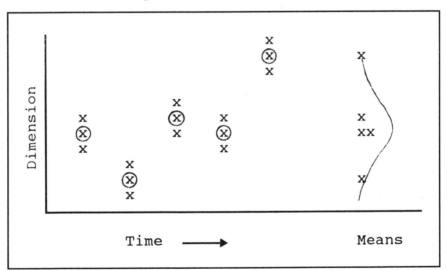

Figure 4.23 Distribution of $\overline{X}$ Values for a Process that Is Not in Statistical Control

The value of $A_2\overline{R}$ calculates how far the $\overline{X}$ values would be spread out if the process was indeed under control. It estimates the spread of the $\overline{X}$ values, by the spread from within the subgroup ($\overline{R}$). This is illustrated in Figure 4.24.

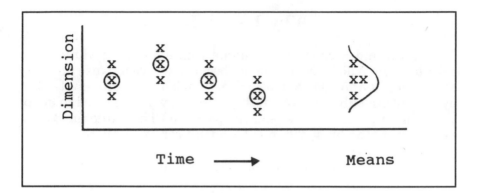

Figure 4.24 Distribution of $\overline{X}$ Values for a Process in Statistical Control

In example 4.12, the $\overline{X}$ and R chart from the harness clamp data, n = 5, illustrates the different results of these two calculations.

Example 4.12

Using the data from Problem 4.13 when $3\sigma_{\overline{x}}$ is estimated by:

$$s_{\overline{x}} = \sqrt{\frac{\Sigma\,(\overline{X} - \overline{\overline{X}})^2}{k - 1}} \text{ (where } \overline{\overline{X}} = 35.7)$$

We get $s_{\overline{x}} = 3.0$. So we estimate $3\sigma_{\overline{x}} = 3\,(3.0) = 9.0$

The control limits would then be:

$$
\begin{array}{cc}
25.7 & 25.7 \\
-9.0 & +9.0 \\
\hline
16.7 & 34.7
\end{array}
$$

Using these limits, all of the points would be within the limits, denoting the process *in control* even though the process wanders and is not stable (Figure 4.25).

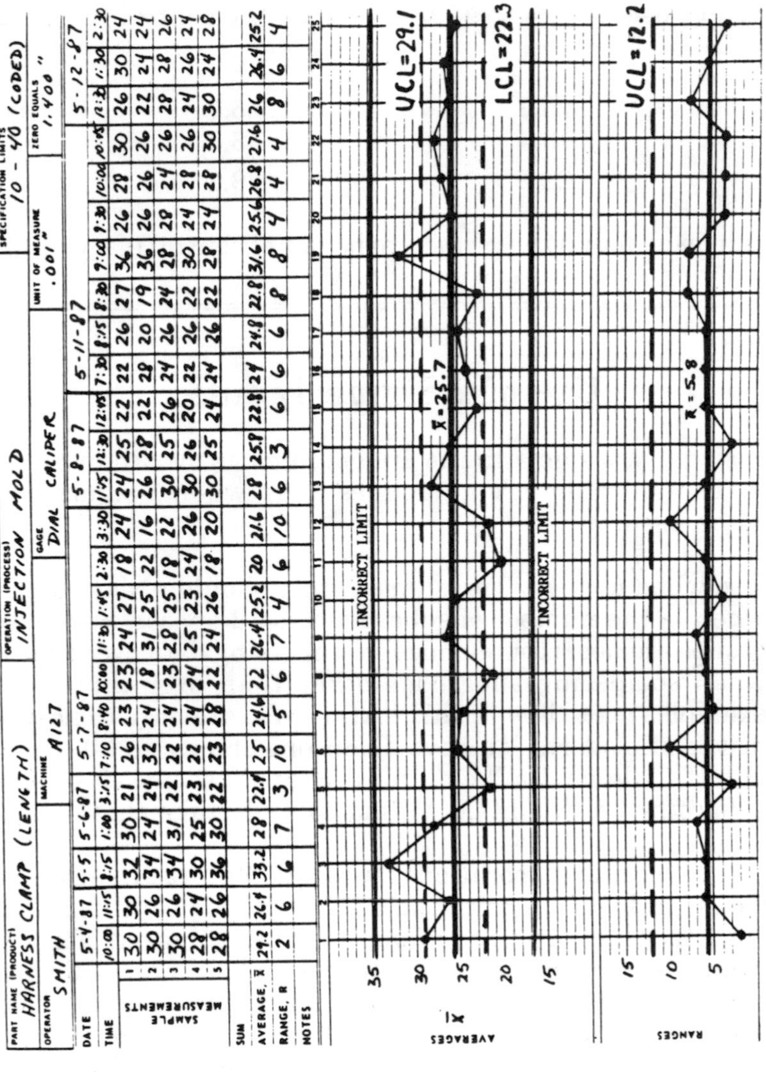

Figure 4.25 Correct versus Incorrect Control Limits

The correct limits, derived from the variability within the subgroups, uses $A_2\overline{R} = .58(5.8) = 3.4$. So the control limits turn out to be:

$$
\begin{array}{cc}
25.7 & 25.7 \\
-3.4 & +3.4 \\
\hline
22.3 & 29.1
\end{array}
$$

And indeed, found the process to be out of control (Figure 4.25).

Use of 2-Sigma Limits

Occasionally, 2-sigma limits are opted for rather than 3-sigma limits. The following are guidelines as to when 2-sigma limits should be used:

1. Use when $k \leq 12$. Two-sigma limits should always be used when k, the number of subgroups, is 12 or less. So few subgroups are not recommended for collecting data over time but when comparing subgroups other than over time. (Short examples over time in this text, recall, are only to keep the arithmetic short.) We have about one chance in 20 of going out of 2-sigma limits by pure chance, so in 12 or fewer subgroups we would be willing to undertake those odds.

2. Use in a critical operation. Two-sigma limits are also sometimes used when monitoring a very critical operation. Again, since they have about one chance in 20 of going out of 2-sigma limits by pure chance, we may go out on more wild-goose chases, looking for trouble when there is none when a point goes out of the 2-sigma limits. However, if the operation is critical we might want to take that chance in the hopes of catching problems (assignable causes) more quickly if there are any.

Unless stated otherwise, 3-sigma limits are assumed. The calculations are illustrated in Example 4.13.

Example 4.13

2-sigma limits for an $\overline{X}$ and R Chart:

$$2\sigma \text{ UCL } (\overline{X}) = \overline{\overline{X}} + 2/3 \,[A_2\overline{R}]$$
$$= 32.6 + 2/3 \,[(1.02) \,(10.25)]$$
$$= 32.6 + 2/3 \,(10.5)$$
$$= 32.6 + 7$$
$$= 39.6$$
$$2\sigma \text{ LCL } (\overline{X}) = \overline{\overline{X}} - 2/3 \,[A_2\overline{R}]$$
$$= 32.6 - 7$$
$$= 25.6$$

D_{42} ("D_4" for 2-sigma limits) and D_{32} ("D_3" for 2-sigma limits) as used below are "shortcut" factors developed by the authors for ease of calculation. They are found in Appendix A. Using this "shortcut" formula:

$$2\sigma \text{ UCL } (R) = D_{42}\overline{R}$$
$$= 2.05 \,(10.25)$$
$$= 21.0$$
$$2\sigma \text{ LCL } (R) = D_{32}\overline{R}$$
$$= 0 \,(10.25)$$
$$= 0$$

The following is an alternate method for calculating 2-sigma limits for the range (the typical approach):

$$
\begin{array}{ll}
3\sigma \text{ UCL } (R): & 26.4 \\
- \ \overline{R} & : \underline{10.25} \\
3\sigma_R & : 16.15
\end{array}
$$

Then $2\sigma_R = 2/3 \,(3\sigma_R) = 2/3 \,(16.15) = 10.77$
so, $2\sigma \text{ UCL } (R) = \overline{R} + 2\sigma_R = 10.25 + 10.77 = 21.0$
$\qquad 2\sigma \text{ LCL } (R) = 10.25 - 10.77 = 0$

These limits are shown in Figure 4.26.

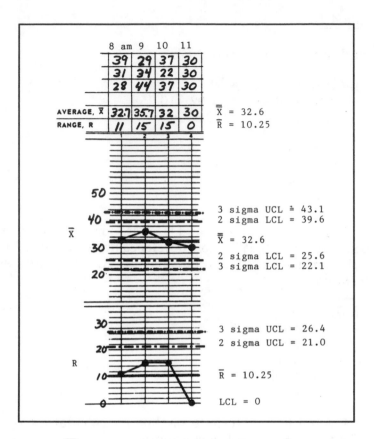

Figure 4.26 $\overline{\mathrm{X}}$ and R Chart with 2-Sigma Limits

Similar factors have been developed for the s chart (B_{42} and B_{32}). The factors can be found in Appendix A. A summary for the calculation of 2-sigma limits is given in Table 4.7.

	Central Tendency	Dispersion	
$\bar{X}$ & R:	2σ UCL($\bar{X}$) = $\bar{\bar{X}}$ + (2/3) $A_2\bar{R}$	2σ UCL(R)	= $D_4{}_2\bar{R}$
	2σ LCL($\bar{X}$) = $\bar{\bar{X}}$ − (2/3) $A_2\bar{R}$	2σ LCL(R)	= $D_3{}_2\bar{R}$
$\tilde{X}$ & R:	2σ UCL($\tilde{X}$) = $\bar{\tilde{X}}$ + (2/3) $\tilde{A}_2\bar{R}$	2σ UCL(R)	= $D_4{}_2\bar{R}$
	2σ LCL($\tilde{X}$) = $\bar{\tilde{X}}$ − (2/3) $\tilde{A}_2\bar{R}$	2σ LCL(R)	= $D_3{}_2\bar{R}$
$\bar{X}$ & s:	2σ UCL($\bar{X}$) = $\bar{\bar{X}}$ + (2/3) $A_3\bar{s}$	2σ UCL(s)	= $B_4{}_2\bar{s}$
	2σ LCL($\bar{X}$) = $\bar{\bar{X}}$ − (2/3) $A_3\bar{s}$	2σ LCL(s)	= $B_3{}_2\bar{s}$

Table 4.7 2-Sigma Limits — Summary

PROBLEMS

4.31 For the data in Figure 4.27, calculate 2-sigma limits for an
$\bar{X}$ and s chart.

$$2\sigma \text{ UCL } (\bar{X}) = \bar{\bar{X}} + \text{⅔ } [A_3\bar{s}]$$
$$= (\quad) + \text{⅔ } [(\quad)(\quad)]$$
$$=$$
$$=$$
$$2\sigma \text{ LCL } (\bar{X}) = \bar{\bar{X}} - \text{⅔ } [A_3\bar{s}]$$
$$=$$
$$=$$
$$2\sigma \text{ UCL } (s) = B_{42}\bar{s}$$
$$= (\quad)(\quad)$$
$$=$$
$$2\sigma \text{ LCL } (s) = B_{32}\bar{s}$$
$$= (\quad)(\quad)$$
$$=$$

Graph these limits in Figure 4.27.

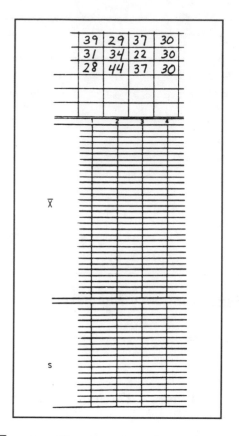

Figure 4.27 $\overline{X}$ and s Chart with 2-Sigma Limits

4.32 For the data in Problem 4.1, compute 2-sigma limits for an $\overline{X}$ and R chart.

4.33 For the data in Problem 4.2, compute 2-sigma limits for an $\overline{X}$ and R chart.

4.34 For the data in Problem 4.7, compute 2-sigma limits for an $\widetilde{X}$ and R chart.

4.35 For the data in Problem 4.19, compute 2-sigma limits for an $\overline{X}$ and s chart.

4.36 For the data in Problem 4.20, compute 2-sigma limits for an $\overline{X}$ and s chart.

Severe Departures from Normality

The data that we obtain for variables control charts can *never* really be distributed normally for the following two reasons:

1. The normal distribution extends from negative infinity to positive infinity, while real process data will, of course, be finite.
2. The normal distribution is a *continuous* distribution, but every measurement taken is a discrete measurement: There exists no ability to obtain or record anything except discrete data.

It follows that all of measurement data departs from normality, and it is the degree of such departure that must be studied.

Shewhart-type variables control charts for $\overline{X}$ and R are robust in the sense that quite broad departures from normality can be tolerated without the control chart losing its ability to do its intended job — to discriminate between assignable and common causes of variation. If, however, the departures of a stable process from a normal distribution become too extreme, the control chart may be rendered ineffective.

Fortunately, the $\overline{X}$ and R chart itself provides a satisfactory warning mechanism to tell when the departures from normality become "severe." The greatest concern is for distributions that are not symmetrical — *skewed* distributions. If the distribution of a stable process has a long tail to the right, we say it is skewed to the right (Figure 4.28a). If the distribution has a long tail to the left, we say that it is skewed to the left (Figure 4.28b).

If the data are badly skewed, the $\overline{X}$ and R charts will show it because the $\overline{X}$ and R charts will be either in phase or 180° out of phase. For example, note that the $\overline{X}$ and R control charts in Figure 4.29 are "in phase," i.e., the R chart goes up when the $\overline{X}$ chart goes up, the R chart goes down when the $\overline{X}$ chart goes down. The histogram (Figure 4.28a) of the data from Figure 4.29 shows that the data are not normal data, but are skewed to the right, i.e., the data trail out to the right.

The histogram of the data in Figure 4.28b shows the data to be skewed to the left. Note that the $\overline{X}$ and R control charts of these data in Figure 4.30 are 180° out of phase, i.e., the R chart goes up when the $\overline{X}$ goes down and vice versa.

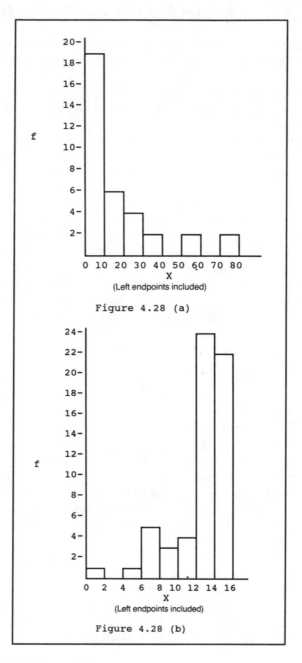

Figure 4.28 Skewed Data

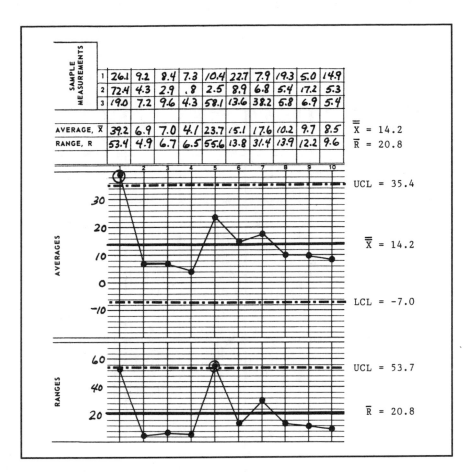

Figure 4.29 X and R Chart "In Phase"

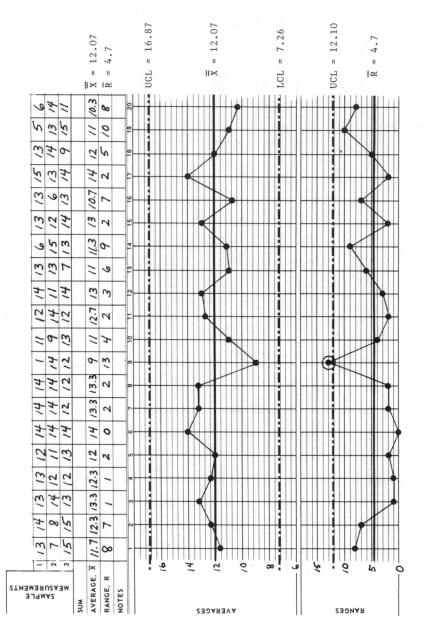

Figure 4.30 $\overline{X}$ and R Chart "180° Out of Phase"

172

To determine that the distribution is by nature skewed rather than skewed in appearance only, we must examine the nature of the process. For instance, TIRs (total indicator runouts) are often skewed to the right because the values are always positive or zero, with zero as the low limit but with no upper limit.

If the X̄ and R charts do not appear to be essentially "in phase or 180° out of phase," it may be assumed that any departures from normality are sufficiently small so as not to interfere with the usefulness of the control charts.

Caution: As noted in the previous paragraph, control charts may be quite usefully applied to data that depart substantially from a normal distribution. This is because control charts are robust in their insensitivity to lack of normality. On the contrary, estimates of process capability that assume normality are very sensitive to departures from this assumption. In Part V it will be seen that this question is entirely circumvented by the use of the probability plot for determining limits, rather than making the assumption of a normal distribution.

Writing Comments on Charts

Comments regarding changes in the process and actions taken on the process are at least as important as the data for problem solving. Comments should always be placed on run charts and control charts when appropriate. To encourage the operator to keep such notes, the chart ideally should be specifically designed for the operation with places to write comments for actions, explanations, and other comments.

Figure 4.31 shows an example of such a chart. The comments on the bottom of the chart are explanations, i.e., why a certain reading was observed. These comments relate to the points, which is why they are lined up with the points. The comments on the top of the chart are actions, i.e., what action was taken on the process. These actions are taken between pieces, so the comments are lined up between the points. It is then more easily discernible as to whether the action was taken before or after the piece was made.

The best chart for a process is one specially tailored to that operation.

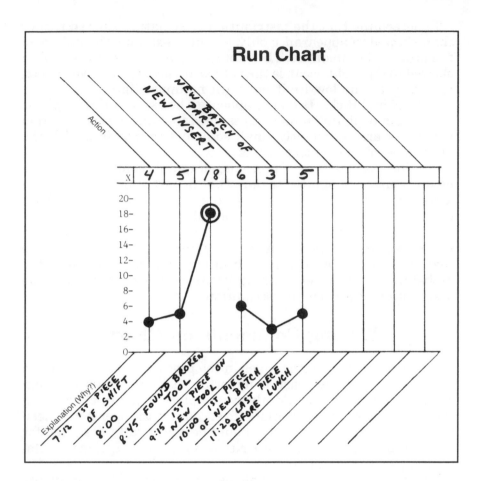

Figure 4.31   Comments on Charts

Process Data Analysis and the Use of Computers

We will first look at the several ways in which process data may be analyzed and then consider the usefulness of the computer for each of these. Process data may be viewed in either of two ways:

1. In the past tense
2. In the present tense

1. Data may be gathered and then studied in the *past tense*.

The objective in the retrospective analysis of process data may be simply an *evaluation* of the process, but more often it is to discover assignable causes of statistical nonuniformity in order to *improve* the process. For this purpose, the same data may be viewed from many perspectives using an assortment of tools.

For example, if there are two machines and four operators, we may make an $\overline{X}$ and s chart on the data subgrouped by the two machines, make another $\overline{X}$ and s chart on the same data subgrouped by the four operators, etc. (as in Problem 4.25). We may make a histogram or probability plot (Part V) on the whole data set to study the distribution of the data, etc. It may also be the case (as in Figures 4.15 and 4.17) that we wish to find out if the second reading does tend to always be lower, so we need to subgroup the data by reading number.

In addition to the selection of "rational subgroups" as noted above, we may opt to study the data in time order, making subgroups of, say, four consecutive pieces using an $\overline{X}$ and R chart. While the objective of process evaluation or improvement may be the reason for this method of data analysis, a control chart on time-ordered data which has already been acquired is also the first step in the use of that chart for ongoing process control.

2. Data may be examined in an *ongoing* manner in the present tense (sometimes called *real time* analysis of the data).

The objective here will be either process maintenance or improvement depending on how well the process meets our needs in its present state.

At any given time, we can expect to improve about 2 percent of our quality characteristics using Shewhart control charts. For this purpose we may use, for example, the $\overline{X}$ and R chart with subgroups of size 4 where the control limits would be found from data in the past tense as mentioned in number 1.

If, however, the objective of our ongoing data analysis is simply the maintenance of a process which is already "good" (the other 98 percent of our quality characteristics), we will *not* use a Shewhart control chart because of our scarce resources, but rather a simple plot of individual measurements gathered over time. These charts will use action limits based on judgment, usually derived from the process specifications (see Part VI).

Let us now examine the usefulness of the computer for the several methods of data analysis described previously.

When looking at process data retrospectively, after it has been gathered, we will want to transform the data in many different ways, and use a number of tools for the examination of both the raw and transformed data. For these purposes, there is no substitute for the use of a computer with excellent software for data transformation and analysis. The examples in this text have used StatScan® software for this purpose.

When looking at data for ongoing process control, we will opt to continue our Shewhart control chart if — and only if — our objective is clearly one of bringing about needed process improvement. Under those circumstances, the plotting of the points and making comments on the control chart is a simple operation best performed with pencil on paper. Indications of lack of statistical uniformity are then less likely to go unnoticed. Moreover, the paramount consideration here is *taking action* on the process after statistical signal; the computer is clearly of no help in this regard.

If we are monitoring the process in "real time" for the primary purpose of process maintenance, we will measure and consider only individuals (not averages of subgroups) and compare these on an ongoing basis with maintenance action limits (see Part VI). It should be noted that these action limits will remain fixed over time, whereas we can expect the limits for a Shewhart control chart to shift constantly — reflecting the shifting nature of the variability of the process. For the objective of process maintenance, where a Shewhart chart is not to be used, the computer may be an ideal helper.

In summary, the computer is an invaluable tool for looking at data in the past tense. It may also be extremely useful for ongoing process control when this control is based on a chart of individual observations with maintenance action limits.

Part V. The Individuals Within the Process

Once the $\overline{X}$ and R charts in time order of manufacture show the process to be in a state of statistical control, the process is *statistically uniform* or *stable*. Only then is the future behavior of the process predictable; only then does the calculation of a "sigma" for the process have meaning. While the process is in control, estimates of its process capability may be made so that tolerance limits may be set intelligently on the engineering drawings. Several methods of estimating the "capability" of the stable process will be discussed.

The philosophy of continuous improvement of the process by ongoing reduction in variability will also be discussed.

Control charts based on process individuals, rather than on subgroup averages, will be investigated and the many advantages of these simple charts will be seen.

Chapter 14 Preliminary Estimates of the Distribution of Individuals: Normal Distribution Assumed

Stability

Control charts determine if the process is in a state of statistical control, statistically uniform, stable. They do not tell if the process is meeting specifications and producing good product.

The most commonly used set of control charts is the $\overline{X}$ and $\underline{R}$ chart. The $\overline{X}$ chart looks at subgroup averages (means). The $\overline{X}$ control limits define the variability of the *means*. The only points plotted on the chart are the means. If these plotted means fall within the control limits (and the R chart also has all the ranges falling within the range control limits), the process is said to be in a *state of statistical control*. Being in a state of control only means that the process is statistically uniform: It is *stable* or *repeatable*. Note that the control limits have *nothing* to do with the specification limits.

Only after the process is in a state of statistical control does it make sense to talk about the capability of the process — where it is centered and how much it is spread. If the process is not in control, it is unstable and unpredictable; thus, saying where the process is centered and how much it is spread would have no meaning.

Preliminary Estimates of the Mean and Standard Deviation of the Process Individuals.

Once the $\overline{X}$ and R chart shows the process to be stable, the location of the process center is estimated by $\overline{\overline{X}}$, the center line of the $\overline{X}$ chart. The spread of the process is harder to estimate. A preliminary estimate based only on the within-subgroup variability is dangerous, but often used. One such method of estimating standard deviation is given by:

$$\text{(a)} \quad \hat{\sigma} = \overline{R}/d_2$$

where d_2 is found in Appendix A for a given value of n. The symbol $\hat{}$ over the σ means that it is an estimate. Note that this formula is only valid *if* the process is stable and the process data are normally distributed.

Note: When working with an $\overline{X}$ and s chart, the formula

$$\text{(b)} \quad \hat{\sigma} = \overline{s}/c_4$$

is used instead, where c_4 is found in Appendix A for a given value of n.

Example 5.1

Using the data from Example 4.1 and using equation (a) we get:

$$\hat{\sigma} = \overline{R}/d_2 = 10.25/1.69 = 6.07$$

where $d_2 = 1.69$ for subgroups of size n = 3.

Preliminary Estimates of the Natural Limits of the Process

If the process is approximately normally distributed, the total spread of the process individuals is estimated to be (a) $3\hat{\sigma}$ up and $3\hat{\sigma}$ down from the center line. Although we may underestimate the spread of the process by using the within-subgroup estimate of sigma, the computational procedure is widely used and the limits $\overline{\overline{X}} \pm 3\overline{R}/d_2$ are commonly referred to as the natural limits of the process individuals. The natural limits are wider than the control limits on $\overline{X}$ because the natural limits define the variability of the *individuals* of the process whereas the $\overline{X}$ control limits define the variability of the subgroup means. It is the natural limits that are to be compared to specification limits because the specifications also refer to *individuals*. If the natural limits do not fall within the specification limits the process is not capable of meeting specifications and defective product will result. Note that it is quite possible that all of the readings for individuals taken for a control chart fall within the specification limits but that the natural limits do not. If there are, for example, 25 subgroups of size 5 giving 125 readings for individuals, one would not expect these observed individuals to include either the largest or the smallest reading which would come from the process. The natural limits compensate for that, estimating the spread of the process for all except a few pieces per thousand.

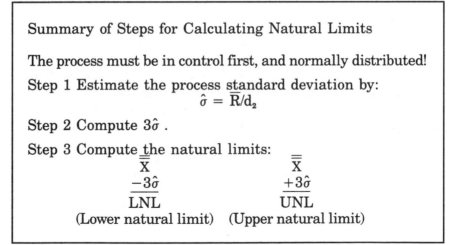

Summary of Steps for Calculating Natural Limits

The process must be in control first, and normally distributed!

Step 1 Estimate the process standard deviation by:
$$\hat{\sigma} = \overline{R}/d_2$$

Step 2 Compute $3\hat{\sigma}$.

Step 3 Compute the natural limits:

$\overline{\overline{X}}$	$\overline{\overline{X}}$
$-3\hat{\sigma}$	$+3\hat{\sigma}$
LNL	UNL
(Lower natural limit)	(Upper natural limit)

Example 5.2

Continuing with Example 5.1 ($n = 3$, $\overline{\overline{X}} = 32.6$, $\overline{R} = 10.25$): The process must be in control first, and normally distributed.

Assuming we had at least 25 subgroups of the type shown in Example 4.1, with no evidence of lack of control, we *act* as if we believe that the process is in control. We assume a normal distribution here, as is commonly done, to illustrate the procedure. Note that this is a risky assumption and not recommended in practice.

1. Estimate the process standard deviation:
   $\hat{\sigma} = \overline{R}/d_2$

   here: $\hat{\sigma} = \overline{R}/d_2 = 10.25/1.69 = 6.07$.

2. Compute $3\hat{\sigma} = 3(6.07) = 18.2$

3. Compute the natural limits

$$
\begin{array}{cc}
\overline{\overline{X}} & \overline{\overline{X}} \\
-3\hat{\sigma} & +3\hat{\sigma} \\
\hline
\text{LNL} & \text{UNL}
\end{array}
$$

here:

$$
\begin{array}{ll}
& 32.6 \qquad\qquad\qquad 32.6 \\
& -18.2 \qquad\qquad\quad +18.2 \\
\text{LNL:} \quad 14.4 \qquad \text{UNL:} \quad 50.8
\end{array}
$$

These limits are illustrated in Figure 5.1a. The natural limits are compared to the control limits previously calculated in Example 4.1 in Figure 5.1b. Recall that the X values (individual readings) are expected to have more spread than the $\overline{X}$ values (averages).

The graph of the individual readings as plotted against the natural limits is an optional step and is illustrated in Figure 5.2.

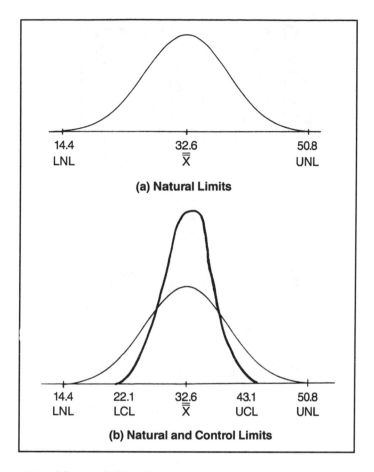

Figure 5.1 Natural Limits

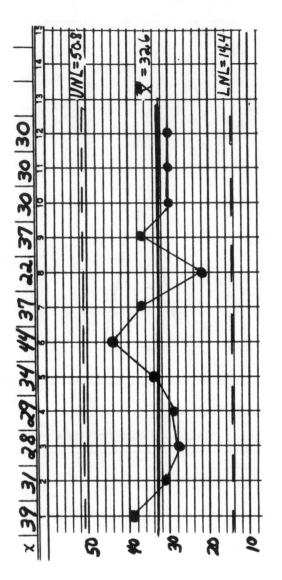

Figure 5.2 Plot of Individuals Against the Natural Limits

PROBLEM

5.1 Make the assumption that the process is in statistical control and normally distributed. Using the data from the following problems, compute the natural limits. Plot the individual readings and show the natural limits.

    a. Problem 4.1
    b. Problem 4.8
    c. Problem 4.5
    d. Problem 4.9

Comparison of Natural Limits and $\overline{X}$ Control Limits

Recall that the $\overline{X}$ control limits show the expected dispersion of the subgroup means. The control limits on $\overline{X}$, along with those on R, are used to determine the *stability* of the process. Natural limits refer to the spread of the individuals. It is the natural limits that may be compared to the engineering specifications. A summary is given in Table 5.1.

LIMITS	COMMENTS
$\overline{X}$ Chart Control Limits	look at spread of subgroup means to determine stability
Natural Limits	look at spread of individuals; can be compared to specification limits
Specification Limits	set by engineering upon individuals

Table 5.1 Summary of the Different Types of Limits

A typical scenario is illustrated in Figure 5.3. Note that the natural limits are inside of the specification limits so the process is capable of meeting specifications and is referred to as a "capable" process. The process in Figure 5.4 shows the natural limits to be

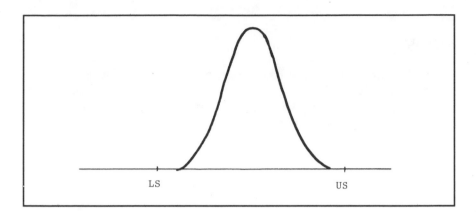

Figure 5.3 A Capable "Process"

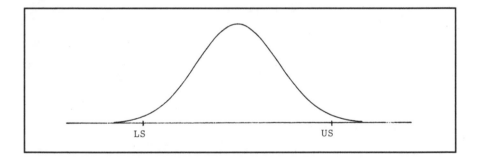

Figure 5.4 A Process that Is Not Capable

outside of the specification limits so it is not capable of meeting specifications. It is not a capable process.

Three comments are in order. First, even though being in a state of control has nothing to do with specifications, it is necessary to get the process in control *and* within specifications because both are needed. The process must meet specifications, but it must also be stable to continuously meet specifications in the future and to decrease variability.

Second, the estimate of σ as $\overline{R}/d_2$ is chosen to calculate control limits because it provides the smallest estimate of σ and hence the tightest and most useful control limits. This formula, widely misused for estimating capability, may underestimate the process spread. Shewhart specifically warned us against the use of such an estimate.

Third, the use of 3-sigma limits on individuals — regardless of how $\hat{\sigma}$ is calculated — is a dangerous method of estimating the limits on individuals because of the critical dependence on the assumption that the process is normally distributed. Although wide departures from normality may be acceptable in making control charts, the estimate of the limits for individuals is hypersensitive to this assumption. As we will see in Chapter 15, the probability plot provides the only safe procedure for the estimation of the distribution of process individuals.

PROBLEMS

5.2 Assuming a normal distribution that is in control and given the following information, is the process capable of meeting specifications? Sketch.

UCL $(\overline{X})$ = 60
LCL $(\overline{X})$ = 40
UNL = 70
LNL = 30
US = 65
LS = 25

5.3 Assuming a normal distribution that is in control and given the following information, is the process capable of meeting specification? Sketch.

UCL $(\overline{X})$ = 50
LCL $(\overline{X})$ = 40
UNL = 53.7
LNL = 36.3
Specifications = 46 $\pm$ 10

5.4 With $n = 5$, recent experience while in statistical control had shown $\overline{X}$ = 50 and $\overline{R}$ = 6. If the product specifications are 50 $\pm$ 10, and the process is assumed to be normal, is the process meeting specification? Use the conventional 3-sigma limits on individuals with $\hat{\sigma} = \overline{R}/d_2$. Sketch.

Preliminary Estimates of the Process Capability

From an $\overline{X}$ and R chart with an ongoing state of statistical control and subject to the assumption that the process is normally distributed, a preliminary estimate of the dispersion of the process individuals has been made as $\overline{\overline{X}} \pm 3\overline{R}/d_2$, and the limits of this spread have been called *natural limits*.

These natural limits may also be called a preliminary estimate of "process capability" — preliminary in the sense that it is an easy estimate to make, but recognizing that such an estimate may be dangerously misleading by underestimating the total spread of the process. Recall that this estimate is based only on the within-subgroup component of variability. If there is an additional between-subgroup component of variability or if the process has even "minor" deviations from normality, this estimate of process capability may lead us astray. The estimate of $\overline{\overline{X}} \pm 3\overline{R}/d_2$ and all of the process capability measures or indices based on it should be regarded only as a crude "quick and dirty" procedure at best. As will be discussed in Chapter 15, any serious estimate of the limits of the process dispersion should be based on a probability plot using only observations taken while the process was shown to be in a state of statistical control. The larger the number of such observations, the better will be the estimate of the process capability. Shewhart recommended at least 1,000 observations to estimate process capability, while accepting only 100 to show a state of statistical control. In practice, 125 or more readings are typically used.

Several methods of expressing the preliminary estimates of process capability, all typically based upon $\overline{\overline{X}} \pm 3\overline{R}/d_2$, will now be reviewed. Note that as companies and, in particular, suppliers, become more discerning, they will begin to base their estimates of σ for process capability indices using the s (overall), the standard deviation of all the readings. This will be discussed in more depth in Chapter 15. We assume that the objective is to center the process on the midpoint of the specifications.

1. $\boxed{\text{PROCESS CAPABILITY} = 6\hat{\sigma}}$

This expression of process capability is a measure of the repeatability of the process and is commonly called the 6-sigma range for individuals, for a system which is in a state of statistical control. This is simply the approximate total spread of the process.

Example 5.3

Say $\hat{\sigma} = 0.01$ inch. The process capability is 0.06 inch. Notice that this type of measure of process capability is limited. We cannot determine whether or not the process has the potential for meeting the specifications until we can compare it to the specification range, which leads to the second method.

---

2. $$\text{PROCESS CAPABILITY RATIO} = \frac{6\hat{\sigma}}{\text{specification range}} \times 100\%$$

where specification range = US − LS.

One method of expressing process capability that is sometimes used in the automotive industry is the *process capability ratio* which divides the 6-sigma process spread by the range of the specifications and expresses this quotient as a percentage. Note that this should properly be called a *process incapability percentage*, but the term process capability ratio is too well established to change.

Note that Examples 5.4 through 5.9:

upper specification limit (US) = 22
lower specification limit (LS) = 10

Example 5.4

Suppose our process is in a state of statistical control and $\overline{\overline{X}} = 16$, $\hat{\sigma} = 1$. Always start with a sketch of the process showing the natural limits compared to the specification limits.

Sketch: UNL $= \overline{\overline{X}} + 3\hat{\sigma} = 16 + 3(1) = 16 + 3 = 19$
LNL $= \overline{\overline{X}} - 3\hat{\sigma} = 16 - 3 = 13$

(See Figure 5.5)

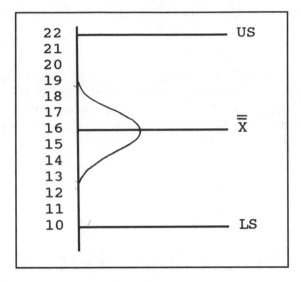

Figure 5.5 Process in Example 5.4

Then, process capability ratio

$$= \frac{6\hat{\sigma}}{\text{specification range}} \times 100\%$$

$$= \frac{6\,(1)}{22 - 10} \times 100\% = \frac{6}{12} \times 100\% = 50\%$$

This means that the process spread is using only 50 percent of its allowable spread — a very good process.

Notice that the process capability ratio completely ignores the location of the process, which may or may not be acceptable as illustrated by Example 5.5.

Example 5.5

Suppose our process is in a state of statistical control and $\overline{\overline{X}} = 20$, $\hat{\sigma} = 1$.

Sketch: UNL $= \overline{\overline{X}} + 3\hat{\sigma} = 20 + 3(1) = 20 + 3 = 23$
UNL $= \overline{X} - 3\hat{\sigma} = 20 - 3 = 17$

(See Figure 5.6)

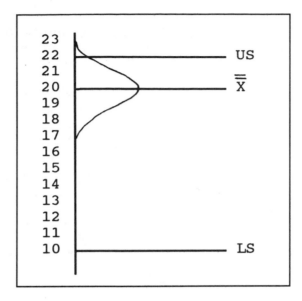

Figure 5.6 Process in Example 5.5

Then, process capability ratio

$$= \frac{6\hat{\sigma}}{\text{specification range}} \times 100\%$$

$$= \frac{6\ (1)}{22 - 10} \times 100\% = \frac{6}{12} \times 100\% = 50\%$$

Note that this is the same process capability ratio as the process in Example 5.4. However, unlike the process in Example 5.4, this process is *not* a good process. Product is being made out of the specification limits.

Note from Examples 5.4 and 5.5 that the process capability ratio only addresses the spread of the process. It only gives an indication as to whether or not the process is *potentially* capable of meeting specifications. It does *not* give an indication as to whether or not the process actually meets the specifications. This need leads to the third method for expressing the preliminary estimate of process capability.

$$3. \quad C_p = \frac{\text{specification range}}{6\hat{\sigma}}$$

Potential Capability (how many bell curves will fit into the specification range)

$$C_{pk} = \frac{\min [Z_U, Z_L]}{3}$$

where $Z_U = \dfrac{US - \bar{\bar{X}}}{\hat{\sigma}}$

$$Z_L = \frac{\bar{\bar{X}} - LS}{\hat{\sigma}}$$

Demonstrated Excellence (compared to specifications)

This pair of indices was borrowed from the Japanese, then modified and introduced into the United States by Ford Motor Company (Kane 1986). We will first discuss the index C_p.

C_p (*potential capability*) is defined as:

$$C_p = \frac{\text{specification range}}{6\hat{\sigma}}.$$

C_p denotes how may $6\hat{\sigma}$ process distributions (bell-shaped curves) will fit into the specification range. C_p not only tells us if the process spread is small enough to allow us to meet specifications, it tells us by what amount (what factor) our process quality has the *potential* ability to show excellence beyond the minimum specification requirement.

Note that the threshold value for C_p is 1. Any value larger than 1 would imply that the natural spread of the process is small enough to meet our prescribed specifications. The larger the value for C_p, the better. Any value for C_p smaller than 1 would imply that the whole process bell curve will not fit into specifications and defective product will certainly be made. Hence, C_p tells whether or not the natural spread is small enough to meet our prescribed specifications, and by what safety factor we are potentially able to make product of quality which is superior to the minimum specification requirements.

Example 5.6

Suppose the process is in control and centered at $\overline{\overline{X}} = 16$, with $\hat{\sigma} = 1$. Then $3\hat{\sigma} = (3)(1) = 3$, so the process readings will get as large as:

upper natural limit (UNL) $= \overline{\overline{X}} + 3\hat{\sigma} = 16 + 3 = 19$

and as low as:

lower natural limit (LNL) $= \overline{\overline{X}} - 3\hat{\sigma} = 16 - 3 = 13$

The process is the same as the one discussed in Example 5.4 and is shown in Figure 5.5.

$$C_p = \frac{\text{specification range}}{6\hat{\sigma}} = \frac{22 - 10}{6\,(1)} = \frac{12}{6} = 2.0$$

A C_p of 2.0 implies two distributions (bell-shaped process curves) will fit into the specification range. The process is centered on the specifications, producing a uniform product, and allowing a "cushion" if the process should change.

Example 5.7

The process is in control with:

$\overline{\overline{X}} = 16, \qquad \hat{\sigma} = 2$

Sketch: UNL $= \overline{\overline{X}} + 3\hat{\sigma} = 16 + 3(2) = 16 + 6 = 22$
      LNL $= \overline{\overline{X}} - 3\hat{\sigma} = 16 - 6 = 10$

This is illustrated in Figure 5.7

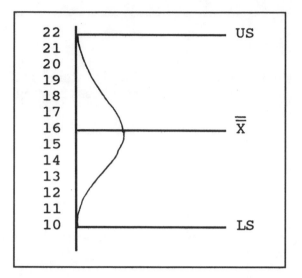

Figure 5.7 Process in Example 5.7

$$C_p = \frac{\text{specification range}}{6\hat{\sigma}} = \frac{22 - 10}{6\,(2)} = \frac{12}{12} = 1.0$$

i.e., only one bell-shaped curve will fit between the specification limits.

PROBLEM

5.5 The process is in control with:

$$\overline{\overline{X}} = 16, \ \hat{\sigma} = 3$$

US = 22
LS = 10.

Sketch and find C_p.

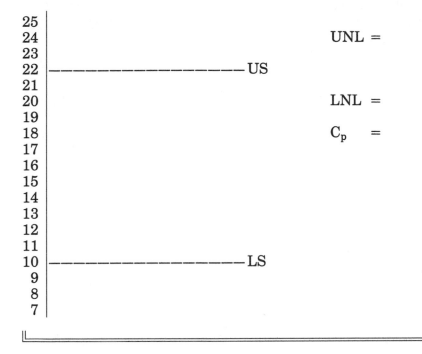

However, the process may not be centered at the midrange of the specification limits as illustrated by the next example.

Example 5.8

Continuing with the process discussed in Example 5.5 and illustrated in Figure 5.6, suppose the process is in control and centered at $\overline{\overline{X}} = 20$ with a spread having $\hat{\sigma} = 1$. Then, as before, $3\hat{\sigma} = 3 (1) = 3$ so:

upper natural limit (UNL) = $\overline{\overline{X}} + 3\hat{\sigma} = 20 + 3 = 23$
lower natural limit (LNL) = $\overline{\overline{X}} - 3\hat{\sigma} = 20 - 3 = 17$

$$C_p = \frac{\text{specification range}}{6\hat{\sigma}} = \frac{22 - 10}{6\,(1)} = \frac{12}{6} = 2.0$$

This is the same C_p value we got in Example 5.6. However, this time the process is not satisfactory because it is making product beyond the upper specification limit. C_p does not reflect this. C_p only reflects whether or not the process spread would be acceptable for a perfectly controlled process. Hence, we need another index to describe how well the process has demonstrated conformity to specifications to tell how well our process has narrowed around the midpoint of the specifications.

The process capability index that accomplishes this is called C_{pk}. C_{pk} is the "demonstrated excellence" of the process. If C_{pk} is equal to or larger than 1, the closest specification limit is far enough from the process center so that virtually no product is being made beyond the specifications. If C_{pk} is less than 1, the process is spreading beyond at least one of the specification limits, so defectives are being made.

The evaluation of C_{pk} may be approached using either an algebraic or a graphical method. We will look at the algebraic method first.

To work through the formula for C_{pk}, it is necessary to understand the concept of a Z-score.

A Z-score is the distance of a specification limit from the process average in terms of the standard deviation of the process. Since the process is assumed to vary $3\hat{\sigma}$ upward from the average and $3\hat{\sigma}$ downward from the average, it is desirable that the specification limits be at least 3 standard deviations away from the average, i.e., that the Z-score be at least 3. The larger the Z-score, the farther the specification limit is from the process average and hence, the tighter the repeatability of the process about target. We will use the formulas:

$$Z_U = \frac{US - \bar{\bar{X}}}{\hat{\sigma}} \quad \text{for the upper specification limit}$$

$$\text{and } Z_L = \frac{\bar{\bar{X}} - LS}{\hat{\sigma}} \quad \text{for the lower specification limit.}$$

For example, if $US = 70$, $\bar{\bar{X}} = 50$, and $\hat{\sigma} = 10$, then we use Z_U and get $Z_U = \dfrac{70 - 50}{10} = \dfrac{20}{10} = 2$.

PROBLEM

5.6 Assuming $\overline{\overline{X}} = 60$ and $\hat{\sigma} = \overline{R}/d_2 = 10$, use the formulas for Z_U and Z_L and find the Z-scores corresponding to the following specification limits.

    a. US = 80
    b. LS = 50
    c. US = 75
    d. LS = 35
    e. US = 70

Z_U (Z upper) is the distance the upper specification limit falls above the process average in terms of standard deviations, $Z_U = \dfrac{US - \overline{\overline{X}}}{\hat{\sigma}}$. Z_L (Z lower) is the distance the lower specification limit falls below the process average in terms of standard deviations, $Z_L = \dfrac{\overline{\overline{X}} - LS}{\hat{\sigma}}$. Note that in the formula for Z_L, $\overline{\overline{X}}$ and LS have been switched around in an attempt to try to avoid negative signs. (If $\overline{\overline{X}} - LS$ is negative, the process is producing more than 50 percent of the product outside of the specification limits. The same is true if $US - \overline{\overline{X}}$ is negative.)

Since we are most concerned with the specification limit that is closest to the process average, C_{pk} addressed the smaller of Z_U and Z_L, represented by Z_{min}.

Z_{min} is then divided by 3 to get C_{pk}. If C_{pk} is smaller than 1, the minimal safety factor has not been achieved — there is no "margin of safety," and defectives are being made.

$$Z_U = \frac{US - \overline{\overline{X}}}{\hat{\sigma}}$$

$$Z_L = \frac{\overline{\overline{X}} - LS}{\hat{\sigma}}$$

$$Z_{min} = \text{smaller of } Z_U \text{ or } Z_L$$

$$C_{pk} = \frac{Z_{min}}{3}$$

C_{pk} is an index that measures how narrow the process spread is compared to the specification spread — tempered by how well the process centers around the midpoint of the specifications. Note that this is implying that the target value for the process is at the midpoint of the specifications. It is a comparative term, so we can monitor C_{pk} increasing as we continuously and forever shrink the process variation around target.

Let us return to Example 5.6 to illustrate the calculation of C_{pk}:

Example 5.6, Part 2

Recall $\overline{\overline{X}} = 16$, $\hat{\sigma} = 1$. The process was illustrated in Figure 5.5.

Recall that $C_p = 2.0$. From Figure 5.5 it appears that C_{pk} is larger than 1 since no defectives are being produced.

By formula:

$$Z_U = \frac{US - \overline{\overline{X}}}{\hat{\sigma}} = \frac{22 - 16}{1} = \frac{6}{1} = 6$$

$$Z_L = \frac{\overline{\overline{X}} - LS}{\hat{\sigma}} = \frac{16 - 10}{1} = \frac{6}{1} = 6$$

$$Z_{min} = \text{smaller of 6 and 6} = 6$$

$$C_{pk} = \frac{Z_{min}}{3} = \frac{6}{3} = 2.0$$

Note that when the process is perfectly centered midway between the upper and lower specification limits, $C_{pk} = C_p$. When the process is not centered midway between specification limits, C_{pk} will be smaller than C_p, a penalty for not being "ideally" centered on the target — the midpoint of the specifications.

Example 5.7, Part 2

Recall $\overline{\overline{X}} = 16$, $\hat{\sigma} = 2$. The process was illustrated in Figure 5.7.

Recall that $C_p = 1$. Since the process is centered on the midpoint of the specifications, $C_{pk} = C_p$, so $C_{pk} = 1$. From Figure 5.7, it also can be seen that $C_{pk} = 1$, since the process is just touching the specification limits.

Calculate:

$$Z_U = \frac{US - \overline{\overline{X}}}{\hat{\sigma}} = \frac{22 - 16}{2} = \frac{6}{2} = 3$$

$$Z_L = \frac{\overline{\overline{X}} - LS}{\hat{\sigma}} = \frac{16 - 10}{2} = \frac{6}{2} = 3$$

so Z_{min} = smaller of 3 and 3 = 1

$$C_{pk} = \frac{Z_{min}}{3} = \frac{3}{3} = 1, \text{ as expected.}$$

Example 5.8, Part 2

In Example 5.8, with $\overline{\overline{X}} = 20$ and $\hat{\sigma} = 1$ (Figure 5.6), we calculated $C_p = 2$ and observed that this did not provide a good measure of process excellence. We will now calculate C_{pk} for this same example.

Continuing with Example 5.8:

$$Z_U = \frac{US - \overline{\overline{X}}}{\hat{\sigma}} = \frac{22 - 20}{1} = \frac{2}{1} = 2$$

$$Z_L = \frac{\overline{\overline{X}} - LS}{\hat{\sigma}} = \frac{20 - 10}{1} = \frac{10}{1} = 10$$

so Z_{min} = smaller of 2 and 10 = 2

$$C_{pk} = \frac{Z_{min}}{3} = \frac{2}{3} = .67$$

Since C_{pk} is smaller than 1, it is noted that the process is producing product out of specification as was previously noted.

Example 5.9

Suppose the process is in control and centered at $\overline{\overline{X}} = 12$ with a spread having $\hat{\sigma} = .5$. Then $3\hat{\sigma} = 3(.5) = 1.5$, so:

upper natural limit (UNL) = $\overline{\overline{X}} + 3\hat{\sigma} = 12 + 1.5 = 13.5$
lower natural limit (LNL) = $\overline{\overline{X}} - 3\hat{\sigma} = 12 - 1.5 = 10.5$

The process is illustrated in Figure 5.8.

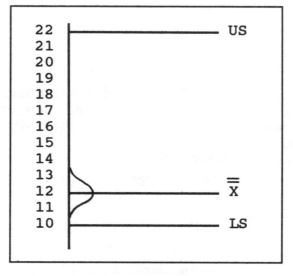

Figure 5.8 Process in Example 5.9

By looking at the graph, C_p looks high (much larger than 1) since many such bell curves will fit into the specification limits. C_{pk} will be larger than 1 since no defectives are being made, but will be much smaller than C_p since the process is so poorly centered in the specification limits.

Calculate:

$$C_p = \frac{\text{specification range}}{6\hat{\sigma}} = \frac{22 - 10}{6\,(.5)} = \frac{12}{3} = 4$$

$$Z_U = \frac{US - \overline{\overline{X}}}{\hat{\sigma}} = \frac{22 - 12}{.5} = \frac{10}{.5} = 20$$

$$Z_L = \frac{\overline{\overline{X}} - LS}{\hat{\sigma}} = \frac{12 - 10}{.5} = \frac{2}{.5} = 4$$

so Z_{min} = smaller of 20 and 4 = 4

$$C_{pk} = \frac{Z_{min}}{3} = \frac{4}{3} = 1.33, \text{ as expected.}$$

Note in Example 5.9 that $C_{pk} = 1.33$. A C_{pk} of 1.33 is often thought of as a minimum acceptable value in production, since this implies a Z_{min} of 4 which gives at least one standard deviation of "cushion" between the natural limits and the specification limits. This reflects uniform product and provides a minimal acceptable allowance for mean shift or increased dispersion. A Z value of 4 rather than 3 also means fewer parts are outside of the specifications. (Recall only around 99.7 percent of the readings are within 3 standard deviations of the mean for a normal distribution.) Decreasing the variability also saves money by incurring less loss as explained in Chapter 16.

A C_{pk} of at least 2.00 should be obtained on a new tool tryout in order to allow for the expected increase of variability in regular production over an extended period of time.

Note that in this example, a simple centering of the process to the middle of the specifications would increase the value of C_{pk} to a value of 4.0.

PROBLEMS

5.7 Given the process is in control with $\overline{\overline{X}} = 16$, $\hat{\sigma} = 0.5$, US $= 22$, LS $= 10$, sketch the process and compute C_{pk}.

```
22 |
21 |                              Z_U  =
20 |
19 |
18 |
17 |                              Z_L  =
16 |
15 |
14 |
13 |                              C_pk =
12 |
11 |
10 |
```

5.8 Continuing Problem 5.5 with $\overline{\overline{X}} = 16$, $\hat{\sigma} = 3$, US $= 22$, LS $= 10$, sketch the process and compute C_{pk}.

```
25 |
24 |                              Z_U  =
23 |
22 |
21 |
20 |                              Z_L  =
19 |
18 |
17 |
16 |                              C_pk =
15 |
14 |
13 |
12 |
11 |
10 |
 9 |
 8 |
 7 |
```

5.9 Given the process is in control with $\overline{\overline{X}} = 19$, $\hat{\sigma} = 1$, US = 22, LS = 10, sketch the process and compute C_p and C_{pk}.

```
26
25                              C_p  =
24
23
22                              Z_U  =
21
20
19                              Z_L  =
18
17
16                              C_pk =
15
14
13
12
11
10
 9
 8
 7
```

5.10 Given the process is in control with $\overline{\overline{X}} = 20$, $\hat{\sigma} = 2$, US = 22, LS = 10, sketch the process and compute C_p and C_{pk}.

```
26
25
24
23
22
21
20
19
18
17
16
15
14
13
12
11
10
 9
 8
 7
```

C_p =

Z_U =

Z_L =

C_{pk} =

5.11 Given the process is in control with $\overline{\overline{X}} = 17$, $\hat{\sigma} = 2.5$, US = 22, LS = 10, sketch the process and compute C_p and C_{pk}.

```
26
25                                C_p  =
24
23
22                                Z_U  =
21
20
19                                Z_L  =
18
17
16                                C_pk =
15
14
13
12
11
10
 9
 8
 7
```

5.12 Your process has been found to be in statistical control. From the control chart, it is found that $\overline{\overline{X}} = 40.2$ and $\overline{R} = 9.3$ for subgroups of size 4. The specifications on this product are LS = 25.0 and US = 43.1. Sketch the process distribution against the specifications. Find C_p and C_{pk}.

Note the relationship between the product specifications and C_{pk} from the graphs in Figure 5.9.

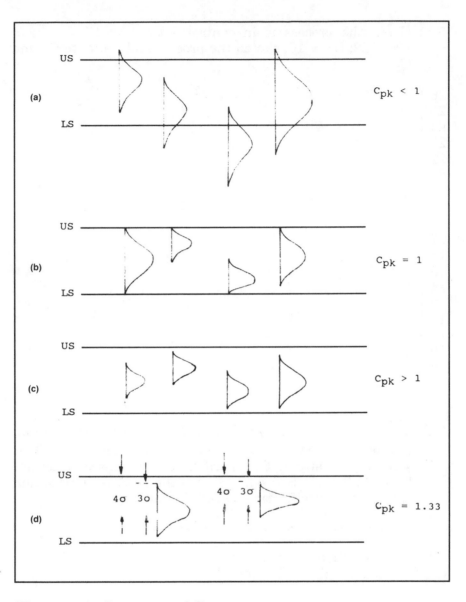

Figure 5.9 Summary of C_{pk}

For a given 6σ spread, C_{pk} can be improved by moving the center of the process toward the midpoint of the specifications, as shown in Figure 5.10. Shifting the process up any further would begin to decrease the value of C_{pk} as we move the process average farther from midpoint of specifications.

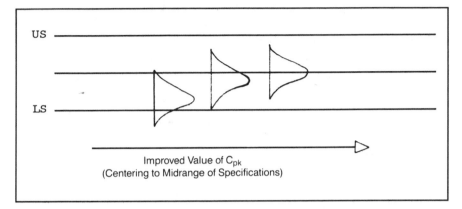

Figure 5.10   Improving the Value of C_{pk}

Once the process is centered at the midpoint of specifications, C_{pk} can be improved only by decreasing the process standard deviation (the spread) as shown in Figure 5.11.

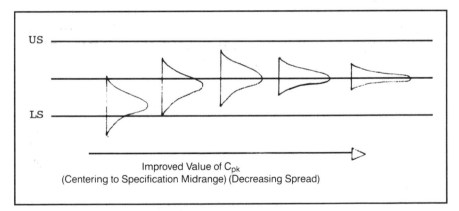

Figure 5.11   Improving the Value of C_{pk}

Note than an increase in C_{pk} resulted from a more uniform product around the midpoint of specifications.

A Graphical Interpretation of C_{pk}

The interrelationship between C_p and C_{pk} may be illustrated graphically as shown in Figure 5.12, where we let

$$A = \text{half specification} = \frac{US - LS}{2}$$

B (for bell) = half bell width $\equiv 3\hat{\sigma}$

C (for closest) = distance from $\overline{\overline{X}}$ to the closest specification limit.

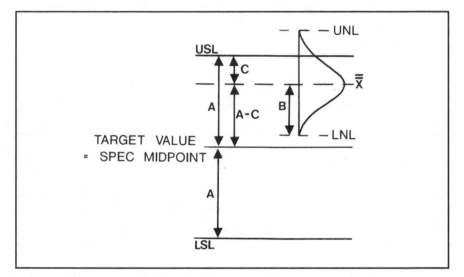

Figure 5.12 Graphical Interpretation of C_{pk}

Consider the dimension "C." It is the distance from the process center, $\overline{\overline{X}}$, to the closest specification, which may be measured, say, in "inches." Note that if we were to measure in units of "standard deviations" instead of "inches," C would be a Z-score. Similarly, if we measure C in units of "half-bell widths," C becomes the measure of demonstrated process quality as compared to specifications, C_{pk}. Following the approach of measuring in units of *half-bell widths* (B = $3\hat{\sigma}$) the following relationships can be shown:

Demonstrated Process Excellence	Distance from $\overline{\overline{X}}$ to = closest specification limit, measured in half bells	$= C_{pk} = \frac{C}{B}$
Mean Shift Demerits	Distance from = specification midpoint to $\overline{\overline{X}}$, measured in half bells	$= MS = \frac{A-C}{B}$

(Sum) Potential (Equals) Process Capability	Half specification = range, measured in half bells	$= C_p \;\; = \frac{A}{B}$

Note again that as the process becomes perfectly centered, the mean shift approaches zero and C_{pk} approaches C_p as an upper limit.

Example 5.6, Part 3

The process is in control with $\overline{\overline{X}} = 16$, $\hat{\sigma} = 1$, US $= 22$, LS $= 10$ (Figure 5.5).

Sketch: UNL $= \overline{\overline{X}} + 3\hat{\sigma} = 16 + 3\,(1) = 16 + 3 = 19$

 LNL $= \overline{\overline{X}} - 3\hat{\sigma} = 16 - 3 = 13$

Half specification $= A = \dfrac{22 - 10}{2}$ $\qquad\qquad = 6.0$

distance from $\overline{\overline{X}}$ to closest specification $= C = 22 - 16 \;\; = 6.0$

$3\hat{\sigma} = $ half bell $\quad = B = 3\,(1)$ $\qquad\qquad\qquad = 3.0$

$$C_{pk} = \quad \frac{C}{B} \quad = \frac{6}{3} = 2.0$$

$$MS = \frac{A - C}{B} = \frac{0}{3} = 0.0$$

$$C_p = \quad \frac{A}{B} \quad = \frac{6}{3} = 2.0$$

Example 5.8, Part 3 (Figure 5.6)

The process is in control with $\overline{\overline{X}} = 20$, $\hat{\sigma} = 1$. Sketch:

UNL $= \overline{\overline{X}} + 3\hat{\sigma} = 20 + 3\,(1) = 20 + 3 = 23$

LNL $= \overline{\overline{X}} - 3\hat{\sigma} = 20 - 3 = 17$

$$\text{Half specification} = \text{A} = \frac{22 - 10}{2} \qquad\qquad = 6.0$$

$$\overline{\overline{X}} \text{ to closest specification} = \text{C} = 22 - 20 \qquad = 2.0$$

$$3\hat{\sigma} = \text{half bell} = \text{B} = 3\,(1) \qquad\qquad\qquad = 3.0$$

$$C_{pk} = \frac{C}{B} = \frac{2}{3} \qquad\qquad\qquad\qquad\qquad = .67$$

$$MS = \frac{A - C}{B} = \frac{4}{3} \qquad\qquad\qquad\qquad = 1.33$$

$$C_p = \frac{A}{B} = \frac{6}{3} \qquad\qquad\qquad\qquad\qquad = 2.0$$

PROBLEM

5.13 The process is in control with $\overline{\overline{X}} = 20$, $\hat{\sigma} = 2$, US $= 22$, LS $= 10$

Sketch: UNL $= \overline{\overline{X}} + 3\hat{\sigma} =$

LNL $= \overline{\overline{X}} - 3\hat{\sigma} =$

Half specification $= \text{A} =$

$\overline{\overline{X}}$ to closest specification $= \text{C} =$

$3\hat{\sigma} = $ half bell $= \text{B} =$

$$C_{pk} = \frac{C}{B} \qquad\qquad =$$

$$MS = \frac{A - C}{B} \qquad\qquad =$$

$$C_p = \frac{A}{B} \qquad\qquad =$$

Use of C_p and C_{pk}

The tool engineer has the primary responsibility for providing tooling that is potentially capable of meeting specifications. The tool engineer's criterion for evaluating the tooling is the measure of *potential process capability*, C_p. Everyone else in the organization should be primarily interested in the *demonstrated excellence* of the process, C_{pk}. Interest in C_p is of a secondary nature.

In communicating information about process capability, C_{pk} should be the standard. Manufacturers at each step in the process must be primarily concerned with their supplier's demonstrated excellence and their own demonstrated excellence as compared to specifications. In practice, a high C_{pk} (say 3.5) shows a "safety factor." This concept of attaining the minimal possible spread from the target value — being better than required by specifications — must become our measure of quality in the future if we are to successfully compete in the world markets.

A simple quantitative measure of demonstrated process quality (C_{pk}) is, indeed, a new dimension in evaluating the "capability" of a manufacturing process. This concept provides a universal yardstick by which we can measure and communicate the elusive concept we know as "quality."

We now know that our quest for quality must be an effort to continuously and forever shrink the limits of variability of the process about our target value, resulting in more uniform product and hence better fitting parts and cost reductions. The factor C_{pk} enables us to quantitatively monitor our progress in this ceaseless endeavor. (See also Chapter 16.)

Caution When Using C_{pk}

Several words of caution are in order here. First, and most important, process capability is not defined until after the process is in a state of control as seen by a control chart. Only then is the process stable and it makes sense to speak of the capability of the process. If the process is not in control, do *not* calculate C_{pk}.

A second word of caution is that the calculation of C_{pk} assumes that the target value for the quality characteristic is located at the midpoint of the specifications. If this is not the case, centering the process on the off-centered target will result in a lower value of C_{pk} as if the process was being "penalized" for centering on target. Some attempts (Kane 1986) have been made to redefine C_p and C_{pk} for off-centered targets, but these attempts have not yet reached a balance between aiming for the off-centered target yet watching how the process is doing compared to specification.

A third caution is that C_{pk} is an arbitrary algebraic formula which may not express the excellence of the process satisfactorily. For example, process excellence as measured by a loss function (Chapter 16) may not be faithfully reflected by C_{pk} (Figure 5.13). Also, in the case of one-sided specifications, although C_{pk} is mathematically defined, a higher value of C_{pk} may not reflect a better process. C_{pk} is best considered as a tentative measure of process excellence which is useful under many circumstances.

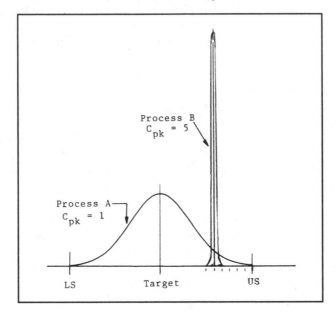

Figure 5.13 C_{pk} Should Not Be Considered Alone: Process A Provides Much Less "Loss," but Process B Has a C_{pk} Five Times as Large (See Chapter 16)

A final word of caution: C_{pk} is not an absolute measure of excellence but only a measure relative to the specification limits, which may change. Specification limits are only arbitrary due to the fact that engineering might put another set of specification limits on the quality characteristic tomorrow. One could always go about improving the value of C_{pk} by obtaining wider limits (or by changing the method by which the process standard deviation is estimated). Such tactics would obscure the meaning of the process capability index. The important point is to track the values of C_{pk} as they increase over time denoting continuous improvement of the process. (See also Chapter 16.) Actually, the sketches of the process curves (as compared to the specification limits) over time provide the *real* information on the (hopeful) improvement of the process.

Estimating the Percent Defective

If the process is approximately normally distributed, the percent of product outside the specification limits can be approximated after the Z-score has been calculated.

PROBLEM

5.14 Complete the following table using the approximations from Figure 5.14.

_____ % will be above + 1σ
_____ % will be below − 1σ

_____ % will be above + 2σ
_____ % will be below − 2σ

_____ % will be above + 3σ
_____ % will be below − 3σ

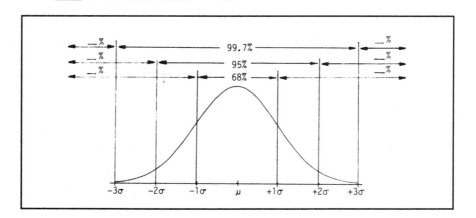

Figure 5.14 Areas Under the Normal Curve

A more extensive table (Appendix B) gives the percentage of the values which falls beyond a given number of standard deviations above the mean. The approximate percent of product that will fall beyond a specification limit may be estimated by using the following procedure.

Procedure for Approximating the Percent of Product Falling Outside of Specifications

Step 1 Compute the Z-score corresponding to the appropriate specification limit using the appropriate formula:

$$Z_U = \frac{US - \overline{\overline{X}}}{\hat{\sigma}}$$

or

$$Z_L = \frac{\overline{\overline{X}} - LS}{\hat{\sigma}}$$

Step 2 Check the signs of the Z-scores. If a Z-score is negative more than 50 percent of the product is beyond the specification limit. The procedure for this case is not given here.

Step 3 Look up the Z-score in Appendix B, finding the integer part and the first decimal along the left column. Go across the table for the second decimal place.

Step 4 Read the value in the body of the table at the intersection of the row and column from Step 3, above. This value is the fraction of product falling beyond that specification limit. Multiply this fraction by 100 percent to obtain the percent of product falling beyond the specification limit.

Step 5 If two specification limits are involved, follow the above procedure for each specification limit independently. Then add the two percents from Step 4 to get the total percent outside of the specification limits as shown in Figure 5.15.

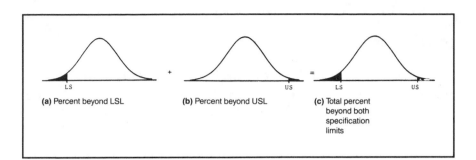

Figure 5.15 Total Percent Outside of Specification Limits

Example 5.10

The process is in control with

$$\overline{\overline{X}} = 60 \qquad \hat{\sigma} = 10.$$

...and US = 80. Then $Z_U = \dfrac{US - \overline{\overline{X}}}{\hat{\sigma}} = \dfrac{80 - 60}{10} = 2.0$

and about 2.5 percent will be above the US (about 2.28 percent from table).

Example 5.11

The process is in control with $\overline{\overline{X}} = 60$, $\hat{\sigma} = 10$,...and LS = 50.
Then $Z_L = \dfrac{\overline{\overline{X}} - LS}{\hat{\sigma}} = \dfrac{60 - 50}{10} = 1.0$; about 16 percent will be
below the LS (about 15.87 percent from the table).

Example 5.12

The process is in control with $\overline{\overline{X}} = 60$, $\hat{\sigma} = 10$,...and US = 75,
then $Z_U = \dfrac{US - \overline{\overline{X}}}{\hat{\sigma}} = \dfrac{75 - 60}{10} = 1.5$; about 6.68 percent will be
above the US.

PROBLEMS

For the specification limits in Problems 5.15 through 5.18, the process is in control and normally distributed with $\overline{\overline{X}} = 60$ and $\hat{\sigma} = 10$. Calculate Z_U or Z_L and estimate the percent of product beyond the specification limit.

5.15 LS = 35 $Z_L =$
5.16 US = 70 $Z_U =$
5.17 US = 72 $Z_U =$
5.18 LS = 42 $Z_L =$

5.19 Given US = 30.1 $\overline{\overline{X}} = 25.3$ $\overline{R} = 9.1$ n = 3, calculate Z_U and estimate the percent of product beyond the specification limit.

Note that these estimates of the amount of product out of specification are used only if the following are true:

- The process is in a state of statistical control and normally distributed.
- The information is somehow useful.

Often knowing the amount of product out of specification is of no real help. As soon as it is known that the process is out of specification, the decision is the same — fix the process.

Chapter 15 Improved Estimates of the Process Capability

In this chapter, as in Chapter 14, an ongoing state of statistical control is assumed, as demonstrated by an $\overline{X}$ and R (or similar) chart. Without this, the words "sigma" or "distribution" have no meaning.

Normal Distribution Assumed

In Chapter 14, a normal distribution of the process individuals was assumed. The estimate of the process standard deviation (sigma) that is most used is $\overline{R}/d_2$, which is correctly identified as the estimate of the within-subgroup component of variability. Shewhart cautioned specifically against using this deliberate underestimate of the total process variability for any purpose except to calculate control limits: $\overline{R}/d_2$ is *not* to be used to calculate process capability, except as a preliminary "quick and dirty" estimate.

If the questionable assumption of a normal distribution is to be retained, an improved estimate of process variability can be obtained by using the more realistic estimate of sigma provided by taking the *overall* single estimate:

$$s \text{ (overall)} = \sqrt{\Sigma(X - \overline{\overline{X}})^2/(N - 1)},$$

where N is the product kn, k being the number of subgroups and n the subgroup size. Note that in practice s (overall) is expected to be larger than $\overline{R}/d_2$.

The estimate of $\hat{\sigma} = s$ (overall) instead of $\hat{\sigma} = \overline{R}/d_2$ is preferred for all estimates relating to the dispersion, capability, etc., for process individuals. It should be noted, however, that any estimate of sigma (and the assumption of normality) is acceptable only for providing a preliminary estimate of the process distribution. The best practice for estimating process capability is to use as many observations as possible, obtained from an ongoing state of statistical control, using a probability plot, which will be discussed later.

Example 5.13

Using the small amount of data from Example 4.1, we will estimate the process standard deviation by s (overall) from the data just to illustrate the concept.

$$s \text{ (overall)} = 5.9$$

where all $N = 12$ observations are considered to be a single large group.

No Assumption of Normality: The Probability Plot

Shewhart (1939) cautioned us that estimates of the type $\hat{\sigma} = \bar{R}/d_2$:

1. Must be used to set control limits.
2. Must *not* be used for estimating process capability.

Whereas Shewhart inferred a state of statistical control from only 100 observations, for estimating process capability (as for the purpose of setting tolerance limits) he looked at the distribution of at least 1,000 points taken while the process was in statistical control. In practice, at least 125 observations are typically used. The familiar histogram can be used to portray these observations. The cumulative sum of the histogram, however, provides the straightforward method of obtaining the needed estimate of process capability. This plot is known as the cumulative distribution plot, or more commonly, as the probability plot.

The Probability Plot

The probability plot is a graph of the cumulative relative frequency of the data. It will be plotted here on normal probability paper.

Normal probability paper is shown in Figure 5.16. The data readings are plotted on the horizontal scale on the X axis. The "adjusted" cumulative relative frequency expressed as a percentage is plotted on the vertical axis or Y axis (see left scale in

Figure 5.16). Note this vertical scale. It is not a regular (linear) scale, but is "stretched" out at the top and bottom so that a plot of normal data will yield a straight line. The scale on the right side is linear. It is the Z-value of the reading from a normal distribution. The right scale is usable only if the distribution is normal. The left scale is always valid.

Although 1,000 points while in control are recommended to obtain a process capability with enough confidence to set tolerance limits, even just a few points on a probability plot may give useful information if judiciously interpreted. Regardless of the quantity of data available, the best estimate of the process capability that can be made from this set of data will come from the probability plot. A plotting procedure is given below including a "plotting convention" for adjusting the Y values (cumulative percent) referred to previously.

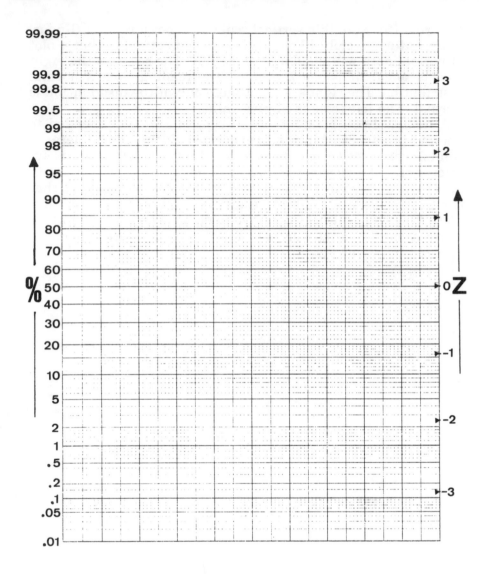

Figure 5.16 Normal Probability Paper

Procedure for Making a Probability Plot

Step 1 Arrange the X values from the smallest reading to the largest reading. The more observations used, the better the plot will be.

Step 2 Assign consecutive integer *order numbers* to the observations, i.e., give them a count number with the count of the smallest reading = 1, the count of the largest reading = N = the total number of readings = nk. Call this count number i.

Step 3 For each reading, calculate $Y = [100 \, (i - 0.5) \, / N]\%$. This is a plotting convention for the cumulative relative frequency expressed as a percent.

Step 4 Set the scale along the horizontal axis to accommodate all the readings.

Step 5 Plot each (X, Y) pair. Note: If there are repeat Y values for the same X value, plot only the highest and lowest Y values.

Step 6 Sketch the "curve" that appears to best fit these points.

Example 5.14

Starting at the bottom of the page of random normal numbers in Appendix C, Table 2 with $\mu = 20$, $\sigma = 5$, 10 numbers are read. They are:

$$13, \ 20, \ 15, \ 23, \ 13, \ 18, \ 26, \ 27, \ 14, \ 24.$$

(This small amount of data is used only as a *short* example.)

Plot the cumulative frequency distribution on normal probability paper using the plotting convention given above.

Making the Probability Plot

Step 1 Arrange the X values from the smallest reading to the largest reading. (These results are displayed in Column 1 of Table 5.2.)

Step 2 Assign consecutive integer order numbers to each observation. (These results are displayed in Column 2 of Table
5.2.)

(1)	(2)	(3)
		$y =$
x	i	$[100 (i - 0.5) / N]\%$
13	1	5
13	2	15
14	3	25
15	4	35
18	5	45
20	6	55
23	7	65
24	8	75
26	9	85
27	10	95

Table 5.2 X and Y Coordinates for Making a Probability Plot

Step 3 For each observation, calculate $Y = [100 (i - 0.5) / N]\%$.
(Here $N = 10$.) (These results are displayed in Column 3
of Table 5.2.)

Step 4 Set the scale along the horizontal axis to accommodate all
the readings. (See the horizontal axis in Figure 5.17.)

Step 5 Plot each (X, Y) pair. (Since no reading appeared more than
twice, all readings are plotted in Figure 5.17.)

Step 6 Sketch the "curve" that appears to best fit these points.
(Since we know the data are normally distributed, we try
to fit the best straight line. See the sketch in Figure 5.17.)

Note that such departures from the best fit line are quite
common when working with so few (only 10) observations.

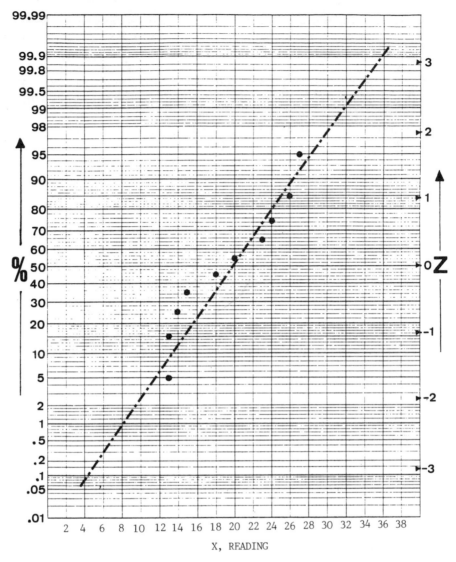

Figure 5.17 Probability Plot

PROBLEM

5.20 On the next few pages, plot the cumulative frequency distribution from four more sets of $N = 10$ numbers continuing from the bottom of the page of random normal numbers with $\mu = 20$ and $\sigma = 5$ using the plotting convention $[100(i - 0.5)/N]\%$. Next plot the cumulative distribution for all 50 numbers (include Example 5.14) taken as a whole. What conclusions do you draw?

Set 2

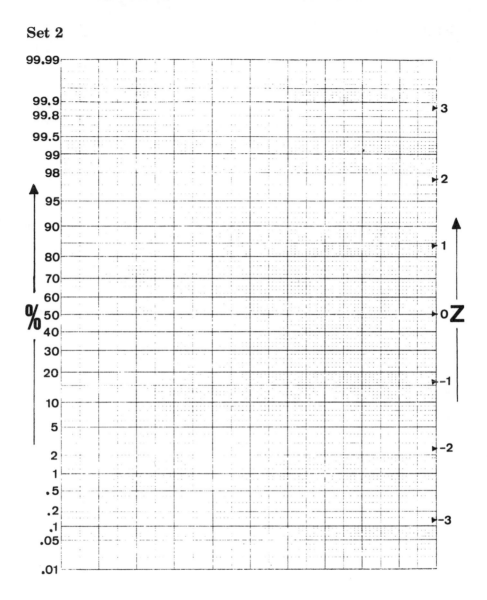

Set 3

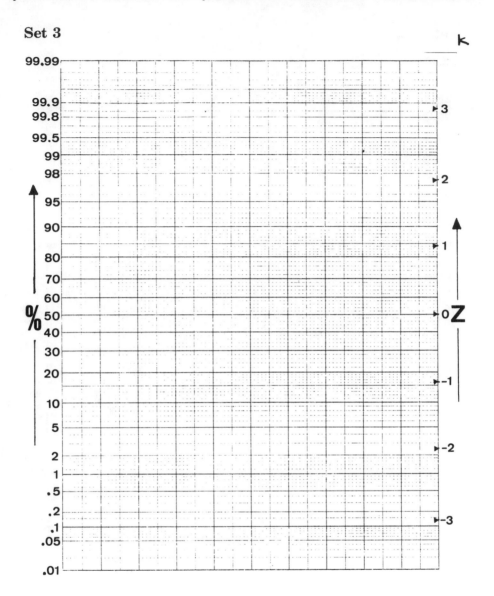

Set 4

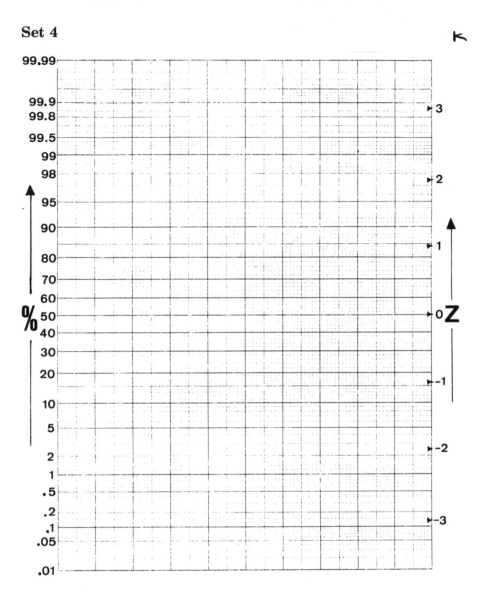

Set 5

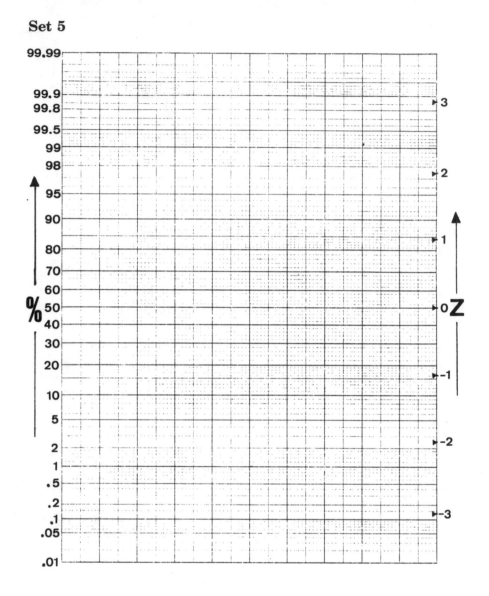

Total Set

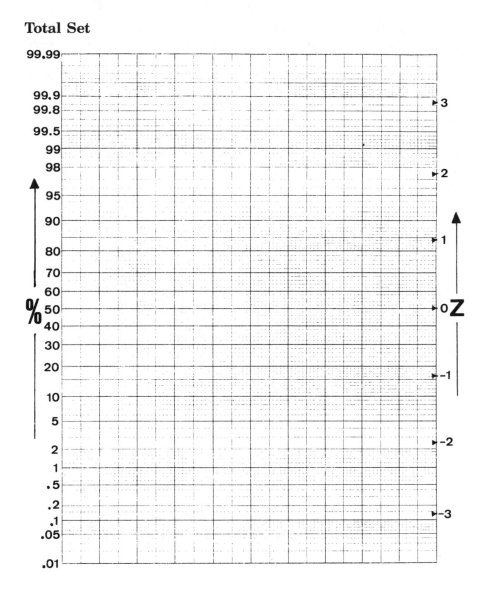

The probability plot, like the histogram, has no meaning if the process is not in statistical control. When used for many engineering purposes, a probability plot may consist of any number of observations, even just a few. For setting tolerance limits, a large number of observations while in control are desired. (Shewhart recommended at least 1,000, although in practice this many observations are seldom used.) The process capability estimate will be only as good as the amount of information available, but no matter how little information is available, the process capability estimate should *always* be based on the probability plot, rather than on the shortcut methods $\bar{\bar{X}} \pm 3\bar{R}/d_2$ or $\bar{\bar{X}} \pm 3s$ (overall).

The advantage of the probability plot is that it uses *all* of the data to best advantage and makes no assumption about normality, or any other distribution assumption.

If the points on the probability plot make a straight line, the normal distribution assumption is good, and the estimate from $\bar{\bar{X}} \pm 3s$ (overall) will probably be in good agreement with the estimate of process capability from the probability plot. If the curve made by the plotted points does not appear to be a straight line, the shape of the probability plot curve will help identify the nature of the distribution, as shown in Figure 5.18.

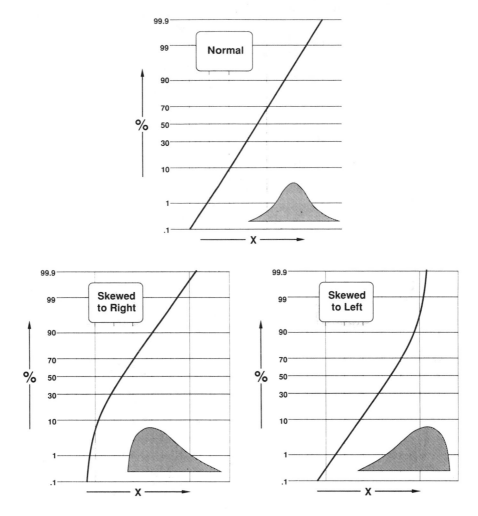

Figure 5.18 Cumulative Probability Plots for Various Types of Distributions (cont. on p. 230)

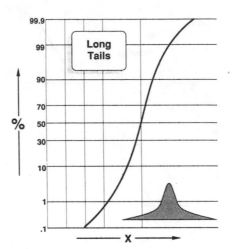

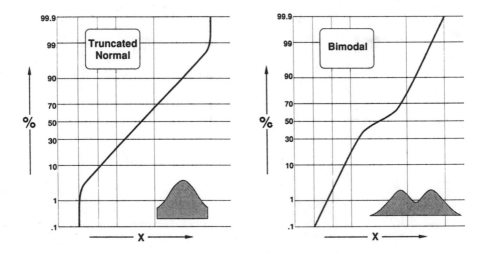

Figure 5.18 (cont.)

Procedure for Estimating the Process Capability from the Probability Plot

Step 1 Draw horizontal lines across the paper at Y = 0.1% and at Y = 99.9%. For the normal distribution, these are approximately at the 3-sigma limits.

Step 2 Where these two lines intersect the probability plot curve, drop vertical lines to the X axis.

Step 3 Read the intercepts $X_{.001}$ and $X_{.999}$ from the X axis.

Technical note: To the closest 0.001%, the 3-sigma limits for a normal distribution yield $X_{.00135}$ and $X_{.99865}$ corresponding to Y = 0.135% and Y = 99.865%. To the closest 0.1% these give the $X_{.001}$ and $X_{.999}$ values noted previously.

Note that the values of $X_{.001}$ and $X_{.999}$ are valid whether or not the probability plot is a straight line. They are the "limits" that leave 0.1% of the distribution in each tail, approximately analogous to 3-sigma limits for a true normal distribution.

Example 5.15

Consider the control chart of TIRs on armature shafts shown in Figure 5.19. The process appears to be in control. The histogram illustrated in Figure 5.20 shows the data to be skewed rather than normally distributed. The departure from normality was not severe enough to destroy the usefulness of the control chart, or for the control chart to clearly signal the nonnormality (although the charts were almost "in phase"). Calculating process capability using conventional methods ($\overline{\overline{X}} \pm 3\overline{R}/d_2$) gives natural limits of -19.0 and 48.4. These limits are not valid, however, because these conventional methods assume a normal distribution, a condition not met here. The probability plot, shown in Figure 5.21, is not a straight line — further evidence the data are not normally distributed. Noting where the plotted data intersects the 0.1 percent and 99.9 percent lines on the vertical axis, the corresponding horizontal axis readings are approximately 0.0 and 48.5. This implies that most all product can be held between these two values,

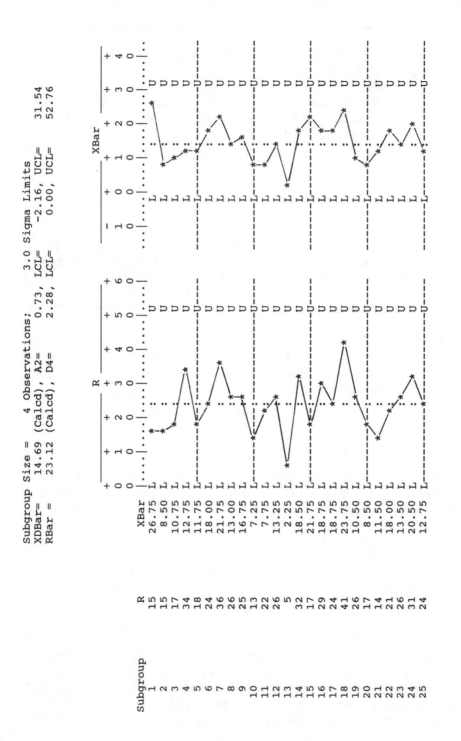

Figure 5.19 Control Chart on T I Rs

```
EACH VERTICAL UNIT IS 1 OBSERVATION(S)
Selected SubGroup s = 25, N   = 100  Observations

      |              X
      |          X   X
      |          X X X
  +15 |          X X X
      |          X X X
      |          X X X X
      |          X X X X       X
      |          X X X X       X
  +10 |          X X X X       X
      |          X X X X   X X
      |          X X X X X X X
      |          X X X X X X X
      |          X X X X X X X
  + 5 |          X X X X X X X
      |          X X X X X X X
      |          X X X X X X X X
      |          X X X X X X X X X X
      |          X X X X X X X X X X
      |.|.|.|.|.|.|.|.|.|.|.|.|.|.|.
       - - - + + + + + + + + + + +
       1 1 0 0 0 1 1 2 2 3 3 4 4 5
       5 0 5 0 5 0 5 0 5 0 5 0 5 0
```

Figure 5.20 Histogram of T I Rs

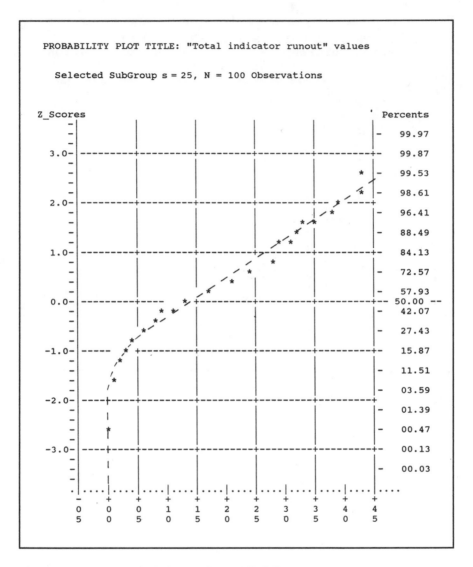

Figure 5.21 Probability Plot of T I Rs

defining the capability of the process. Note how far different the limits calculated in the conventional way were from the limits calculated in the proper way.

The control chart, histogram, and probability plot were obtained using StatScan® software.

PROBLEMS

5.21 The following data are displayed in an $\overline{X}$ and R chart in Figure 5.22. The cumulative frequency table is shown in Table 5.3. Complete the probability plot (Figure 5.23) and then estimate the process capability by

    a. $\overline{\overline{X}} + 3\overline{R}/d_2$
    b. $\overline{\overline{X}} + 3s$ (overall)
    c. $(X_{.001}, X_{.999})$

Compare.
Recall that the rows marked with an asterisk in Table 5.3 do not have to be plotted. (Why?)

Subgroup 1	0	11	12	20	2
Subgroup 2	32	13	−1	8	7
Subgroup 3	20	−1	−14	−10	−6
Subgroup 4	7	18	5	−5	−3
Subgroup 5	13	−6	16	9	15
Subgroup 6	29	12	13	12	17
Subgroup 7	6	−5	−9	21	12
Subgroup 8	6	4	17	17	13
Subgroup 9	18	−1	0	−21	20
Subgroup 10	1	13	18	11	−3

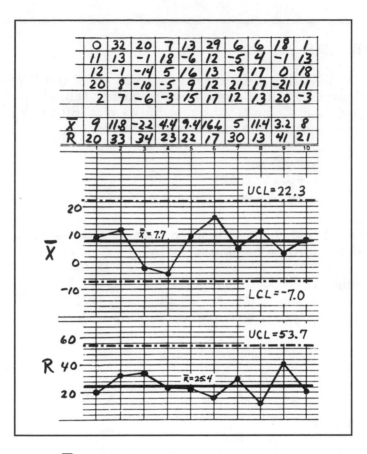

Figure 5.22 $\overline{X}$ and R Chart for Data in Problem 5.21

Order Number	Ordered X	$Y = [100\,(i - .5)\,/N]\%$
1	−21	1
2	−14	3
3	−10	5
4	−9	7
5	−6	9
6	−6	11
7	−5	13
8	−5	15
9	−3	17
10	−3	19
11	−1	21
12*	−1	23
13	−1	25
14	0	27
15	0	29
16	1	31
17	2	33
18	4	35
19	5	37
20	6	39
21	6	41
22	7	43
23	7	45
24	8	47
25	9	49
26	11	51
27	11	53
28	12	55
29*	12	57
30*	12	59
31	12	61
32	13	63
33*	13	65
34*	13	67
35*	13	69
36	13	71
37	15	73
38	16	75
39	17	77
40*	17	79
41	17	81
42	18	83
43*	18	85
44	18	87
45	20	89
46*	20	91
47	20	93
48	21	95
49	29	97
50	32	99

Table 5.3 Cumulative Frequency Table for Data in Problem 5.21

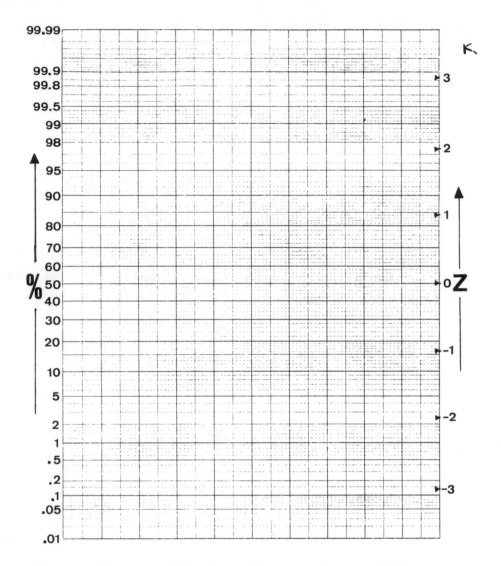

Figure 5.23 Probability Plot of Data in Problem 5.21

Process Capability Estimates for Problem 5.21

Method

1. $\overline{\overline{X}} \pm 3\overline{R}/d_2$

2. $\overline{\overline{X}} \pm 3s$ (overall)

3. From the probability plot:
   $(X_{.001}, X_{.999}) =$

5.22 The following data are displayed in an $\overline{X}$ and R chart in Figure 5.24. The cumulative frequency table is shown in Table 5.4. Complete the probability plot (Figure 5.25) and then compute the process capability three ways as in Problem 5.21. Compare these data and their results to the data and the results in Problem 5.21

Subgroup					
1	0	11	12	20	2
2	32	13	1	8	7
3	20	1	14	10	6
4	7	18	5	5	3
5	13	6	16	9	15
6	29	12	13	12	17
7	6	5	9	21	12
8	6	4	17	17	13
9	18	1	0	21	20
10	1	13	18	11	3

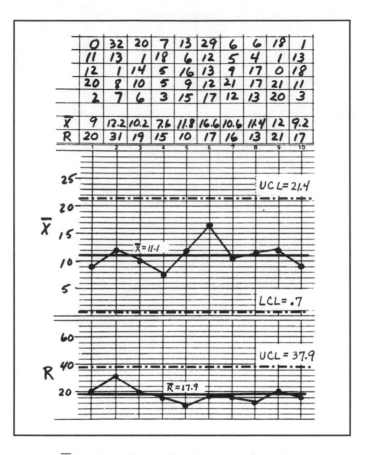

Figure 5.24 $\overline{\text{X}}$ and R Chart for Data in Problem 5.22

Order Number	Ordered X	Y = [100 (i − .5) /N]%
1	0	1
2	0	3
3	1	5
4	1	7
5	1	9
6	1	11
7	2	13
8	3	15
9	3	17
10	4	19
11	5	21
12	5	23
13	5	25
14	6	27
15	6	29
16	6	31
17	6	33
18	7	35
19	7	37
20	8	39
21	9	41
22	9	43
23	10	45
24	11	47
25	11	49
26	12	51
27	12	53
28	12	55
29	12	57
30	13	59
31	13	61
32	13	63
33	13	65
34	13	67
35	14	69
36	15	71
37	16	73
38	17	75
39	17	77
40	17	79
41	18	81
42	18	83
43	18	85
44	20	87
45	20	89
46	20	91
47	21	93
48	21	95
49	29	97
50	32	99

Table 5.4 Cumulative Frequency Table for Data in Problem 5.22

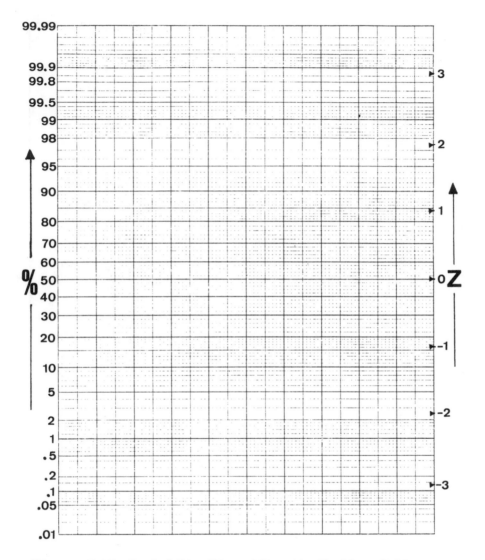

Figure 5.25 Probability Plot of Data in Problem 5.22

Process Capability Estimates for Problem 5.22

Method

1. $\overline{\overline{X}} \pm 3\overline{R}/d_2$

2. $\overline{\overline{X}} \pm 3s$ (overall)

3. From the probability plot:
   $(X_{.001}, X_{.999}) =$

5.23 You have identified the critical quality characteristic you wish to monitor. Arrange the following in the order in which you would do them.
   State of control
   Run chart
   Process capability index
   Control chart
   Natural limits

Chapter 16 Continuous Improvement: The Utility and Loss Functions

The reduction of *variability about target* for a given quality characteristic is, and should be, the ultimate goal for quality improvement. This reduction of variability begins with eliminating the assignable causes of variability and bringing the process into control. But this is *not* enough. On an ongoing basis, further ongoing improvement in the process is needed through the reduction of the variability due to common causes. These efforts must achieve the never-ending pursuit of "continuously and forever" shrinking the limits of variability about target.

The traditional view of loss from product is illustrated in Figure 5.26. All product falling within the specifications has been judged as equally good, resulting in no loss to the company. Product falling outside of specifications was considered bad, resulting in the loss of the cost of scrap or rework. This viewpoint does not seem realistic because from experience it is known that not all product within the specification is equally good. Product just within the upper specification limit is not as good as product at target. Similarly, product just outside the upper specification limit is not much different from product just within the upper specification limit.

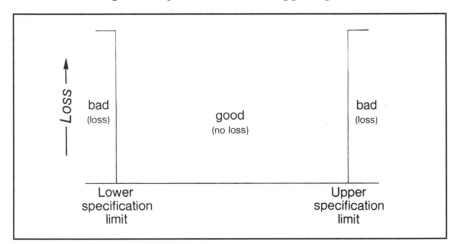

Figure 5.26 Traditional View of Loss

Burr (1967) discussed the need for specifying the desired distribution rather than just the specification limits. He considered two "utility" or "usefulness" curves as shown in Figure 5.27. Burr

(1967, p. 95) comments on these curves as follows. In curve (a)...

> The parts outside the limits are thought to be unusable and thus of zero utility (until reworked or "material review approved"). Meanwhile, those parts anywhere between the specification limits are all equally useful and in a sense perfect...The other utility curve (b) of (Figure 5.27) gives a more realistic picture. The utility must be at its maximum around the middle of the tolerance range, gradually diminishing in each direction, but not hitting zero until well outside the typical limits. Isn't this curve much more realistic and practical?

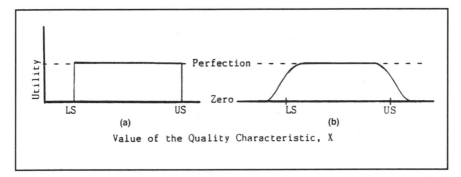

Figure 5.27 Two Utility or Usefulness Curves

Taguchi and Wu (1979, p. 1) and Taguchi (1981, p. 1) defined quality "as the losses a product imparts to the society from the time the product is shipped." Taguchi also states that the loss function is U-shaped, quadratic. He first presented this concept in Tokyo in 1960.

The loss function can be illustrated by a quadratic function as illustrated in Figure 5.28. The more the product deviates from the target value, the more loss is incurred.

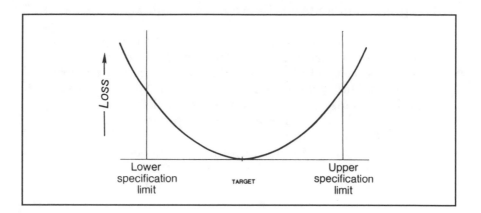

Figure 5.28 A More Realistic Loss Function

The process in Figure 5.29 is meeting specifications but the process is still incurring a loss represented schematically by the shaded area. As the process is improved by elimination of some common causes of variability, less loss is incurred (Figure 5.30).

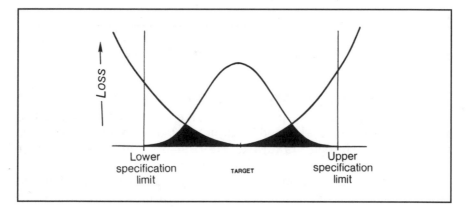

Figure 5.29 Product with a Normal Distribution

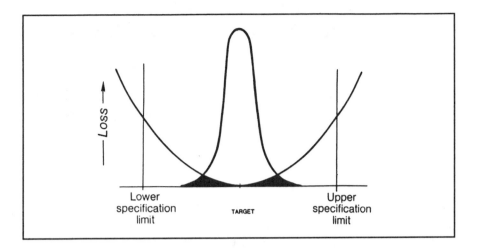

Figure 5.30 Product with a Narrowed Normal Distribution

Technical note: The relative loss generated by a process is really the product of the height of the process normal curve at each reading times the height of the loss function at that reading summed over all readings.

Jessup (1985) concluded that industry's long-term competitive viability depends on how effectively it uses its economic resources to serve market needs. To be effective, three things are needed. At each step of the process, suppliers must:

1. Recognize that customers (downstream processes and end-item users) have needs and expectations that often differ from their own.
2. Learn those needs to be able to set target values for quality characteristics to fill those needs. Recognize the penalties for deviating from those targets.
3. Find and implement ways to reduce process variation from the target.

Jessup (1985, p. 6) states that a loss function "may provide the necessary economic decision framework to support continuing improvement."

The loss function has been useful to depict varying degrees of excellence in the process. Much work remains to be done to put this concept to practical use and to overcome the drawbacks C_{pk} exhibits.

Chapter 17
Control Charts for Individuals
Building on the Run Chart

Shewhart (1931) pointed out that the optimum size subgroup would be one for an ongoing control chart in the presence of a changing chance cause system. The obstacle at that time was the lack of a method for estimating process variability if the subgroup size, n, was dropped below 2. Shewhart's wisdom has been confirmed many times over by the realization that run charts, so highly recommended by Deming, provide a strikingly powerful and simple tool for process improvement. The control charts for individuals described below take the run chart one step forward to provide control limits on the variability of the individuals.

The X and MR Chart for 100 Percent Inspection on Long Runs

The chart for individuals (X) and moving range (MR) is simple and useful for the case where 100 percent inspection is used on long production runs. This is particularly true when the production rate is low. For example, with the manufacture of large components with a production rate of six or seven per day, it would be common to take measurements on each one. The readings can be correctly subgrouped into nonoverlapping subgroups of any constant size. Following Shewhart, we note that when the chance-cause system changes over time, the smallest possible subgroup size will give the smallest, hence best, estimate of sigma. The smallest group from which an estimate of sigma can be obtained is n = 2. This defines the optimum subgroup size under 100 percent inspection (or for any other detection scheme intended to detect the occurrence of a changing chance-cause system). An additional benefit of a chart for individuals in a slow process is that we are able to determine after each observation whether or not that reading is still within the limits of natural variability with no assignable causes present.

Under conditions of 100 percent inspection, a control chart on individuals may be preferred to one for averages.

The most common control chart for individuals is the X (individual) and MR (moving range) chart. It is not considered a "Shewhart chart" by some people because:

1. It does not use *independent* subgroups to estimate dispersion.
2. It plots individuals rather than averages.

Computations for the X and MR Charts

Steps for Constructing an X and MR Chart

Step 1 Collect the individual readings.
Ideally, 30 or more readings should be collected. (Preliminary estimates may be obtained with 10 observations.)

Step 2 Calculate the MR values.
A moving range (MR) value is the difference between the current reading and the previous reading, high minus low. An MR value is always greater than or equal to zero. Note that the first of a series of sequential observations will not have a corresponding MR value.

Step 3 Find the center lines for the two charts: the mean of all the X values to obtain $\overline{X}$, and the mean of all the MR values to obtain $\overline{MR}$.

Step 4 Calculate the control limits for the charts.
For the X chart:
UCL (X) = $\overline{X}$ + [2.66 $\overline{MR}$]
LCL (X) = $\overline{X}$ − [2.66 $\overline{MR}$]

For the MR chart:
UCL (MR) = 3.27 $\overline{MR}$
LCL (MR) = 0

Step 5 Plot the center lines and control limits.
Plot two separate charts, one for the X values (called an X chart) and one for the MR values (called an MR chart). Using an appropriate scale on each chart, draw the center lines, $\overline{X}$ and $\overline{MR}$, and the control limits. Label these lines with the appropriate values to ease reading of the chart.

Step 6 Plot the points.
Plot the X and MR values from each observation. (Note that the first reading does not have an MR value.) The X values and the MR values are usually connected by lines to help the visual display of the pattern. All indications of lack of control should be clearly marked to point them out immediately to the reader.

Example 5.16

The following are coded data for the dimensions of shaft journals on large hydroelectric turbine rotors. In order to set up trial control limits, 10 readings are taken.

Step 1 Collect the individual readings.
The 10 readings are:

| 39 | 31 | 28 | 32 | 45 | 31 | 25 | 32 | 30 | 46 |

Step 2 Calculate the MR values.

X	39	31	28	32	45	31	25	32	30	46
MR		8	3	4	13	14	6	7	2	16

Step 3 Find the center lines for each chart.

$$\overline{X} = \frac{339}{10} = 33.9$$

$$\overline{MR} = \frac{73}{9} = 8.11$$

Step 4 Calculate the control limits for the charts.
For the X chart:

$$\text{UCL (X)} = \overline{X} + [2.66\ \overline{MR}] = 33.9 + [(2.66)(8.11)]$$
$$= 33.9 + 21.6$$
$$= 55.5$$

$$\text{LCL (X)} = \overline{X} - [2.66\ \overline{MR}] = 33.9 - 21.6$$
$$= 12.3$$

For the MR chart:

$$\text{UCL (MR)} = 3.27\ \overline{MR} = [3.27\ (8.11)\ ]$$
$$= 26.5$$

$$\text{LCL (MR)} = 0\ (\text{always})$$

Step 5 Plot the center lines and control limits.
See Figure 5.31.

Step 6 Plot the points.
See Figure 5.31.
Note that no evidence of lack of control is found.

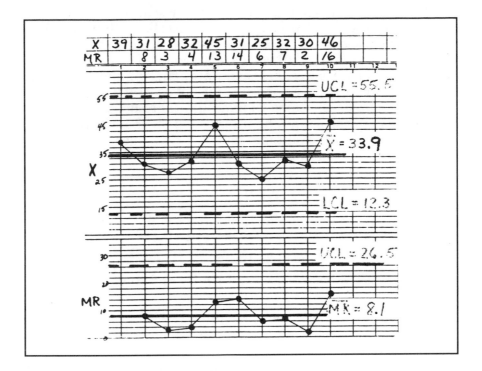

Figure 5.31 X and MR Chart

Note that when working with X and MR charts, the control limits are the natural limits.

The 2-sigma control limits are given by the following formulas:

$$2\text{-sigma UCL (X)} = \overline{X} + [1.77\ \overline{MR}]$$
$$2\text{-sigma LCL (X)} = \overline{X} - [1.77\ \overline{MR}]$$
$$2\text{-sigma UCL (MR)} = 2.51\ \overline{MR}$$
$$2\text{-sigma LCL (MR)} = 0\ \text{(always)}$$

Advantages and Disadvantages of the X and MR Chart

In theory, one disadvantage of the X and MR chart is its dependence on an underlying normality assumption. If a point goes out of the limits on the X chart it is difficult to tell whether it means the process is out of control with an assignable cause or if the underlying distribution is highly skewed. A second theoretical disadvantage is that you lose the sensitivity that X has to process shifts. In fact, the X and MR chart does an excellent job of detecting assignable causes in real processes. A third disadvantage of this chart is the fact that the MR values are correlated, since successive MR values share 50 percent of their data. This implies that some of the usual criteria for evidence of lack of control (such as 2 out of 3 points outside the same 2-sigma limit) are not valid for the MR chart. Patterns cannot be interpreted on the MR chart.

A summary of the advantages and disadvantages of the X and MR chart is given in Table 5.5.

ADVANTAGES

1. Simple to use and understand; just a half-step beyond a run chart.

2. Easy to calculate control limits.

3. No confusion between control limits and limits for individuals; they are one and the same.

4. Plotted points can be compared directly with specifications. (Your specifications are almost always on individuals, not on averages.)

5. Results for a single observation can be plotted as soon as they are obtained. You don't have to wait to aggregate a subgroup.

6. Usually give smallest, hence best, estimate of sigma (just like $\overline{X}$ and R with n = 2).

7. Gives a better look at what is really happening with the individuals in time order.

DISADVANTAGES

1. Seldom useful except for 100 percent inspection (if you *must* use subgroups of size one without 100 percent inspection, X and MR is no worse than other control charts).

2. Poor with skewed data.

3. Gives no notice of skewed data.

4. Some of the usual criteria for evidence of lack of control are invalid for MR charts.

5. Poor for detection of shifts in level of process.

Table 5.5 Advantages and Disadvantages of X and MR Charts

PROBLEMS

5.24 Make an X and MR chart for the following data.

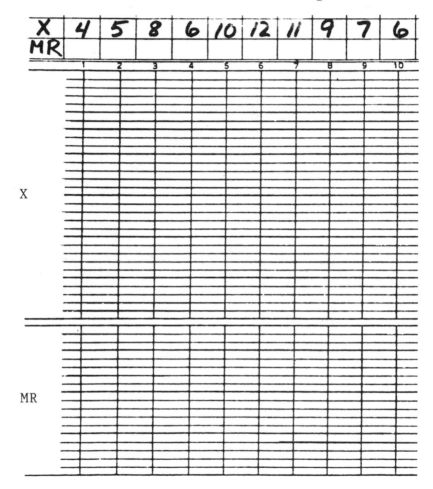

| X | 4 | 5 | 8 | 6 | 10 | 12 | 11 | 9 | 7 | 6 |
| MR | | | | | | | | | | |

5.25 Make an X and MR chart for the following data. Note that these are the same readings as in Problem 5.24, but in a different order.

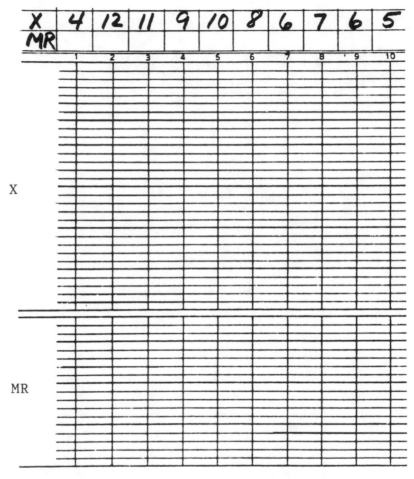

X	4	12	11	9	10	8	6	7	6	5
MR										

5.26 For the following data, find if there is evidence of lack of control, using X and MR charts with 2-sigma limits.

 50   51   63   34   49   32   17   23   24

5.27 The following data give the number of orders filled daily for the last 30 days. Find if there is evidence of lack of control, using X and MR charts (reading across).

14	24	27	14	22	16	21	25	15	22
15	14	19	17	16	32	18	17	15	23
14	24	21	19	21	27	23	23	23	22

The Discontinuous X and MR Chart

Under some circumstances, consecutive observations may be taken only for a small number of consecutive pieces, followed by an interruption in the continuity of the process. This could result, for example, in short runs of data, such as the following:

| | 4 1 7 | 5 0 4 9 | 3 | 1 5 | |

This condition could exist because:

1. Only a few pieces of a particular part were needed and made at any one time.
2. Tool adjustments were made at irregular intervals after only a few pieces.
3. Data were gathered in this way because those were the pieces the operator considered to be of interest.

Whatever the reason, data gathered in short runs can result in a series of X and MR values and plots (Figure 5.32).

It is essential to note the discontinuous nature of the X and MR charts. In this case, $\overline{X} = 39/10 = 3.9$ and $\overline{MR} = 27/6 = 4.5$. The discontinuous X and MR chart provides an extremely powerful and versatile tool.

The RX Chart: A Special Case of the X and MR Chart

If the short runs of the X and MR chart were deliberately kept to a constant length of $n = 2$, a special chart results, which we will call the RX chart. It is a chart for ranges (R) of consecutive pairs and for the individuals (X) that make up those pairs.

The RX chart has all of the advantages of the X and MR chart listed above, but eliminates most of the disadvantages. The R chart is identical with the R chart for an $\overline{X}$ and R chart with subgroups of size 2, but in the case of the RX chart, the individuals instead of the averages are plotted. This leads to a considerable simplification in plotting and experience has shown that there is no loss in efficiency in detecting assignable causes. An example is illustrated in Figure 5.33

Note: A similar chart for individuals could be made for $n = 3$, 4, etc.

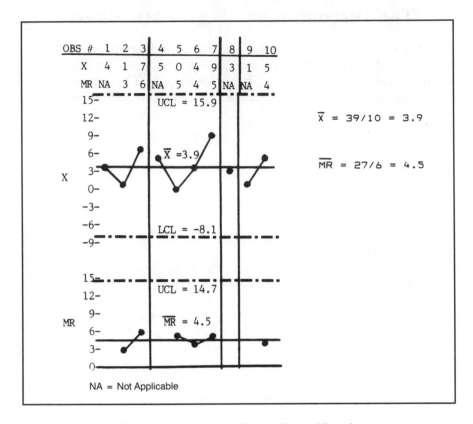

Figure 5.32 Short Run Data, Same Part Number

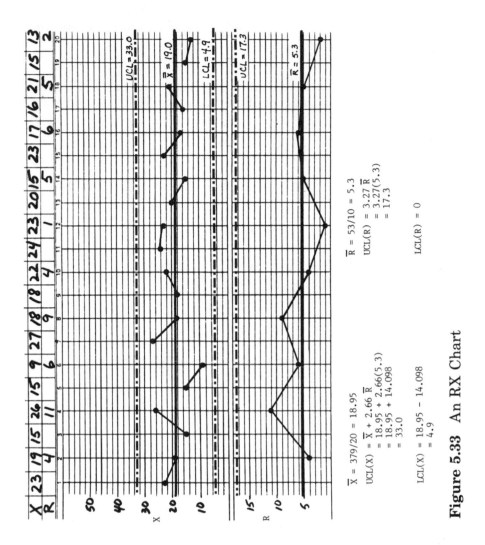

$\bar{X} = 379/20 = 18.95$

$UCL(X) = \bar{X} + 2.66\,\bar{R}$
$\quad = 18.95 + 2.66(5.3)$
$\quad = 18.95 + 14.098$
$\quad = 33.0$

$LCL(X) = 18.95 - 14.098$
$\quad = 4.9$

$\bar{R} = 53/10 = 5.3$

$UCL(R) = 3.27\,\bar{R}$
$\quad = 3.27(5.3)$
$\quad = 17.3$

$LCL(R) = 0$

Figure 5.33 An RX Chart

PROBLEMS

5.28 Calculate trial control limits and make an X and MR chart for the following lengths of part number 526, taken in short runs:

3   2   9   0   6   ¦ 2   4 ¦   5   4   1

5.29 Calculate trial control limits and make an RX chart for the following data:

4   5   8   6   10   12   11   9   7   6

5.30 Make an RX chart for the following data (reading across):

14	24	27	14	22	16	21	25	15	22
15	14	19	17	16	32	18	17	15	23
14	24	21	19	21	27	23	23	23	22

Part VI. Process Maintenance

Continuous improvement is the ideal for all processes. However, due to the restriction of scarce resources (people, time, and money) we are forced to reserve our greatest attention to those processes for which process improvement is the most important. For the vast majority of the processes, where we must restrict our activity to maintenance, a less demanding tool than a control chart is needed. Run charts on individual observations provide an effective tool for process maintenance on this "98 percent" of our quality characteristics.

Chapter 18 Process Maintenance

Continuous improvement in product (goods or services) is accepted today as a condition precedent to competing in the world markets. However, it is essential that this be recognized as continuous *selective* improvement. The improvement process must be viewed in the following light: Given the conditions at this time, how should we allocate our resources so as to best address the needs for improvement as viewed by our customers? If the answer to this question is the same today as it was yesterday, we are probably falling behind.

There is broad agreement that the Shewhart control chart should be used for only a small fraction of the quality characteristics under consideration. This is because the tremendous demands of the Shewhart chart are not in the area of *detection* of excessive variation, but in *responding* to this signal. This response typically requires prompt and intensive managerial action, imposing heavy demands on a scarce and costly resource. Bicking and Gryna (1974, p. 23-5) state that "control charts are justified for only a small minority of the quality characteristics." For instance, on a certain part there may be 200 dimensions, but of these, five dimensions may account for 95 percent of the trouble — and the troublesome dimensions have typically already been identified. Shewhart control charts will be appropriate on only these few troublesome dimensions, and then only intermittently as the need arises. The question remaining is, how should the bulk of the dimensions be monitored? If we restrict the use of Shewhart control charts to the critical two percent of our quality characteristics, what do we do for the other 98 percent? Without doubt, the answer to this question is to use a graphical time series representation of the individual measurement values from the process, the *run chart*. If Deming does not deserve the sole credit for the use of the run chart, he certainly qualifies as the single person most responsible for recognizing its worth.

Shewhart control charts should be used for process improvement, and run charts should be used for process maintenance. This is a nice rule of thumb, but unfortunately it is an oversimplification. Many processes are not suited to the use of standard Shewhart control charts that are based on the assumption that the process "should be" a generator of normally distributed data which are random. Processes that inherently will not fit this description include those with linear trends (such as tool wear or change in potency of a chemical solution over time), continuous processes such as the material flow into a plastic injection molding operation, and "two-stage" processes such as a batch process where batch-to-batch variability is superimposed on within-batch variability. For applications such as these, run charts of individual values provide a practical alternative to Shewhart control charts for ongoing process control. Other approaches using modifications to standard Shewhart control charts are shown in Part VIII.

The run chart can take on many forms, three of which are:

1. One hundred percent inspection.
2. Small subgroups of consecutive pieces taken at more or less regular intervals, as for an X bar and R chart.
3. Isolated observations (subgroups of size one) that are never recommended for X bar and R charts.

We will consider each of these three types of run charts in turn, but first it should be noted that whatever form of run chart is used, there are important advantages of plotting individuals instead of plotting "subgroup averages."

- Averages *always* result in loss of information about individuals.
- Specification limits may properly be shown on plots of individuals, whereas they create endless confusion when shown on plots of averages.
- Individual observations may be plotted immediately, without even waiting to aggregate a number of observations to make a subgroup.
- The computations required to find the average are avoided.
- Because of the simplicity and obvious practicality of the plot of individual points, the operator quickly assumes "ownership" of the run chart, using it to good advantage.
- Experience has shown that, in fact, problems are often solved easily with run charts.

1. *Run charts for 100 percent inspection.*
Typically, the use of 100 percent inspection is not recommended. If, however, it takes a substantial amount of time to complete a single piece, and/or the cost of a single piece is high, 100 percent inspection may be quite appropriate. Since the run chart for 100 percent may be regarded as a limiting case of either of the other two types of run charts, comments made below for those charts will also be valid here.

2. *Run charts using small subgroups.*
The use of run charts using small subgroups of consecutive pieces provides an opportunity to maintain a process in a simple way, but it also provides an effective, if informal, means for process improvement without the demanding consequences of a Shewhart control chart. (Our thanks to Mr. Thomas Lewis for his insight into this application, based on work which had been done at Mercury Marine.)

To illustrate this concept, consider the several time-ordered subgroups of size 2 in Figure 6.1a. Based only on judgment, and not on any calculations, does it appear that the within-subgroup variation is reasonably consistent from subgroup to subgroup? (Almost everyone answers this question in the affirmative.) Does it appear that the between-subgroup variation is more than might reasonably be explained by the variations within the two pieces of a subgroup? (There is broad agreement that this answer is also yes.)

Now consider the run chart shown in Figure 6.1b, noting that only one point is different from the preceding figure. If the question is now asked, "Does it appear that the within-subgroup variation is reasonably consistent from subgroup to subgroup?", the answer is clearly no. It is also quite clear that the within-subgroup variability, being inconsistent, provides no basis for judging subgroup-to-subgroup variation. Run charts on subgroups of consecutive pieces not only can provide a means for improving the process, they also demonstrate the essence of the philosophy of the Shewhart control chart method.

The effectiveness of run charts of this type for process improvement will be directly dependent on the skill used in determining the timing (spacing) of the subgroups. A subgroup of observations should be taken immediately before and immediately after each discontinuity in the process, such as shift change, tool change, lunch break, etc.

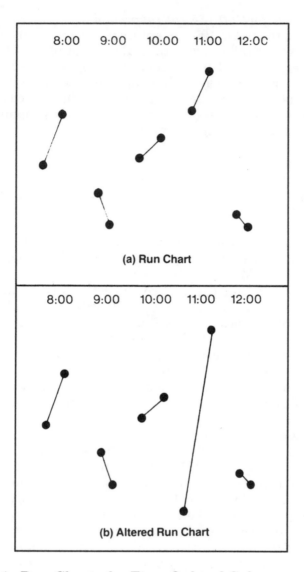

Figure 6.1 Run Charts for Time-Ordered Subgroups of Size 2

3. *Run charts using isolated individual observations.*
   Run charts that are strictly for ongoing process maintenance
   (as opposed to the objective of process improvement) will usually
   employ only isolated individual observations taken at more or
   less regular intervals. It is this type of process data on which
   the entire engineering science of process control is built, involv-
   ing such concepts as feedback and feedforward control. The

remainder of this chapter will be restricted to the consideration of run charts which use isolated individual observations.

The objective of process maintenance implies that the process has, at least informally, shown itself to be reasonably stable and comfortably within specifications. Consider, for example, a process with a normal distribution, perfectly centered on the target value, at something more than 4 standard deviations from each specification limit. Under these circumstances, fewer than 30 parts per million would be out of tolerance in each tail. To *maintain* this process near this state of excellence requires a two-step maintenance action plan:

1. Establish a set of *action limits* to use in determining when the process has wandered too far.
2. Establish a formal *procedure* telling when to take corrective action on the process, based on these action limits.

Procedure for a Maintenance Action Plan

Step 1 Establish two sets of action limits on the process, *outer maintenance limits* at four standard deviations on each side of the target value, and *inner maintenance limits* at two standard deviations on each side of the target value.

Step 2 Take corrective action whenever a point falls outside of the outer action limit and/or whenever two consecutive points fall beyond the same inner action limit.

Using this procedure, as long as the process remains stable, the signal for corrective action would be a rare event.

Maintenance action limits set in the manner described previously should not be confused with limits which might come from two other sources: a Shewhart control chart or the specification limits. The type of maintenance action limits discussed here include some of the elements of each of the other two types. Like Shewhart limits, these proposed *maintenance* limits would reflect the demonstrated variability of the process, but unlike Shewhart limits, the maintenance limits would stay stable over time while "minor" changes might occur in the process center and/or dispersion. Like specification limits, the maintenance limits would stay stable over time, and hopefully "out of the way," i.e., not trouble us too often. Unlike specification limits, the maintenance limits might cause action to be taken on the process long before the limits imposed by specifications were approached, in keeping with the inherent ability of the process.

Run charts on individuals, sampling only isolated individuals (say every twentieth piece), will often be the most convenient tool for process maintenance. When accepting this procedure one gives up two important sources of information, no matter how the action limits are set: information on the process "capability" and information on how to improve the process are both lost when the decision is made to use this approach.

Example 6.1

Background: The quality policy of this company is "selective continuous improvement," employing the Pareto principle to allocate available resources for quality improvement in accordance with the severity of the need. This means that the use of Shewhart control charts must be restricted to those few characteristics where an intense effort will be made to improve the process.

The quality characteristic of interest here comes from a process in a state of statistical control with a C_p and a C_{pk} each at approximately 5.3. This process does not qualify for the use of a Shewhart chart since it is already doing well and the company needs to concentrate its efforts and energies on other processes which are not doing well. However, it is considered necessary to maintain the process at a high level of quality, and to prevent deterioration of the process at a minimal expenditure of resources. It is decided to use a run chart, measuring one piece during each half shift. Action limits on the individuals have been found from a probability plot such that no more than 30 parts per million will be found in each tail. These outer maintenance (action) limits will be at the 4-sigma limits for this characteristic which is approximately normally distributed. The inner maintenance limits will be at the 2-sigma limits.

Upper specification limit = 90
Target value (aim point) = 50
Lower specification limit = 10
Upper outer maintenance (action) limit = 60
Lower outer maintenance (action) limit = 40
Upper inner maintenance limit = 55
Lower inner maintenance limit = 45

As shown in Figure 6.2, the process stayed well within the action limits, as expected, for six or seven shifts, then wandered out of the limits. This signaled the need for corrective action on the process. The maintenance chart had the desired effect. The process was left undisturbed for an extended period of time, with action only being taken when the need arose.

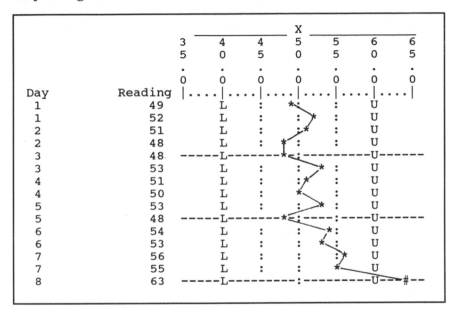

Figure 6.2 Run Chart for Process Maintenance

Classroom Exercise

We are dealing with coded data on our process, which has been found to be in control with:

Upper specification limit = 12.85
Target value (aim point) = 3.5
Lower specification limit = −5.85
$\overline{\overline{X}}$ = 3.5
$\hat{\sigma}$ = 1.7 yielding C_{pk} = 1.83
Upper outer maintenance (action) limit (OML) =
Lower outer maintenance (action) limit (OML) =
Upper inner maintenance limit (IML) =
Lower inner maintenance limit (IML) =

Phase I   Roll one die 10 times and plot the results on the chart below. Indicate when action would be needed, if at all.

Phase II Roll two dice 10 times and plot the results on the chart below. Indicate when action would be needed, if at all.

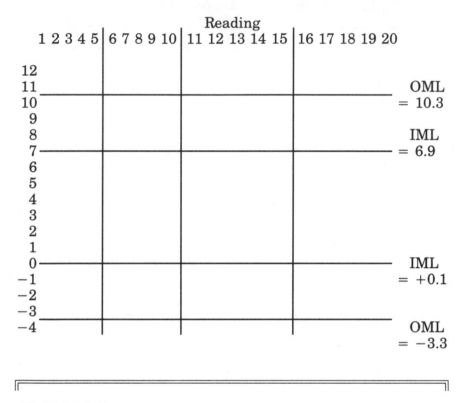

PROBLEMS

6.1 A normally distributed process is centered on the target value of 50, with a standard deviation of 3.5 and a $C_{pk} = 3.4$. It has been decided that, due to limited resources and more pressing problems elsewhere, the process need only be maintained at this high level.

a. Set up outer maintenance limits at 4-sigma and inner maintenance limits at 2-sigma.
b. Given the following data, does action need to be taken on the process?

Reading	Value
1	53.4
2	56.9
3	52.2
4	49.7
5	47.0
6	51.2
7	49.4
8	45.7
9	49.9
10	48.9
11	41.1
12	47.0
13	50.1
14	45.2
15	56.2
16	52.9
17	49.6
18	51.1
19	49.2
20	48.6

6.2 A normally distributed process is centered on the target value of 62, with a standard deviation of 2.8 and a C_{pk} = 2.6. It has been decided that, due to limited resources and more pressing problems elsewhere, the process need only be maintained at this high level.

a. Set up outer maintenance limits at 4-sigma and inner maintenance limits at 2-sigma.
b. Given the following data, does action need to be taken on the process?

Reading	Value
1	54.7
2	61.7
3	64.1
4	62.3
5	60.2
6	61.4
7	61.4
8	61.9
9	65.2
10	62.6
11	62.5
12	58.1
13	57.0
14	62.4
15	61.1
16	59.6
17	68.3
18	69.2
19	60.0
20	64.2

Chapter 19 Precontrol

We have considered the use of Shewhart action limits at length in earlier chapters. We will now consider another approach which is important because of its historical interest and because it is still used today by some companies. A formal approach to the use of run charts with isolated individual observations where the action limits come from the *specification*, has been called precontrol. The procedures for plotting a basic version of the precontrol chart follows. For variations on this theme and the statistical justification of the procedures, see Putnam (1962, pp. 19-1 - 19-9). We will return to the question of how maintenance limits on the process might best be set after we look in some detail at how the well-established method of precontrol actually works.

In order for precontrol to be effective, two assumptions must be met:

1. The target value or aim point for the process must be at the specification midpoint.
2. The process must be able to meet the specifications.

There are two different types of precontrol charts. The same plotting instructions may be used for both.

1. For the first type of precontrol chart, called a variables precontrol chart, the special run chart just mentioned is used. The measured values are plotted at their appropriate locations and the action limits, called precontrol limits, are set halfway between the specification midpoint and the specification limits.
2. For the second type of precontrol chart, called a zone precontrol chart, the individual data readings are not plotted; points are simply plotted in the "zones" in which the values fall.

Zone Precontrol Chart

A zone precontrol chart is set up by putting precontrol limits halfway between the midpoint of specification and the specification limits, giving a lower precontrol limit (LPL) and an upper precontrol limit (UPL). This results in a chart with five zones, as shown in Figure 6.3. The zones are often color-coded, zone 3 as green (good, hence go), zones 2 and 4 as yellow (caution, measure the next piece), and zones 1 and 5 as red (defective, stop and fix the process). The color-coded zone precontrol chart is sometimes referred to as stoplight gauging.

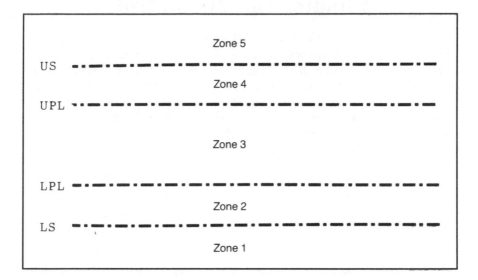

Figure 6.3 Zone Precontrol Chart

Procedure for Plotting a Precontrol Chart

A. 100 percent inspection

Step A1 Demonstrate that the process is able to meet the specifications. Note: It is assumed that the target value or aim point for the process is at the specification midpoint.

Step A2 Set up the precontrol chart with precontrol limits halfway between the specification midpoint and the specification limits.

Step A3 Start (or restart) 100 percent inspection.

Step A4 Measure a piece and plot its point with the symbol X.

Step A5 If the plotted X falls:
- Out of specification limits, reset the process at the specification midpoint and go to Step A3.
- Outside of a precontrol limit but inside of the specification limits, go to Step A6.
- Within the precontrol limits, go to Step A7.

Step A6 Measure the very next piece and plot. If the plot X falls:
- Out of specification limits, reset process at specification midpoint and go to Step A3.
- Outside the same precontrol limit as preceding piece, investigate and take corrective action on the process as required. Reset the process to the specification midpoint and go to Step A3.
- Outside the opposite precontrol limit from the preceding piece, investigate and take corrective action on process to reduce variability and go to Step A3.
- Within the precontrol limits, go to Step A7.

Step A7 Measure the very next piece and plot with the symbol X. If the plotted X falls:
- Outside of specification limits, reset process at specification midpoint and go to Step A3.
- Outside of one of the precontrol limits, go to Step A6.
- Within the precontrol limits, go to A7 until five consecutive X's fall within the precontrol limits. Then start measuring only every Mth piece and go to Step B1. M may initially be set arbitrarily at say, 10 or 20.

B. Sampling Inspection

Step B1 Counting from the piece just measured, measure and plot the Mth piece (see note below) with the symbol 0. If the plotted 0 falls:
- Out of specification limits, reset process at specification midpoint and go to Step A3.
- Outside of one precontrol limit, go to Step B2.
- Within precontrol limits, go to Step B1.

Step B2 Measure and plot the very next piece with the symbol X. If the plotted X falls:
- Out of specification limits, reset process at specification midpoint and go to Step A3.
- Outside of the same precontrol limit as the preceding piece, investigate and take corrective action on the process as required. Reset the process to the specification midpoint and go to Step A3.
- Outside of the opposite precontrol limit, investigate and take corrective action to reduce the process variability and go to Step A3.
- Within the precontrol limits, go to Step B1.

Note: It is recommended that, if possible, the sampling interval, M, be altered by trial and error to obtain only an occasional point outside of the precontrol limits separated by runs of 20 or more points within the precontrol limits.

The method is best shown by way of a simulated example, where properties of the process distributions involved are known. In all cases, the signals from the precontrol chart to take corrective action in the process are ignored in this example. This provides an undisturbed tally of how many signals for action would be received under only the prescribed changes to the process. Two examples will be considered using these data.

1. A zone precontrol chart on a process with
   C_{pk} = (approximately) 1.
2. A variables precontrol chart on a process with
   C_{pk} = (approximately) 2.

Example 6.2

Phase I
A set of data is simulated by rolling three dice (Table 6.1). Process specifications are given by LS = 2.5 and US = 18.5. Note that the zone precontrol chart could have been made from *either* variables-type or attribute-type data. That is, it would be sufficient for this purpose to have one pair of go/no-go gauges for the specification limits and one pair of go/no-go gauges for the precontrol limit.

(a) Phase 1. Sum of three dice.

9	11	15	16	15	10	12	14	14	9
8	6	9	10	13	10	7	11	12	13
11	14	7	7	7	11	14	11	9	5
9	7	11							

(b) Phase 2. Sum of four dice.

10	16	17	14	7	17	12	12	18	5
17	18	15	13	12	14	19	18		

(c) Phase 3. Sum of three dice, again.

9	11	8	13	12	9	14	13	11	11
10	10	10	5	13	16	7	13	17	10
10	7	14	13	11	8	8	11	10	16
9	11	12							

(d) Phase 4. Sum of two dice.

7	6	4	5	7	6	10	9	6	7
4	6	9	5	9	4	10	4		

Table 6.1 Measurements for Precontrol Chart (Reading *across* within each phase)

Step A1 Demonstrate that the process is able to meet the specifications and that the target value is centered on the specification midpoint.

The specifications for this process are given at LS = 2.5 and US = 18.5. Hence, this process will always be able to meet specifications ($C_{pk} \geq 1$) which was one of the conditions necessary for precontrol to be applicable. In this example, the process is just meeting specifications, so C_{pk} is approximately 1. Note that 10.5 is both the midpoint of the specifications and the expected value of the sum of three dice, so both required conditions are met.

Step A2 Set up the precontrol chart with precontrol limits halfway between the specification midpoint and the specification limits.

The upper specification limit (US) is 18.5 and the midpoint of specifications is 10.5. The upper precontrol limit (UPL) is set halfway between at 14.5. Similarly, lower specification limit (LS) is 2.5, so the lower precontrol limit (LPL) is set halfway between at 6.5. These limits are illustrated in Figure 6.4.

Step A3 Start 100 percent inspection.

Step A4 Measure a piece and plot its point with the symbol X. The first number in Table 6.1a tells us that the first piece measured 9, so an X is marked in zone 3 on the chart (Figure 6.2a).

Step A5 Since 9 fell within the precontrol limits, we go to Step A7 and the next piece is measured. The second piece measured 11 and is marked within the precontrol limits so the next piece is measured. The third piece measured 15 which is marked outside of the upper precontrol limit but inside the specification limits, so we go to Step A6 and measure the next piece.

Step A6 The fourth piece measured 16 and is marked in zone 4. Since this falls outside the same precontrol limit as the preceding piece, the process would be investigated and corrective action taken if needed to reset the process to the specification midpoint. We would return to Step A3 and continue in like manner. (This would have been a case of random variability giving us a false signal, because no change had occurred in the process.)

Piece number 5 (15) was also outside the precontrol limits, but pieces 6 through 10 (10, 12, 14, 14, 9) all fell within the precontrol limits. That gives five pieces in a row within the precontrol limits.

Step A7 Since we would have had five pieces in a row we would be able to switch from 100 percent inspection to sampling inspection, sampling every Mth piece. As noted above, M will be arrived at by trial and error.

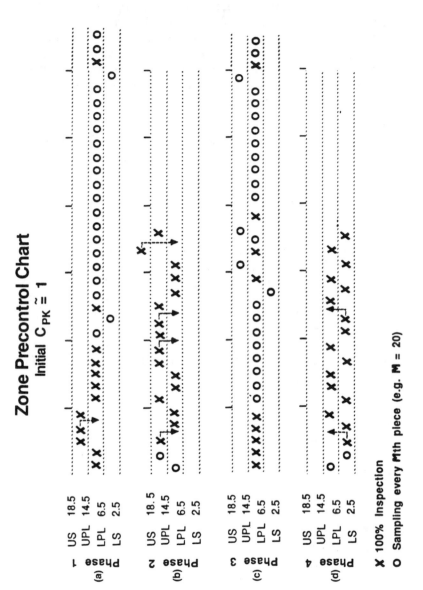

Figure 6.4 Zone Precontrol Chart
Initial $C_{pk} \cong 1$

Step B1 Start sampling. Say we decided to measure every twenty-fifth piece. The twenty-fifth piece made since we decided on sampling inspection was measured and plotted. From Table 6.1, we will use the measurement 8. Measuring a piece 25 pieces later (the fiftieth piece), we measure and plot a value of 6. Since this is outside a precontrol limit, we go to Step B2.

Step B2 The very next piece (piece number 51 after beginning sampling) measured 10. It is marked with an X between the precontrol limits, and sampling is resumed (Step B1).

Figure 6.4a illustrates the plotting of the points from Table 6.1a.

Phase II
Suppose a change occurred in the process resulting in an upward shift in the process level and an increase in dispersion simulated by switching to the roll of four dice. This might have been due, for instance, to a new shipment of raw material coming into the process stream. A random set of values for the sum of four dice is given in Table 6.1b. The plot of these points on the precontrol chart is continued in Figure 6.4b. Note that the precontrol scheme promptly reverted to 100 percent inspection with repeated signals to take corrective action.

Phase III
Suppose the process now returned to the initial conditions, again simulated by the sum of three dice. The results are given in Table 6.1c and plotted in Figure 6.4c. Note the resulting change from 100 percent inspection back to sampling.

Phase IV
Suppose another change occurred in the process, this time resulting in a downward shift in the process level and a decrease in dispersion simulated by the sum of two dice. The results are given in Table 6.1d and plotted in Figure 6.4d. Note that the precontrol scheme again promptly reverted to 100 percent inspection with repeated signals to take corrective action.

The results of Figure 6.4 show that the initial process conditions, depicted in phases 1 and 3 by the sum of 3 dice, would have called for only one unnecessary correction (when there was really no fault with the process) in 66 observations. Following the precontrol procedure would efficiently lead to the use of sampling inspection (rather than 100 percent inspection) if the process remained in its initial conditions.

Phases 2 and 4 in Figure 6.4 show that for the process changes considered, the precontrol scheme would promptly revert to 100 percent inspection with repeated signals to take corrective action on the process.

It works!

The method of precontrol has been proven to provide a practical method of maintaining processes within specification limits, where the process can readily be operated in such a way as to make good product. The precontrol method is totally untroubled by the fact that the process is not a random normal number generator, as is required for the use of a Shewhart control chart; such process peculiarities as tool wear don't interfere with the use of precontrol at all.

In spite of its usefulness, precontrol is not an appropriate tool in this enlightened era without some modifications. We simply cannot accept "just meeting specifications" if the process is inherently able to do better than that even in a "maintenance" mode. A practical solution to this problem is to substitute the use of maintenance limits based on the demonstrated variability of the process, as described earlier, provided that these limits fall within the specification limits. If they do not, the process is a candidate for "improvement," not just "maintenance." An important extension to the use of 4-sigma action (outer maintenance) limits comes from the use of the probability plot. If a sample of, say, 1,000 pieces is taken from past production, and if judgment indicates that this past performance can be duplicated in the future, then the "4-sigma equivalent" action (outer maintenance) limits for the process can be read from the probability plot. Note that the linear Z-scale will have to be extended to ± 4. Note that there are absolutely no assumptions made about the distribution of the process, only that it be stable over time. Regardless of the shape of the curve on the probability plot, the points where that curve would cross the 4-sigma limit lines for a normal distribution give the desired action limits for the variable, X. The 2-sigma inner action limits are found in an analogous manner.

Variables Precontrol Chart

If the objective is simply one of maintenance and of meeting specifications on an ongoing basis, and the process is capable of doing this, the simple zone precontrol chart will accomplish the stated purpose. A better chart will be required, however, if more information is desired, such as:

1. An estimate of the process capability.
2. Signals of changes in the process which may signal trouble, even though no bad product is made.
3. Information providing help on how to improve the process.

A conventional run chart, or a *variables precontrol chart* as used in Example 6.3 will assist in each of these three categories.

Example 6.3

For this example, we use the same process data as in Example 6.2, but assume a specification change to provide a process capability index, C_{pk}, of approximately 2.0. This gives the limits shown in the variables precontrol chart of Figure 6.5. A cursory inspection of Figure 6.5 shows that the additional information of three items mentioned previously would be provided by this chart. The sole contribution of the precontrol concept in this example is the addition of the precontrol limits in Figure 6.5, which provide little, if any benefit beyond a simple run chart. Note further that a zone precontrol chart for Example 6.3 would be of little interest, with very few points (one point from Table 6.1) falling outside of the precontrol limits and even fewer, if any, signals to take action on the process.

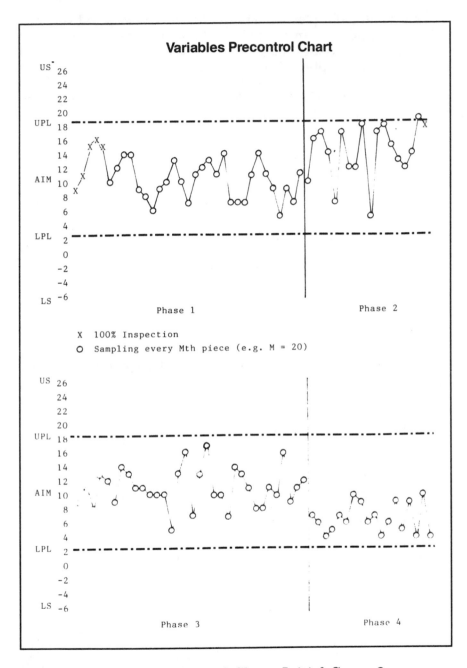

Figure 6.5 Variables Control Chart, Initial $C_{pk} = 2$

The procedure for plotting a precontrol chart (Steps A1 through A7 and B1 and B2) can be modified to accommodate the process maintenance procedure based on maintenance limits discussed earlier in this chapter. This procedure would be more desirable than precontrol since it would be based on the variability of the process, not on specification-derived limits. This would help keep the process from deteriorating.

Summary

The zone precontrol chart used as specified will help to meet specifications, but that is all. The variables precontrol chart will provide additional important benefits and is always at least as good as the less formal run chart. The procedure for using process maintenance limits based on the variability of the process is the best procedure. It will keep the process at its current level.

PROBLEMS

6.3 For the following specification limits, set up precontrol limits:

a. LS = 10, US = 30
b. LS = 8, US = 12
c. LS = 0, US = 7
d. LS = −2, US = 10
e. LS = −2, US = 8

6.4 For the following specification limits, set up precontrol limits:

a. LS = 20, US = 60
b. LS = 16, US = 24
c. LS = 0, US = 5

6.5 Would precontrol charts be useful for the following four processes as they are now?

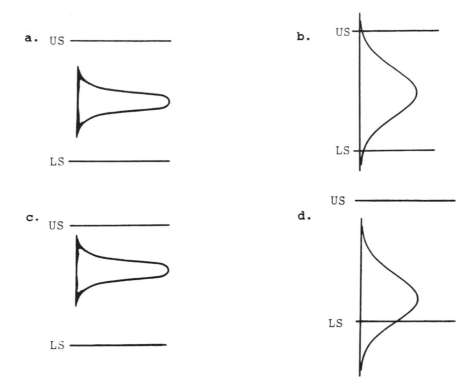

6.6 For cut-to-length pipes having a specified length of 20 inches ± .0050 inch, prepare a zone precontrol chart and plot the following readings (coded zero = 20 inches and coded unit = .0001 inch; read across). Every thirtieth piece has been measured.

−22	12	8	−14	−20	22	22	21	−20	19
28	−24	−26	20	−30	−16	21	−32	−23	30
18	−19	−15	−19	−21	18	18	21	15	22

6.7 For the stem diameter of a valve with specifications of 1.1250 inches ± .0015 inch, every twenty-fifth piece has been measured. Prepare a zone precontrol chart and plot the following readings (coded zero = 1.1200 inches and coded unit = .0001 inch; read across). When sampling was justified, every twentieth piece was measured.

46	52	45	56	52	44	56	50	51	53
48	60	49	45	51	56	45	67	53	56
58	57	52	48	51	53	53	43	42	45
61	53	41	57	46	49	48	49	50	49

6.8 For the data in Problem 6.6, prepare a variables precontrol chart.

Part VII. Attribute Charts

Sometimes, rather than working with measurements on a piece of product, we are only interested in whether or not that piece of product is acceptable. As an alternative, we may be interested in how many defects or errors there are in each piece of product. In these cases, we are working with attribute data for which attribute control charts are used.

Chapter 20 Types of Attribute Data

Sometimes product inspections that could have been made by taking measurements are instead made on a "go and no-go" gauge, only telling whether or not the product met the specifications. For some product inspections, such as the quality of a painted surface, no measurement may be possible. Here the paint finish may be judged to be acceptable or not. In these cases, we must analyze the fraction defective or the fraction nonconforming.

Sometimes we inspect a defective or nonconforming piece of product to count the number of defects (nonconformities, errors) on it. For example, we may be counting the number of errors in a purchase order or the number of scratches in a plate of glass. In these cases, we must analyze the number of defects (nonconformities) per unit.

The control charts used for "fraction defective" are different from those used for "defects per unit." To understand this, consider the manufacture of transparency sheets. If each sheet is inspected and is classified as either acceptable or not, we are concerned with those sheets that are "defectives." If each sheet is inspected and the number of scratches on that sheet is counted, we are concerned with "defects." If these sheets are shipped out in boxes of 10, what is the largest number of defectives that can be found in the box? (Answer: 10) What is the largest number of defects that can be found in the box? (Answer: There is no limit.) Since the number of defectives is limited by sample size but the number of defects is not, they are governed by different "probability distributions" and are plotted on different control charts.

The fraction of product which is defective is plotted on a p chart. If the subgroup size is always constant, it is feasible to compare only the number defective, np, (rather than fraction defective, p) and an np chart may be used as a shortcut.

The number of defects per unit is plotted on a u chart. If the subgroup size is always constant, the number of defects (per subgroup) can be monitored using a c chart. The four attribute control charts (p, np, u, c) will be discussed in this chapter.

Chapter 21   Varying Subgroup Sizes

When using attribute data, subgroup size should be large, for instance n = 50, 100, or even larger. When using attribute data, the subgroup size may vary from subgroup to subgroup.

The fraction defective from a large subgroup will tend to be closer to the true fraction defective of the process than will the fraction defective from a small subgroup. Consequently, for a constant true fraction defective the fraction found defective from large subgroups will vary less then the fraction found defective from small subgroups. Accordingly, large subgroups will have narrower control limits than small subgroups. The control limits when using varying sample sizes will not be the same all across the page as was the case for $\overline{X}$ and R charts where the sample size was always held constant.

Classroom Exercise

Let each student flip a coin 10 times and record the results below (H or T). Let a head be called a defective. Expected percent defective = _____

Toss Results:

Number of defectives = _____ for this student.

Percent defective = 100% X _____ /10 = _____ % for this student.

Summary of results for entire class:

Lowest percent defective = _____

Highest percent defective = _____

Class total number of defectives = _____

Total number of students in class = _____

Total number of tosses = _____

Overall percent defective = _____ for the entire class.

Moral of the story: (Fill in the words "much" or "little"; "wide" or "narrow")

Small Samples	Large Samples
_____ variability	_____ variability
_____ control limits	_____ control limits

Chapter 22 Basic Attribute Charts

p Charts

When monitoring the fraction of defective (nonconforming) product, a p chart is used. The value p represents the number of defective product divided by the number inspected, usually expressed as a decimal, sometimes as a percent.

Steps for Setting up p Charts

Given for each subgroup:

Number defective (np)
Number inspected (n)

Step 1 Calculate $\bar{p} = \dfrac{\text{total number defective from all subgroups}}{\text{total number inspected (all subgroups)}}$

Step 2 Evaluate the numerator in the formula for $3\sigma_p$,

$$\text{where } 3\sigma_p = \frac{3\sqrt{\bar{p}\,(1 - \bar{p})}}{\sqrt{n}}$$

Step 3 Evaluate $3\sigma_p$ for each different value of subgroup size n.

Step 4 Calculate upper and lower control limits for the various values of n:

$$\begin{array}{cc} \bar{p} & \bar{p} \\ - 3\sigma_p & + 3\sigma_p \\ \hline \text{LCL} & \text{UCL} \end{array}$$

Negative lower control limits are taken to be at zero.

Step 5 Calculate the p from each subgroup, where

$$p = \frac{\text{number defectives in the subgroup}}{\text{number inspected for the subgroup}}$$

Step 6 Set a scale on the p chart which will cover all control limits and p values.

Step 7 Plot the p values from Step 5 and connect them.

Step 8 Plot the center line, $\bar{p}$, and the control limits for each subgroup.

Step 9 Evaluate the chart for evidence of lack of control (lack of statistical uniformity). Record your conclusions.

Example 7.1

In a machining operation, the following data were collected. Each entry is the number of defective pieces out of a subgroup of size 50. We will prepare a control chart by time order, subgrouped into days of the week.

Operator	M	T	W	Th	F	
A	12	9	6	12	8	
B	7	11	6	9	11	
C		9	9	9	5	
D		4	5	11	3	Totals
Number defective	19	33	26	41	27	146
n	100	200	200	200	200	900

(See Figure 7.1 for solution.)

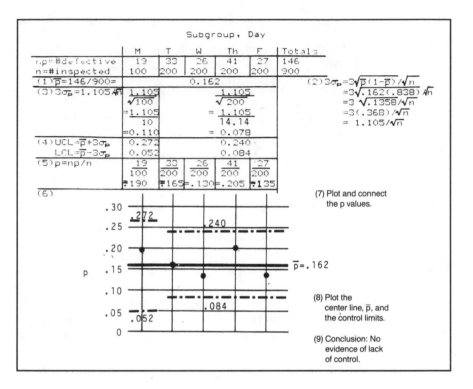

Figure 7.1 p Chart

Procedure

Step 1 Calculate $\bar{p}$ = total number defective/total number inspected.

Step 2 Evaluate the numerator in the formula for $3\sigma_p$.

Step 3 Calculate $3\sigma_p$ for each different subgroup size n.

Step 4 Calculate UCL = $\bar{p} + 3\sigma_p$ and LCL = $\bar{p} - 3\sigma_p$ for each n.

Step 5 Calculate the fraction defective for each subgroup, p = np/n.

Step 6 Set a scale on the p chart which will cover all control limits and p values.

Step 7 Plot the p values from Step 5 and connect them.

Step 8 Plot the center line, $\bar{p}$, and the control limits for each subgroup.

Step 9 Evaluate the chart for evidence of lack of statistical control (uniformity). Record your conclusions.

Classroom Exercise

Using beads of two colors, define one color as defective. Have three inspectors take samples of size 50 for each day of the week and record the number defective in each sample following. Analyze the data on a p chart.

p Chart, by Day

operator	day				
	M	T	W	Th	F
np=number defective						TOTAL
n=number inspected					

(1) $\bar{p} =$

(3) $3\sigma_p = \quad /\sqrt{n}$

(4) UCL$=\bar{p}+3\sigma_p$
   LCL$=\bar{p}-3\sigma_p$

(5) p = np/n

(6)

p

	.30	---------------------
	.25	---------------------
	.20	---------------------
	.15	---------------------
	.10	---------------------
	.05	---------------------
	0	---------------------

(2) $3\sigma_p=3\sqrt{\bar{p}(1-\bar{p})}/\sqrt{n}$

$=3\sqrt{(\quad)(\quad)}/\sqrt{n}$

$=3\sqrt{\quad}/\sqrt{n}$

$=3(\quad)/\sqrt{n}$

$=\quad /\sqrt{n}$

(7) Plot and connect the p values.

(8) Plot the center line, $\bar{p}$, and the control limits.

(9) Conclusions.

Classroom Exercise

Take the data from the previous classroom exercise and analyze it by subgrouping by the three operators.

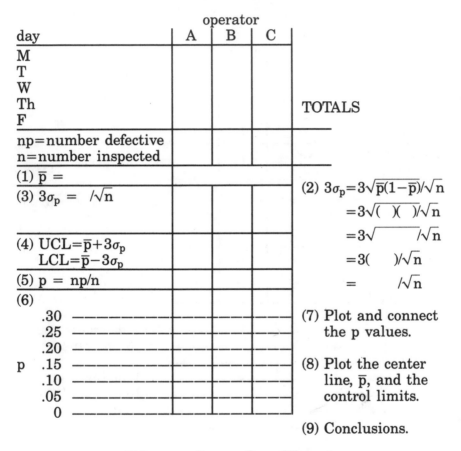

p Chart, by Operator

day	operator			
	A	B	C	
M				
T				
W				
Th				TOTALS
F				
np=number defective n=number inspected				
(1) $\bar{p}$ =				
(3) $3\sigma_p$ = $/\sqrt{n}$				
(4) UCL=$\bar{p}$+$3\sigma_p$ LCL=$\bar{p}$−$3\sigma_p$				
(5) p = np/n				

(2) $3\sigma_p = 3\sqrt{\bar{p}(1-\bar{p})}/\sqrt{n}$

$\quad = 3\sqrt{()()}/\sqrt{n}$

$\quad = 3\sqrt{}/\sqrt{n}$

$\quad = 3()/\sqrt{n}$

$\quad = /\sqrt{n}$

(6)

p .30 ------------------------
   .25 ------------------------
   .20 ------------------------
   .15 ------------------------
   .10 ------------------------
   .05 ------------------------
    0 ------------------------

(7) Plot and connect the p values.

(8) Plot the center line, $\bar{p}$, and the control limits.

(9) Conclusions.

Discussion of p Charts

A process displaying a state of statistical control (statistical uniformity) on a p chart only implies that the process is stable; the variations in the fraction defective could be explained by chance variation. If one is not happy with the overall fraction defective generated by the chart, it is management's responsibility to take corrective action to improve the process. Such improvement might take the form of getting more uniform incoming material, improving the design to make it more easily manufacturable, overhauling the machinery, better training, etc.

Shewhart pointed out that success in attaining process improvement would be directly related to expert knowledge of the process so as to know how to select rational subgroups. These methods of subgrouping are in addition to subgrouping by time. Note that the data in the classroom exercise were subgrouped by time order and that the same data were divided into rational subgroups by operator. Possible ways of forming rational subgroups (Table 7.1) are by shift, operator, machine, supplier, etc. By analyzing the data several different ways, it may be possible to find one method of subgrouping, say by supplier, which shows evidence of lack of control (uniformity). If one supplier has more defectives than might reasonably be attributed to chance cause, we may then be able to lower the overall proportion defective by working with that supplier to lower the supplier's proportion defective. Conversely, if one supplier shows fewer defectives than may reasonably be attributed to pure chance (and if we have verified that the inspection was valid) we want to discover what methods the supplier used to do so well. We may want to make this supplier our sole supplier, or at least have other suppliers make use of this supplier's preferred procedures.

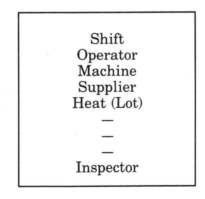

Table 7.1 Possible Ways of Forming Rational Subgroups in Addition to Subgrouping by Time

PROBLEMS

7.1 The following data were collected over three shifts. Do the shifts appear to have product quality in a state of statistical uniformity?

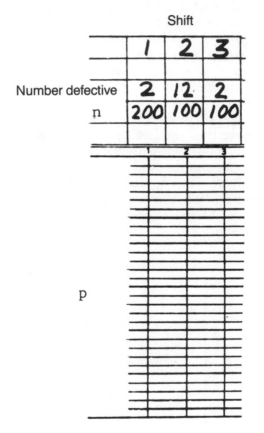

	Shift		
	1	2	3
Number defective	2	12	2
n	200	100	100

Discussion of Problem 7.1

When the proportion defective is above the upper control limit, as seen here for the second shift, it is easy to jump to the conclusion that more defectives were made by shift number 2 than were explainable by chance. It appears that the second shift is less skilled. It could be, however, that only the second shift has valid inspection data. The inspectors from shifts 1 and 3 might not have identified the defectives, but simply let them pass as good. Only investigation will reveal the real reason for lack of statistical uniformity, and this does no good until appropriate corrective action is actually taken.

7.2 Analyze the following data from four different vendors.

Vendor	W	X	Y	Z
number defective (np)	97	13	1	6
number good	903	87	149	144

Discussion of Problem 7.2

It is possible to have evidence of lack of statistical uniformity by getting a point below the lower control limit. This implies that the subgroup is different from the overall fraction defective and the difference is apparently *not* due to chance. This supplier's own incoming material may have better quality, or this supplier's material may be processed only on your best machine. The real reason will only be discovered after investigation. If this supplier's product is really better, contemplate purchasing all the incoming material from this vendor.

7.3 Analyze the following data from three different machines.

Defectives by Machine

Machine	A	B	C
number defective (np)	3	37	12
number inspected (n)	9	400	144

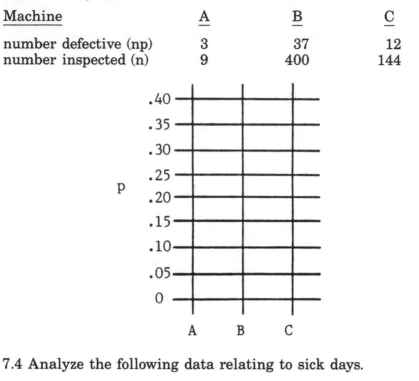

7.4 Analyze the following data relating to sick days.

Employee	A	B	C	D	E	F	G	H	I
number sick days = np	2	4	3	5	18	2	3	0	2
number days available for work = n	200	232	232	232	182	232	213	210	232

np Charts

Sometimes the subgroup size remains constant from subgroup to subgroup and the step of calculating the fraction defective for each subgroup can be omitted. We simply compare the number defective, np, in each subgroup. The steps are similar to those of the p chart, except for Steps 2 and 5, which are deleted. Note: $3\sigma_{np} = 3\sqrt{n\bar{p}(1-\bar{p})}$.

Example 7.2

In a plastic injection molding operation, data are collected on each of four days from one shot of a 50-cavity mold. Each entry is the number of defective pieces out of a sample of size 50.

| Day | Subgroup (Day) | | | | |
	T	W	Th	F	Totals
np, number defective	4	5	11	3	23

Step 1 Calculate $\bar{p}$ and $n\bar{p}$.

$$n\bar{p} = \frac{\text{total number defective}}{\text{number of subgroups}} = \frac{23}{4} = 5.75$$

$$\bar{p} = \frac{\text{total number defective}}{\text{total number inspected}} = \frac{23}{200} = .115$$

(Note: $n\bar{p} = (n)(\bar{p})$, i.e., $5.75 = (50)(.115)$)

Step 2 Skip this step.

Step 3 Calculate $3\sigma_{np}$

$$\begin{aligned} 3\sigma_{np} &= 3\sqrt{n\bar{p}\,(1 - \bar{p})} \\ &= 3\sqrt{5.75\,(1 - .115)} \\ &= 3\sqrt{(5.75)\,(.885)} \\ &= 3\sqrt{5.089} \\ &= 3\,(2.26) \\ &= 6.78 \end{aligned}$$

Step 4 Compute control limits.

$$\text{UCL (np)} = n\bar{p} + 3\sigma_{np} = 5.75 + 6.78 = 12.53$$
$$\text{LCL (np)} = n\bar{p} - 3\sigma_{np} = 5.75 - 6.78 = -1.03$$

Say LCL (np) = 0, since we cannot have a negative number of pieces defective.

Step 5 We will work directly with the np values, the *numbers* defective for each subgroup. There is no need to calculate the *fraction* defective for each subgroup.

Step 6 Provide a scale on the np chart that covers all np values and the control limits.

Step 7 Plot the np values from each subgroup and connect them.

Step 8 Plot the center line, $n\bar{p}$, and control limits.

Step 9 Evaluate the control chart, seeking evidence of lack of statistical control (uniformity). This process appears to be in control.

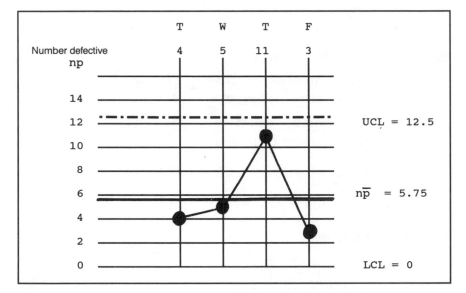

Figure 7.2 np Chart

PROBLEMS

7.5 Make an np chart for the following data on the number of defective cylinders from a sequence of 16 cylinder engines.

Engine S/N	472	473	474	475	476	477	478	479
Defective number of cylinders (out of 16)	0	2	1	0	1	4	2	2

7.6 Make an np chart for the following data on the numbers of sick days where all employees were employed for the whole year, with 232 work days.

Employee	A	B	C	D	E	F	G	H	I	J
Number sick days	11	15	4	8	0	9	8	23	4	5

Probability Distributions

It is worthwhile to note that the control charts we made for vaiables type data were based on the assumption that the data were approximately *normally* distributed. The p and np charts assume that the data are distributed approximately as a binomial distribution. The next two charts, the u and c charts for number of defects, assume a *Poisson* distribution. In every case, the shape of the distribution has no meaning unless the process is stable (i.e., in a state of statistical control).

u Charts

Inspection of a unit of product may continue until the first defect (nonconformity) is detected and the inspection then stopped with the product declared defective (nonconforming), in which case we would use a control chart for fraction defective or number defective. If instead the inspection is continued until all defects are found, it is appropriate to chart the number of defects per unit. We will first look at the u chart, which is similar to the p chart; varying subgroup sizes are acceptable.

Let

$$u = \frac{\text{number of defects found}}{\text{number of units inspected}} \text{ for each subgroup.}$$

A "unit" is any arbitrary unit of production.

The procedures for making a u chart are similar to those for making a p chart. The formula for $3\sigma_u$ is:

$$3\sigma_u = \frac{3\sqrt{\bar{u}}}{\sqrt{n}}$$

The steps are illustrated in Example 7.3

Example 7.3

The u chart shown in Figure 7.3 is for the number of defects in a television set. Note that in this example a "unit" is one television set. As with Example 7.1 for the p chart, note that we are subgrouping by time order with the subgroups being one day.

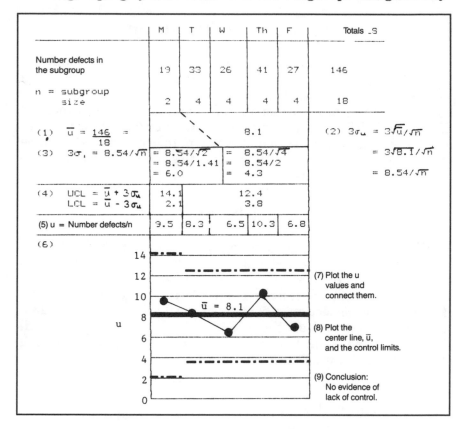

Figure 7.3 u Chart

PROBLEMS

7.7 Make a u chart for the blemishes in coiled steel, given by the following data.

Coil	1	2	3	Totals
Number defects in subgroup	6	10	4	
Coil length, hundreds of linear feet, n*	2.5	5.0	3.5	

(1) $\bar{u} =$

(3) $3\sigma_u = /\sqrt{n} =$

(4) $UCL = \bar{u} + 3\sigma_u$
$\quad LCL = \bar{u} - 3\sigma_u$

(5) u = number defects in subgroup/n

(6)

$$
\begin{array}{c}
6 \\
5 \\
4 \\
u \quad 3 \\
2 \\
1 \\
0
\end{array}
$$

(2) $3\sigma_u = 3\sqrt{\bar{u}}/\sqrt{n}$
$\quad = 3\sqrt{\ }/\sqrt{n}$
$\quad = 3(\ )/\sqrt{n}$
$\quad = \ /\sqrt{n}$

(7) Plot the u values and connect them.

(8) Plot the center line, $\bar{u}$, and the control limits.

(9) Conclusion:

*Note that the unit of production has been taken here to be 100 linear feet. It could just as properly have been selected as 1 linear foot or 1,000 linear feet as long as we were consistent within this one example.

7.8 Make a u chart for the following accident records in 1981.
(a) Use 1,000,000 man-hours as the *unit of production*.

	Number injuries	Million man-hours of exposure
January	11	.175
February	4	.178
March	5	.175
April	8	.210
May	7	.150
June	8	.180
July	2	.186
August	9	.202
September	12	.175
October	5	.184
November	4	.179
December	7	.167

(b) Use 10,000 man-hours as the *unit of production*.

7.9 Make a u chart for the following key punch verification results. Carefully select and record what you are using as your *unit of production*.

Operator	Number cards verified	Number errors
A	4,280	49
B	5,620	72
C	8,219	36

c Charts

If the subgroup size, n, is always constant, a c chart can be used as a shortcut instead of the u chart. We look at the *number* of defects found in each subgroup, which is called c.

The steps are similar to those of the previous charts with

$$3\sigma_c = 3\sqrt{\bar{c}}.$$

The steps are illustrated in Example 7.4

Example 7.4

The following are the total number of defects found each day, inspecting 10 cars each day. Note that each entry is the number of defects *per unit of 10 cars.*

T	W	Th	F	Total
4	5	11	3	23

Step 1 Calculate $\bar{c}$.

$$\bar{c} = \frac{\text{total number of defects}}{\text{number of subgroups}} = \frac{23}{4} = 5.75$$

Step 2 Skip Step 2.

Step 3 Calculate $3\sigma_c$.

$$3\sigma_c = 3\sqrt{\bar{c}}$$
$$= 3\sqrt{5.75}$$
$$= 3\,(2.40)$$
$$= 7.2$$

Step 4 Compute control limits.

$$\text{UCL (c)} = \bar{c} + 3\sigma_c = 5.8 + 7.2 = 13.0$$
$$\text{LCL (c)} = \bar{c} - 3\sigma_c = 5.8 - 7.2 = 0$$
(LCL is reset to zero.)

Step 5 Skip Step 5. We will work with the c values as they are.

Step 6 Provide a scale on the c chart which covers all the c values and the control limits (Figure 7.4).

Step 7 Plot c (the number of defects) from each subgroup and connect them.

Step 8 Plot the center line, $\bar{c}$, and the control limits (Figure 7.4).

Step 9 Evaluate the control chart, seeking evidence of lack of statistical control (uniformity). Record your conclusions.

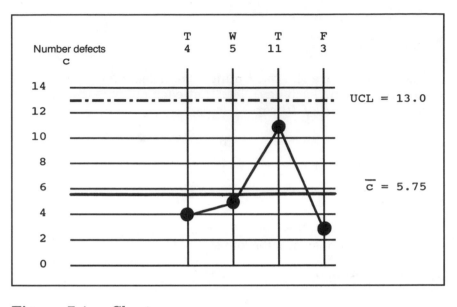

Figure 7.4 c Chart

Example 7.5*

The processing of products often involves mistakes which lead to considerable avoidable cost. A statistical approach to the analysis of these mistakes may provide the key to substantial quality improvement and cost avoidance. Consider, for example, the case of 40 operators doing similar work. A total of 240 mistakes occurred where the number of mistakes per operator varies from a maximum of 24 to a minimum of zero. The data are shown in Figure 7.5 along with the control chart for mistakes per operator. The operating procedure was performed a large number of times during the time period, and we assume they were equally divided among the operators.

The mistakes may be classified into several categories:
1. Wrong part number.
2. Wrong quantity.
3. Wrong procedure.
4. Miscellaneous.

---

*Used by permission of *Quality.* Adapted from "Analyzing Service Operations." *Quality* (June 1985): 33-34.

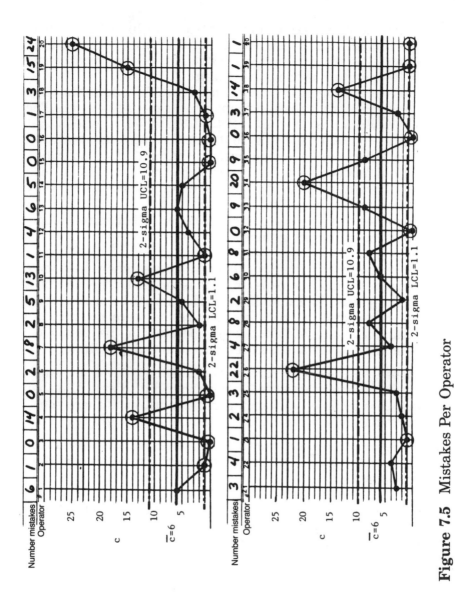

Figure 7.5 Mistakes Per Operator

One method of analyzing this problem is to lump all types of mistakes together and construct a c chart, where c is the number of total mistakes for each operator for the time period. Such a chart for the 40 operators is shown in Figure 7.5.

The interpretation of the chart in Figure 7.5 shows that the average number of mistakes per operator is $\bar{c} = 240/40 = 6$. The standard deviation is $\sqrt{\bar{c}} = \sqrt{6} = 2.45$, from which it is seen that the 2-sigma limits are 1.1 and 10.9 mistakes per operator. If all operators were equally competent, our sample of 40 operators should yield "about" one operator with 11 or more defects. Instead we find 12 operators below the limit and eight above, with only 20 performing "as expected."

We do not have a single group of operators, all of equal competence, but three distinct groups:

1. Those operators with 11 or more mistakes, where help (or a transfer to another department) is needed. The use of a 3-sigma upper limit would be in order here to be more certain that the operators with the poor record were not just the victims of chance. Six of the seven operators in this group have 14 or more defects, which is above the 3-sigma limit.

2. Those operators with zero or one mistake. These operators should be investigated to see why they did so well. Did they have less troublesome work assignments, or is there something in their work methods that should be taught to others?

3. Those operators with two to 10 mistakes, who represent the "system" within which we might expect almost all operators to perform.

Without the benefit of a control chart for guidance, it might have been "policy" for each operator to receive a citation each time a mistake occurred. It is difficult to know whether the demoralizing effect of such notices would be worse for the operator with a single mistake (who is performing significantly better than the "system" would dictate) or for the operator with 24 mistakes (to whom no constructive help has been offered).

The use of statistical methods provides the manager with insights into the "system" as it exists, and with practical methods to help improve the quality of the operators' performance.

PROBLEMS

7.10 Given:

Total number of mistakes = 328
Number of typists = 76
Calculate control limits for the number of mistakes per typist.

7.11 The following numbers are the number of defects found in the 32 pieces from one shot of a 32-cavity mold. Is there any evidence of lack of control?

Date	1/23	1/23	1/23	1/23	1/24	1/24
Time	8:00 am	1:00 pm	5:00 pm	11:00 pm	8:00 am	2:00 pm
Number defects	17	27	14	20	42	13

Control Limits Using "Standard Given" with Attribute Charts

For np charts and c charts the subgroup size is constant, as it was with $\overline{X}$ and R charts. This means that when the chart center line is extended forward as standard given the control limits may be extended forward also. For p charts and u charts, the subgroup size may vary. Only the chart center line is extended forward for standard given: The control limits must be calculated for each subgroup and depend on the subgroup size.

Use of 2-Sigma Limits for Attribute Charts

When using a small number of subgroups (say 12 or fewer subgroups) or in the case of a critical process, 2-sigma limits can be used instead of 3-sigma limits. The calculation of the control limits is only affected by multiplying the standard deviation (σ) by 2 instead of 3. The calculations are given in Table 7.2.

Chart	2-Sigma Calculations
p	$\dfrac{2\sqrt{\bar{p}(1-\bar{p})}}{\sqrt{n}}$
np	$2\sqrt{n\bar{p}(1-\bar{p})}$
u	$\dfrac{2\sqrt{\bar{u}}}{\sqrt{n}}$
c	$2\sqrt{\bar{c}}$

Table 7.2 2-Sigma Calculations

Which Attribute Chart to Use

When deciding which attribute control chart to use, two issues must be addressed:

1. Are data looking at defectives or defects?
2. Is the sample size constant?

An easy way to answer the first question is to decide whether the count is limited by sample size. If yes, the data are looking at "defectives." If no, the data are looking at "defects."
The summary of what chart to use is given in Table 7.3.

	Defectives	Defects
n varies	p	u
n constant	np	c

Table 7.3 Summary of Attribute Charts

PROBLEMS

7.12 For the following problems, which attribute control chart should you make? Use the shortcut charts, np and c, if possible. (Optional: Make the indicated calculations.)

a. Four ports in a housing may each have dimensional errors. Prepare a shop chart for the number of unsatisfactory ports and plot the following data:

S/N	Number bad	S/N	Number bad
A417	2	A720	3
A456	0	A801	2
A523	0	A1020	0
A617	1	A1182	1

b. Prepare a chart for the following pump inspection results:

Date	2/7			2/8			2/9		
Shift	1	2	3	1	2	3	1	2	3
Number defects	7	18	9	4	3	7	12	2	6
Number inspected	48	82	58	15	19	27	43	28	32

c. Tardiness records for 372 employees for last year show the following:

Employee number	1	2	3	372	total
Times late	12	0	4	2	1,218
Days worked	240	240	173	240	74,451

Prepare an appropriate control chart showing the above employees, and comment on their individual tardiness record.

d. The following are the number of breakdowns in successive lengths of 1,000 feet each of coated wire:

Length number	1	2	3	4	5	6	7	8	9	10
Number breakdowns	2	1	1	8	7	1	2	10	1	1

Prepare an appropriate control chart.

7.13 Which attribute control chart should you make for the following problems? Use the shortcut charts, np and c, if possible. (Optional: Make the indicated calculations.)

a. The following table lists the number of coils of steel produced on a daily basis and the total number of defects in each day's production. Compute control limits from these data with no standard given.

Day	Coils of Steel Produced	Number of Imperfections
1	32	39
2	33	36
3	32	42
4	32	40
5	32	38
6	31	39
7	34	49
8	33	31
9	40	51
10	32	36

b. A company that manufactures coils of wire uses a chart to monitor the number of imperfections found in each coil. A total of 143 imperfections were found in the last 20 coils inspected. The following table shows the five highest and lowest totals per coil.

Count the Imperfections

Highest	Lowest
11	2
9	3
9	3
7	4
6	4

Calculate 3σ limits for this process. Is this process in control?

c. The following table gives the number of missing welds found at final inspection of an automobile.

Auto number	Number of missing welds	Auto number	Number of missing welds
1	4	14	4
2	3	15	9
3	6	16	3
4	2	17	5
5	10	18	4
6	8	19	9
7	4	20	11
8	3	21	6
9	5	22	1
10	7	23	6
11	11	24	4
12	7	25	2
13	6		

Compute control limits and plot a control chart. Is there any evidence of lack of statistical uniformity?

d. A company that manufactures light bulbs has been having difficulty with one type of bulb. Data collected over the past 20 days are given in the following table. Compute 3σ control limits. One hundred bulbs are inspected each day.

Day	Bulb type A fraction rejected	Day	Bulb type A fraction rejected
1	.19	12	.31
2	.29	13	.39
3	.27	14	.10
4	.17	15	.21
5	.21	16	.23
6	.16	17	.27
7	.16	18	.30
9	.25	20	.27
10	.21		
11	.23		

e. A chart is to be used to control a paper towel line. End product is produced in rolls of varying length 12 inches wide. Nonconformities include tears, improper printing, improper perforations, etc. The control statistic is nonconformities per 100 sheets with one roll constituting a sample. After 26 rolls have been inspected, the total count of nonconformities is 220 in a total of 8,000 sheets inspected.

   i. Find the value of nonconformities per 100 sheets
   ii. Set up the formulas for 3σ control limits and reduce them to the most convenient form for calculating specific limits.
   iii. Find the control limits for the following three representative samples and determine if the points are in control:

Length of roll (sheets)	Count of nonconformities
200	5
400	29
100	11

f. A large number of samples of 150 items each are taken from a process that has a percentage nonconforming of 12 percent.

   i. What is the expected average of nonconforming units per sample?
   ii. Find the 3σ control limits.

g. A firm that manufactures stereo units has specifications set for the clarity of sound produced by the finished unit. Approximately 150 units are produced and subjected to a final inspection daily. At the end of 15 days 120 units have been rejected out of 2,300 units produced and inspected. Calculate 3σ control limits based on the estimated average daily production of 200 units.

h. A chart is used to monitor the number of surface imperfections on sheets of aluminum. The chart presently is set up based on an average number of surface imperfections of 1.9 per sheet.

Find 3σ control limits for this process.

i. A certain product is given 100 percent inspection as it is manufactured, and the results are summarized by day. In the following table, results for 12 days are recorded. Calculate the varying control limits and note any days that are out of control.

Day	Number units inspected	Number units outside specs
1	50	4
2	47	3
3	32	2
4	45	6
5	47	1
6	42	1
7	49	3
8	50	0
9	41	2
10	36	4
11	48	3
12	51	6

j. Past performance has shown an average of 1.5 percent nonconforming product. Each day 1,300 units are produced and three days of runs are combined to form a shipping lot. A control chart is to be kept by day using a sample of 300 units each day.

Find the 3σ control limits for this purpose.

k. The start-up procedure for new products at a manufacturing plant requires 100 percent inspection for the first three months, or until process control is established at an acceptable level. Six hundred units were found to be defective in the first 15 days. The total number of units produced during this time period was 28,435.

Calculate trial control limits based on the average number of units produced per day.

l. Daily inspection records are maintained on production of a special-design sonar device. For the past 19 days 150 items have been inspected each day with a total of 534 nonconforming items. The four highest and four lowest daily numbers of nonconforming units are shown below.

Is there any evidence of lack of control?

Highest	Lowest
48	16
39	17
37	21
35	23

m. A parts manufacturer requires that 100 percent final inspection be performed during the first four weeks of production on any new or modified part. A total of 690 pieces were found not meeting specifications in the first 40 lots of a new part which is produced in lots of 600 pieces each. Make a control chart using 3σ control limits to receive an entry at the completion of each lot.

n. A plant supervisor wishes to operate a control chart on defects per unit. Each point on the chart represents 100 percent inspection for the day. The production in this shop varies from 600 to 1,200 units per day. The average for the past four months has been 2.9 defects per unit.

   i. Set up a general formula for 3σ control limits for this process for any value of daily production (n).
   ii. Calculate the control limits for a day during which 750 units are produced.

o. An item is made in lots of 300 each. The lots are given 100 percent inspection. The record sheet for the first 30 lots inspected showed that a total of 175 assemblies did not meet specifications. Determine trial control limits on a chart for defective assemblies per lot.

p. The service department at an auto dealer maintains records of complaints on work done by their mechanics. A control chart is kept on each mechanic based on a random sample of two service jobs per day. Because the difficulty and extent of the service jobs vary widely, the number of customer complaints on the service job selected is tabulated along with the number of standard man-hours for that service job. The statistic plotted each day on the control chart for the sum of two randomly selected jobs is complaints per standard man-hours. Which attribute chart should be used?

Solution of a Steel Mill Quality Problem Using p Charts*

As Shewhart pointed out, we would like to use "variables" or "measurement" data wherever possible to get a pair of control charts: one for level and one for dispersion (e.g., $\bar{X}$ and R charts). However, if we do not have "measurement" data available, but only "attribute" data (i.e., go or no-go), then we must make the best of it with an appropriate type of chart, such as a chart for fraction defective (a p-chart). These are the circumstances of the steel mill quality problem discussed here; only attribute data were available so a p-chart was used for problem solving.

Regardless of the type of control chart to be used, we recall from Shewhart's teachings that the degree of success to be attained in using control charts is directly proportioned to how well the rational subgroups are chosen.

Recall that:

1. Our objective is to portray the data so that we can get points out of control if this is in any way possible. (This allows us to readily identify assignable causes of excessive variability so they may be eliminated.)
2. To find out-of-control conditions, we need the tightest legitimate estimate of the control limits which implies the minimum estimate of the population standard deviation.
3. The estimate of population standard deviation comes only from *within* the subgroups. To get the smallest estimate of population variability, we need to find the subgrouping scheme that provides the least variability *within* the subgroups — we seek subgroups that are as homogeneous as possible.

When using control charts as a process improvement (as opposed to a maintenance) tool, we should choose our subgroups in many different ways. We should analyze the same data repeatedly, gaining different information as we subgroup it differently. It might be well to think of "order of production" as the "default" value for subgrouping. It should not exclude other subgrouping methods since it is not always the best, but it is always worth a try.

It is around this theme of multiple choices for subgrouping data that this case study evolved. Shewhart cautioned us that a state

---

*Used by permission of *Quality*. Adapted from "Steel by Shewhart." *Quality* (June 1984): 66-69.

of statistical control does not come automatically. A state of statistical control is a mathematical abstraction which can only be approached in our processes by working hard at the removal of assignable causes. We should *not* expect to just discover a process in a state of statistical control. If our control chart shows no evidence of lack of control, the conclusion that the process is in control is generally not correct. More often, the better conclusion is that we have not yet chosen our subgroups properly.

In a typical U.S. steel mill, one of the end products is cold rolled steel in coil form, for use in such applications as automobile hoods. To make the final coils, a steel slab goes through three steps:

1. Heating and rolling into a "hot band" in a "hot strip mill."
2. Pickling of the hot band to remove surface scale which had formed during hot strip mill rolling operation.
3. Cold rolling the pickled steel for further reduction in thickness.

During the first of these three steps, near the end of the hot strip mill, the steel band is cooled by water spray and then coiled. The nature of these operations is such that a layer of oxide is produced on the surface. This oxide, or scale, must be removed by an acid bath to "pickle" the steel.

In high volume operations, the steel coils (i.e., the hot bands) are welded together to make one infinitely long continuous band; hence the operation is known as the "continuous pickle."

Poor hot strip mill practices will produce oxides that are difficult to remove in the pickling process. When such practices exist, we have a classic example of what Deming calls "you burn the toast and I'll scrape it." You put severe scale on the hot band and I'll spend additional time and money to remove that scale. After pickling, the continuous band is again cut into coils. However, the original coil identity is lost; the new coils may include, somewhere along their length, the welds which were introduced to join the hot bands together. It is the coil-to-coil welding operation in the continuous pickle operations which provides the quality problem which is the subject here.

Prior to the acid bath, it is necessary to weld the tail of one coil of the head to the next. To do this the two coil ends are trimmed, then forced together while an electric current is passed through the interface. The resulting electric resistance weld has two blobs of melted and resolidified metal along the length of the weld, one along the top of the weld, and another along the bottom. These two strips of material are planed off and the result is one continuous band of constant thickness across the weld.

Even a weld of poor quality is usually strong enough to survive the pickling operation. However, this is not the case in the next operation, the cold rolling or cold reduction process. In the cold rolling operation, the weld, like the parent metal of the strip, is reduced in thickness and stretched to many times its original dimension along the length of the coil. Unless the weld has high ductility, it will fracture during the cold rolling operation. It was this fracture mode that constituted the worst quality problem of the steel mill's continuous pickle process.

At the steel mill, the cold rolling division is the customer of the continuous pickle operation. The complaints of this customer made it clear that all too often the welds did not have enough ductility to survive the severe gauge reduction that occurred in the cold rolling process.

As a problem-solving tool, it would have been most desirable to obtain a good measurement of weld quality, both for those welds that survived and those welds that failed. For example, we would have liked to measure "percent elongation" of a standard tensile specimen where the axial dimension of the test specimen went *across* the weld and was centered on the weld. Unfortunately, we did not have access to these kind of data. The evaluation of weld quality was confined to a functional test performed from time to time at the weld station. This test has, for years, been performed in the following manner:

After the weld was completed, and the bulbs of previously molten metal have been planed off, a test piece of steel sheet which included the weld was cut out for weld quality evaluation. This was done four times each turn. (In the steel mill a "turn" is an eight-hour shift. The mill may have run, for example, 16 or 18 turns per week.) The test piece was approximately 12 inches wide, six inches on each side of the weld. The length of the test piece was the full width of the coils being joined together. If the coil width was 60 inches, we had on hand a test piece about 12 by 60 inches, with a 60-inch long weld running along the center line.

The standard test to evaluate weld quality was to press a tool steel ball down until a bulge of a prescribed depth was attained. For instance, a 1¼-inch steel ball might be pressed down until a spherical "bulge" 5/8-inch high was raised on the bottom of the sheet. After the bulge had been made, the weld was evaluated as either failed or not failed. Three conditions were possible:

1. No crack — not failed.
2. Cracked, but no portion of the crack running *parallel* to the weld — not failed. (The logic here is that the weld was stronger than the parent metal; hence, it was not deemed a weld failure.)
3. Cracked with some portion of the crack running parallel to weld — failed.

We had only go and no-go or pass-fail information on the weld quality. We had only this attribute data with which to evaluate the weld, not the measurement type data that we would have liked to have.

Besides the problem of only getting failed or not failed information on weld quality, the bulge test left us with a whole host of unanswered questions of a metallurgical and mechanical engineering nature. Perhaps the most important of these was the question of correlation between the bulge test results and the observed weld failures in the cold reduction mill. We were left with little choice but to gather and evaluate weld bulge test data on the tentative hypotheses that the data would be useful. We assumed that welds that passed the test were good welds and welds that failed the test were bad welds. Fortunately, this turned out to be a viable assumption.

Before considering how to gather and analyze data from the weld operation, it was necessary to consider in some detail the nature of the weld operation itself.

After the head and tail of the mating coils were trimmed, the tail of the leading coil was firmly anchored and the head of the trailing or movable coil automatically positioned parallel to it and at a prescribed distance away. The head of the movable coil was then advanced to a prescribed velocity until contact was made with the tail of the anchored coil. An electric current was then passed through the junction while the advance of the movable coil was carefully controlled. In all, there were perhaps a dozen mechanical and/or electrical parameters that completely defined the weld process. The weld operators set these parameters using control knobs on a console. Immediately below this battery of knobs was a space for a strip of card stick, or "card," on which each knob setting was prescribed. Different weld process parameters were specified for thin gauge steel sheet than for thick gauge sheet. The steel gauges' thickness variability was grouped into four categories from thin to thick with a separate "card" for each. Card A was for the thinnest gauges, card B next, then card C, and finally card D for the thickest gauges. Hence there was a one-to-one correspondence between "card" and "gauge."

At the inception of our efforts, it was not unusual for several bulge tests to be made on a weld, and for *all* of them to fail. When welds failed the bulge test, the operators would "adjust" the weld parameters as they saw fit. No formal record was kept of the weld parameters that "worked" or those that did not, nor was any record kept of the number of bulges which passed or failed the test. In fact, it was common knowledge that all weld operators had their own "vest pocket" set of weld parameters they used and shared with no one. Everyone did his or her own thing, with total disregard for specifications. (Hopefully, this condition does not exist in your plant.)

It is against this backdrop of complete anarchy that we decided to gather and analyze, in control chart form, the fraction of bulge tests defective. Our first step had to be an educational process to try to get each weld operator to do the same thing — to follow the weld parameter specifications, at least on a sustained trial basis.

It was also necessary for us to establish and enforce standard procedures for making the bulge tests, so the following ground rules were established:

Every two hours a completed weld would be tested using the standard bulge test procedures. Six reasonably well-spaced bulges would be made along the length of the weld. Starting at the north side, these bulges would alternate toward the top of the sheet, then the bottom, then the top, etc. This alternation was done in case there turned out to be a problem which had a preference for the top or the bottom of the sheet, such as might be introduced by differences in planing off the top and the bottom "bulbs" of previously molten metal.

After establishing standard procedures for the weld and for the bulge test, we were ready to consider the various methods of subgrouping which we might use to study the test results. In any process, we look at order of production as a potential source of variability — we know from experience that the process may wander with time, and we use 3-sigma limits on a control chart to detect out-of-control conditions. In choosing order of production as a basis for forming rational subgroups we may sometimes forget the basic philosophy of the Shewhart method:

1. We want to choose "rational subgroups" so that items within the subgroup are as much alike as possible (not just by order of production).
2. Our success in troubleshooting will be directly related to our wisdom or good fortune in selecting rational subgroups.

3. We need not restrict ourselves to one choice of subgrouping method. We may choose many different ways to regroup the *same* data to analyze them in different ways (not just by order of production).

The key to the improvement in weld quality was the detection and elimination of sources of excessive variation. This was accomplished by listing the possible sources of variations, based on expert knowledge of the operation, and then making fraction defective control charts with first one set of subgroups and then another. The following potential sources of variability, and hence of subgrouping, were identified:

Turn	Was the third shift really worse than the overall average?
Crew	A crew consisting of both operators and inspectors worked together as a single team, with rotating shift assignments. A crew might work part of a week on first turn and part of a week on second or third turn. Was one particular crew significantly better or worse than average?
Grade	There were some 200 different grades or chemistry of steel. Were one or more particular grades significantly better or worse than the overall average?
Card (Gauge)	Were the thin (or thick) gauges significantly different from the overall average?
Coil Width	Do narrow coils weld better than average?
Top versus Bottom	Do significantly more than half of the failures occur on bulges toward the top of the strip? (This could possibly be due to the operation of planing off the bulbs by previously molten metal.)
Position of Bulge	Do certain bulge positions across the weld (numbered 1 through 6) or certain combinations of positions have significantly more (or less) than their pro rata share of defective bulges?

For a chart on fraction defective, a decision must be made as to the time period within which data will be "bunched." An important consideration here is that within this time period, all trace of order of production is lost. We chose a time period of one operating week, which meant that any processing changes introduced, whether accidentally or deliberately, could only be evaluated on the basis of whole operating weeks. One week was a natural unit of time, since between operating weeks the mill shuts down for maintenance.

To facilitate the gathering of the raw data, one data sheet was provided for each turn, as shown in part in Figure 7.6. In addition to providing the relevant identification information, the data sheet enabled the bulge test results to be readily portrayed: An "X" was drawn through each bulge that failed. Suppose that for a given week, the mill had run 18 turns. Then the number of bulges inspected would have been:

$$
\begin{aligned}
\text{Number inspected} &= 18 \text{ turns} \\
&\times 4 \text{ welds/turn} \\
&\times 6 \text{ bulges/weld} \\
&= 432 \text{ bulges}
\end{aligned}
$$

If there had been, say 73 failed bulges, the overall fraction defective for the week would have been:

$\bar{p}$ = number failed/ number inspected = 73 / 432 = 0.17, or 17 percent defective.

Note that the 17 percent defective was an intrinsic property of the week; no matter how we chose to subgroup the data, $\bar{p}$ would not change. Except for order of production, each of the methods of subgrouping would result in the analysis of a *fixed* quantity of data — the bulge tests' results for one week. We would use 3-sigma limits when subgrouping by order of production where the number of subgroups would constantly increase without limit. However, 2-sigma limits would be a better choice for all methods of subgrouping where the number of subgroups was small (12 or fewer).

After we had obtained the data on bulge test failures for the first week, we could make a different p chart for each proposed method of subgrouping. Week after week we could compare these charts seeking evidence of assignable causes of excessive variability — points outside of the control limits — particularly those which would repeat for more than one week.

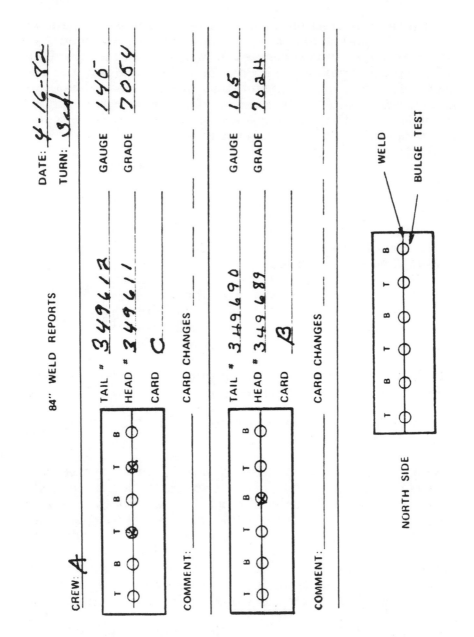

Figure 7.6 Weld Reports

320

Often one finds that a good place to look for trouble is the night shift. This suspicion did not prove fruitful for the weld problem. We could find no evidence of lack of control when the data were subgrouped by turn. (Note in Figure 7.7 that the third turn was manned less than the first or second, so its control limits were wider.) In the absence of evidence of lack of statistical control, we do *not* conclude that we are in control, but rather that we have not yet chosen our subgroups properly.

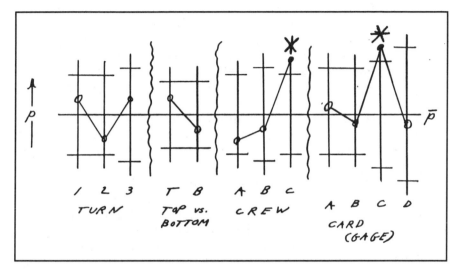

Figure 7.7 Control Charts for Rational Subgroups

We looked at the data again, this time subgrouped by "top" versus "bottom." Half of the bulges inspected were in each of the two categories. This provided a larger sample size than for any other method of subgrouping provided, hence it had the narrowest 2-sigma control limits. Again we found no evidence of lack of control; we had not yet chosen our subgroups correctly to identify our problems.

At this stage in our study, we side-stepped any attempts to subgroup by grade (i.e., steel chemistry). This was done in desperation, since there were over 200 different grades of steel produced and we did not know how to start. We also neglected the opportunity to subgroup by coil width; this decision was made based on engineering judgment that it would not be an important source of variability in weld quality.

Our first success in identifying an assignable cause for excessive variability in weld quality came unexpectedly when we subgrouped the data by crew, as seen in Figure 7.7. The first week showed crew C to be out of control. Crew C showed a significantly higher fraction defective (using 2-sigma limits) than did the overall average. One point out of control proves little, but when it happened two weeks in a row it was convincing evidence that crew C was doing something differently than were crews A and B.

Note that we could not conclude that crew C was "bad." Indeed, it may have been the only crew that was "good" — perhaps the inspectors on crews A and B were not properly reporting their bulge test failures. What we could conclude was that the three crews were not performing the welding operation and/or the bulge test process in the same manner. We had identified a significant source of excessive variability, which had to be removed. Week after week we tried to educate the operators and inspectors to the need for uniform conformance to standard procedures, but week after week crew C continued to show a fraction defective above the 2-sigma limits. One of the significant advantages of the control chart method over other statistical approaches is that anyone can look at a control chart and intuitively grasp and *believe* the message that an out-of-control point conveys. After a number of weeks the excessive variability between crews disappeared. We learned years later that the crew C operators all finally started using the specified weld parameters. We had eliminated a major source of variability in the weld quality and we saw a decrease in the number of actual weld fractures reported in the cold rolling division.

When we subgrouped the weekly data by card (or gauge), we found that sometimes one subgroup would be out of control, and sometimes another. We could take no corrective action and tentatively concluded that our problems were being masked by other, more important factors.

Subgrouping the data by bulge position along the weld (positions 1 through 6) showed ample evidence of lack of control, but gave little indication of the root cause. The first p chart in Figure 7.8 shows a peculiar pattern across the six positions, rather like an irregularly shaped letter "M." Although we were not smart enough to read the message, the process was certainly trying to tell us something, for the next week the p chart had a very similar pattern, which repeated week after week.

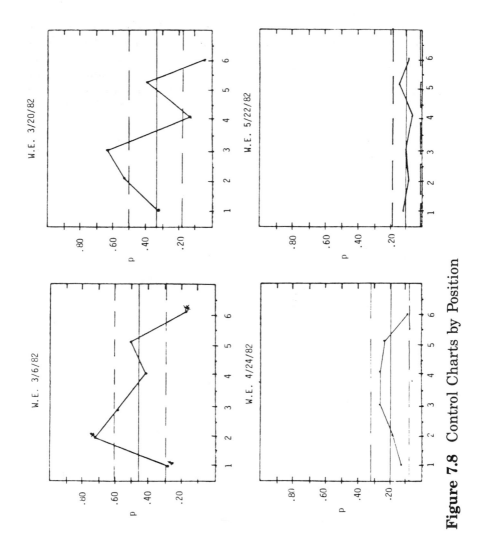

Figure 7.8 Control Charts by Position

The problem was finally solved, not by tremendous insight, but by trial and error. We tried regrouping the data so that positions 1, 2, and 3 (the north half of the coil) formed one single subgroup, and positions 4, 5, and 6 (the south half of the coil) formed another. As seen in Figure 7.9, week after week we found the north side to have too many failures and the south side to have too few. This was our first technological success.

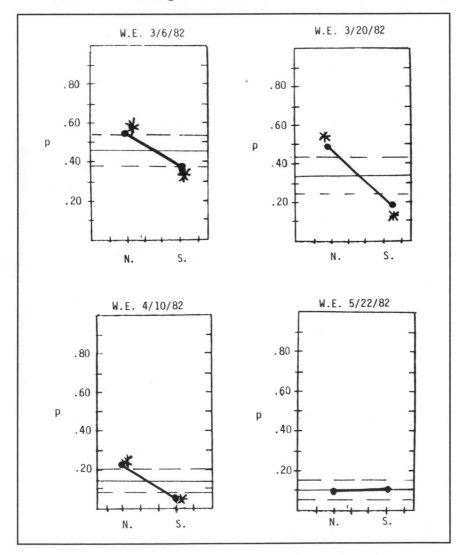

Figure 7.9 Control Charts by North versus South

After the first two or three weeks of results showing a preference for one side of the coil, we asked maintenance personnel to look for an out-of-square condition in the welding equipment. We were looking for something that would allow the two pieces to repeatedly come together cocked toward the same side, rather than butting up squarely, one to another. Diligent efforts by maintenance turned up nothing — measurements taken between the two pieces showed them to be coming together perfectly aligned. However, week after week the preference for the same side showed up on the p charts. We clearly had to look at the equipment again, and this time look more carefully. The second effort by maintenance brought success; it was discovered that one corner of the coil tail, one which should have been firmly anchored, was slipping under load when the head end of the other coil was forced against it.

Repair procedures to assure that the anchored coil tail was securely fastened in place corrected the problem, but the most impressive result was the impact of the experience on the maintenance crew. They were suddenly completely convinced of the power of the control chart — it had accurately pinpointed a serious problem which they otherwise would not have discovered.

By this time we had been working on the problem for about 10 weeks. As noted on the p charts, the average fraction of bulges defective had been greatly reduced. Of far more importance, the failures in the cold reduction mill had virtually disappeared. However, continued study of our p charts each week showed that we still had a problem in position-to-position variability in bulge test results. We were now able to see that there were significantly more failures near the center of the weld than at the two extremities. (This might have been detectable earlier, but as noted in Figure 7.8, the effect had been pretty well masked.) By now maintenance personnel were true believers in the control charts and they were able to quickly find and correct the problem. The dies for trimming the coil ends had been designed with a slight bow, but this condition was corrected by regrinding them to a simpler, straight shape. An important message here is that engineering must be done by "listening to the process."

Although the cold reduction mill quality problem had been corrected, we continued to study the weld bulge test results. Now for the first time we looked at the data by order of production, setting 3-sigma limits based on the results of the most recent two weeks. We prepared a chart for number of defective bulges in each weld (i.e., zero to six defective bulges plotted on an np chart). We immediately discovered that all of the points above the upper control limit came from only eight out of the total of over 200 grades of steel. These eight grades were subsequently identified by metallurgical consultants as "hard-to-weld" grades which inherently suffered from low ductility after welding. New weld parameters were established especially for this one family of steels.

The weld quality problem had been successfully solved through the sequential use of different methods of subgrouping, using the same data each time. It was a step-by-step process of identification and elimination of sources of excessive variability in weld quality. The job would have been easier with measurement data, but in the absence of the preferred method, attribute charts served us very well. The successful use of statistical process control methods was of inestimable value for its impact on the thinking of the steel mill personnel. Fortunately, these efforts are gathering momentum. For the U.S. steel industry to be competitive, the use of statistical process control methods must play a central role.

Postscript: There is an adage that says, "A computer program that has been debugged is one for which the input to make it malfunction has not yet been generated." Perhaps a corollary is, "A manufacturing process that is in a state of statistical control is one for which the proper rational subgroups have not yet been selected."

Chapter 23 Detecting and Correcting Manufacturing Problems

In assembly line manufacturing operations, problems of poor quality are frequently transient in nature. For this reason improvement can only be made by continuously monitoring the process and *responding promptly* by taking corrective action when the need arises. An effective mechanism for monitoring the process will be described in this chapter, but it must be kept in mind that the best monitoring methods become only an idle exercise *unless corrective action is taken when needed.*

A primary roadblock to process improvement is lack of timely information on manufacturing problems. All too often management is totally unable to answer the following questions:

- On the proceeding shift what was the percent defective (or defects per unit?
- What types of problems were causing this scrap and rework?

The prerequisite to process improvement is the ability to define opportunities to improve, sometimes called "problems." The first line of defense for management is timely, accurate information on manufacturing problems. As defects arise, they should first be tallied in real time. To do this effectively requires the development and use of tally sheets (discussed in Part II) appropriate to the process. This frequently calls for the use of a number of different tally sheet forms, each one tailored to a specific area on the shop floor. At regular intervals (no less often than the end of each shift) the data on one tally sheet are summarized and transcribed to a single column of a spreadsheet which may appropriately be called a *percent defective* (or *defects per unit) summary chart*. Figure 7.10 shows an example of a tally sheet and Figure 7.11 shows a *percent defective summary sheet.*

As seen in Figure 7.10, the tally sheet shows the accumulation during the shift of several types of the defects. In addition, the total number of defects, the total number run and the percent defective for that shift are shown on the tally sheet. On each shift, one person must be assigned the task of completing the tally sheet and posting the results onto the percent defective summary chart. Since this information is not completely available until the end of the shift, it means the person responsible for posting the data might (start and) end his or her work period 30 minutes later than the regular shift.

The results from the tally sheet of Figure 7.10 are transcribed into the first column of the percent defective summary chart of Figure 7.11, and the percent defective is plotted on the graph. In

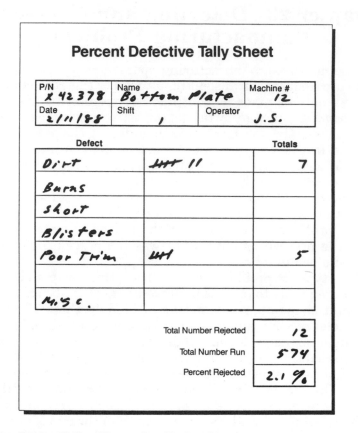

Percent Defective Tally Sheet

P/N	Name	Machine #
X 42378	Bottom Plate	12

Date	Shift	Operator
2/11/88	1	J.S.

Defect		Totals
Dirt	ЦНТ II	7
Burns		
Short		
Blisters		
Poor Trim	ЦНТ	5
Misc.		

Total Number Rejected	12
Total Number Run	574
Percent Rejected	2.1 %

Figure 7.10 Tally Sheet for Defectives

this example, the shift number was used as the plotting symbol. Whatever procedure is used, when multiple shifts are plotted on the same chart, a distinctive symbol must be used for each. This is an application of the general rule that when unlike things are plotted on the same chart, the plotting symbols must clearly identify the particular classifications.

As shown in Figure 7.11, the percent defective summary chart is *not* a Shewhart control chart. It is simply a tabular summary of manufacturing problems that is updated religiously at the end of each shift, supplemented by a graph that shows the overall fraction defective (or number of defects per unit) for that shift. There is neither a center line nor a control limit shown on the graph; the emphasis here is on the overview of process performance rather than on potentially tedious statistical calculations.

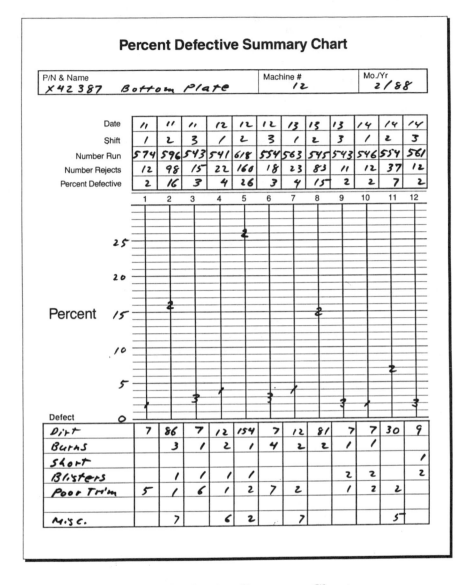

Percent Defective Summary Chart

P/N & Name		Machine #	Mo./Yr
X42387 Bottom Plate		12	2/88

Date	11	11	11	12	12	12	13	13	13	14	14	14
Shift	1	2	3	1	2	3	1	2	3	1	2	3
Number Run	574	596	543	541	618	554	563	545	543	546	554	561
Number Rejects	12	98	15	22	160	18	23	83	11	12	37	12
Percent Defective	2	16	3	4	26	3	4	15	2	2	7	2

Defect	1	2	3	4	5	6	7	8	9	10	11	12
Dirt	7	86	7	12	154	7	12	81	7	7	30	9
Burns		3	1	2	1	4	2	2	1	1		
Short												1
Blisters		1	1	1	1				2	2		2
Poor Trim	5	1	6	1	2	7	2		1	2	2	
Misc.		7		6	2		7				5	

Figure 7.11 Percent Defective Summary Chart

Two important results are immediately clear from the percent defective summary chart in Figure 7.11:

1. Dirt is the biggest problem.
2. The problem is on the second shift.

The percent defective summary chart is intended to be a *problem-identification* tool, not a *problem-solving* tool. However, often the clear identification of the problem leads immediately to the solution. Such was the case in the real example shown here. The process was plastic injection molding. Attention was given to shift-to-shift differences in the processing techniques, and the dirt problem was greatly improved. Moreover, after the assignable cause of shift-to-shift differences was removed, it became clear that there was another problem of tool maintenance that had previously been masked. This problem, once it was in clear focus, was also solved. After that, defects ran at only about 1 percent with more improvements continually being made as they became more visible.

Of all the techniques used to maintain and improve processes, the percent defective summary chart is the most fundamental, simplest, and most useful. It will tell when to go upstream for more in-depth detective work (run charts and control charts) to discover and remove the root causes for the detected symptoms.

Part VIII. Introduction to "Special Situations" Charts

The basic control charts apply in repetitive manufacturing situations where individual pieces are being made. Many manufacturing and nonmanufacturing situations do not fit into that mold so the basic control charts don't apply. In those cases, modifications of the basic charts apply. Part VIII will provide a brief introduction to some of these control charts that are appropriate for special situations.

Chapter 24   Situations Handled by Basic Control Charts

The Shewhart control chart is a simple but powerful statistical tool, but it must be understood that the *only* circumstance under which it is applicable is the unique condition when the within-subgroup variability is a useful estimator of the between-subgroup variability. This is equivalent to saying that the process *must* be, in effect, a random normal number generator.

The truth is that many processes are *not* suitable for the application of a Shewhart control chart. Attempts to use such a chart when it is not appropriate may be devastating and such misuse is often responsible for the feeling that Shewhart charts don't work. There may be dozens of good reasons why a process is not simply a random normal number generator. The primary job of a person trying to improve his or her process is to understand that nature of the variability of the process and how to monitor and control it. Too often the would-be statistician thinks that his or her job is simply to walk around with an X̄ bar and R chart and find someplace to hang it.

Chapter 25 Special Situations

The following (in brief) are some special situations where the basic control charts do not apply and the modifications of the charts that are necessary to handle these situations.

Continuous Processes

In a continuous process, the product is not discrete individual pieces. It then makes no sense to take a subgroup of readings.

Examples Coils of steel, bolts of cloth, liquid chemicals, temperatures in an oven.

Procedure Instead of taking multiple readings in a row, one reading is taken every now and then — one reading of thickness or width every so many feet, one ph level or temperature reading every hour, etc. The best chart to handle this situation is a control chart for individuals, typically the X and MR or RX charts discussed in Part V.

Short Runs

Short runs (i.e., processes where few parts of a given kind are made) do not lend themselves directly to the use of Shewhart control charts. However, many parts have similar operations, only using different dimensions. It is on this common thread that data for a Shewhart control chart may be analyzed. As Deming (1982, p. 59) notes:

> There are, in any job shop, repeated operations, turning, welding, riveting, stitching. Productivity can be improved in these operations by the methods of process control.

Where Applicable Short runs with similar parts, similar operations, but *different dimensions*.

Examples Journal diameters on five different shafts with similar configurations, but different journal diameters.

Procedure

Step 1 For each piece calculate the quantity "X" by which the measurement is in excess of the "target" dimension (i.e., X = reading − target dimension). Note that the X value, or deviation, may be positive or negative depending on whether the reading is larger than or smaller than the target dimension, respectively.

Step 2 Make a *run chart* of the X values.
Plot every deviation on a run chart from the first piece on until you can see that the deviations are stable.

Step 3 When the process appears stable, a Shewhart control chart may be used. Either a discontinuous X and MR chart or a chart for averages and dispersion of small subgroups could be used. For instance, measure three consecutive pieces and calculate their $\overline{X}$ values every half hour until the run is finished. Very short runs may have only one subgroup, longer runs will have more subgroups.

Example 8.1

An example is given in Figure 8.1. It is important to use a different symbol for different parts, or at least a different symbol for each category of parts such as parts under 200 inches versus those over 200 inches, as in Figure 8.1.

In this example, coils of steel are decoiled and cut to "print dimension." The target value for each part number is "set length." The X values are the deviations from target recorded in sixteenths of an inch. The X values recorded for the first subgroup are 0, −1, and −1. This subgroup has a target value or "set length" of 185-3/4. (From this information we can infer that the measured lengths on the first three pieces were 185-3/4, 185-11/16, and 185-11/16, but we really have no use for this information.)

Pieces 200 inches long and over have been plotted using a large triangle. Pieces under 200 inches have been plotted using a small dot. Since the triangles seem to be randomly dispersed (not systematically different from the dots) we conclude that the long and short pieces are behaving in similar fashions. The charts show that the process as a whole (with long and short pieces) is in a reasonably good state of control.

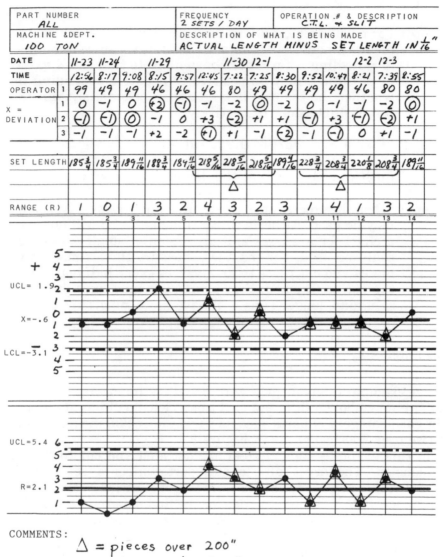

COMMENTS:

$\triangle$ = pieces over 200"
● = pieces under 200"

Figure 8.1 Short Runs

PROBLEM

8.1 Complete the control chart for the following short runs:

SHORT RUN PROBLEM

DATE		NOV 2	NOV 2	NOV 3	NOV. 4	NOV. 4	NOV. 7	NOV. 9	NOV. 9	NOV. 9	NOV. 11
PART NUMBER		603	603	112	115	115	218	814	814	814	603
PRINT DIMENSION		12	12	13	10	10	15	11	11	11	12
READINGS	1	11	13	12	10	10	13	11	11	13	12
	2	14	13	13	11	9	13	10	10	13	11
	3	12	10	11	9	9	16	9	12	11	11
EXCESS OVER	1										
PRINT	2										
	3										
	$\tilde{X}$										
	R										

$\overline{\tilde{X}} =$ $\overline{R} =$

$UCL_{\tilde{X}} =$ $UCL_R =$

$LCL_{\tilde{X}} =$ $LCL_R =$

Tool Wear and Other Linear Trends

Figure 8.2 shows an $\overline{X}$ and R chart made on actual data that have been taken from a machining operation. Each data entry is the depth of a machined recess in mils. Each of the $k=17$ subgroups consist of $n=5$ successive pieces taken from the assembly line.

A glance at the raw data shows that the values within each subgroup never increase; no value is larger than the one above it. This implies a tool wear problem, which is completely masked by the $\overline{X}$ and R chart. The use of the Shewhart method on the raw data is not only worthless, it is misleading. The run chart in Figure 8.3 of the individual readings reveals a downward trend between tool adjustments, disclosing the severe tool wear situation.

Examples Tool wear, contamination level in chemical baths.

Procedure Use a simple run chart on the individual readings or some modification thereof, with action limits derived from the specifications. For purposes of an engineering study of the process (as opposed to ongoing process control) it is possible to make a control chart on the "tool wear increments." These methods are beyond the scope of this text.

Skewed Data

Data that are badly skewed by nature can sometimes be recognized from the control chart as pointed out in Part IV. If the data are so badly skewed as to show up on the control chart, the control chart will not be effective.

Examples Moisture content of coke, impurities in a chemical process.

Procedure Typically, if it's known that by their nature the process data are skewed, a "transformation" of the data are necessary to make the data approximately normal so the control chart will apply. Most commonly a logarithmic transformation of the original data is used. The control chart is then made on the transformed data. These techniques are beyond the scope of this text.

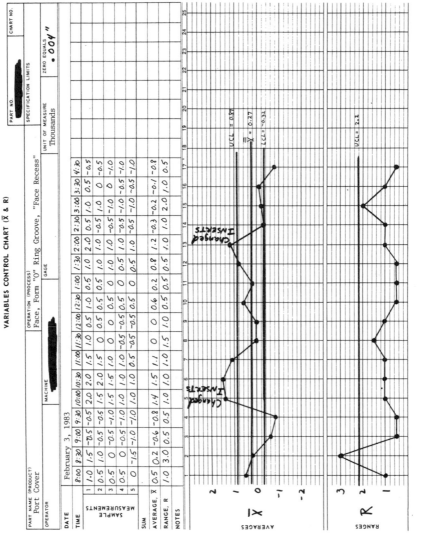

Figure 8.2 X bar and R Chart from Machining Operation

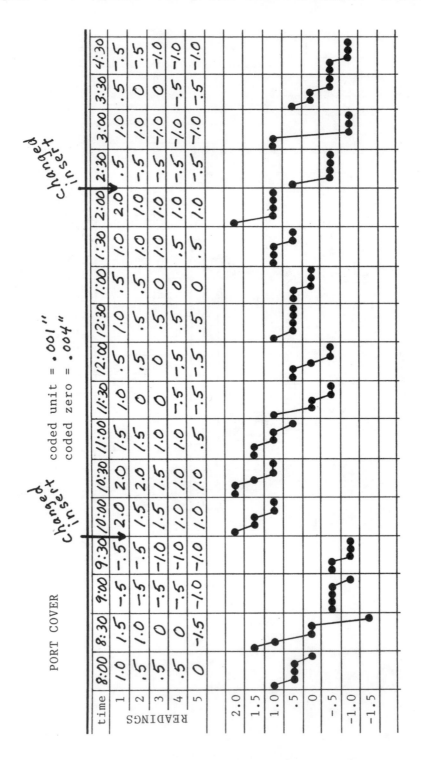

Figure 8.3 Run Chart Showing Tool Wear

Batch Processes

When working with a batch process, we expect the data within a batch to be very much alike, but we expect the data to be different from batch to batch. In this case, it is *not* feasible to use the within-subgroup variability to estimate the between-subgroup variability.

Examples   Paint made in batches, stamping washers out of different coils of steel.

Procedure   Make an RX chart or an $\overline{X}$ and R chart, using the overall average range from all the subgroups for R, but using the grand average from each specific batch for the $\overline{X}$ for that batch as illustrated in Figure 8.4. Other techniques can be used to control batch means, but the details are beyond the scope of this text.

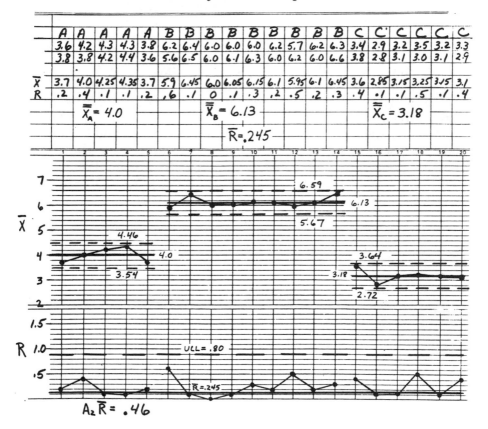

Figure 8.4   Control Chart on Batch Process Data

Measurement Error

When an $\overline{X}$ and R chart on manufactured product indicates a state of statistical control, we have said that $\overline{R}/d_2$ provides an estimate of the standard deviation — sigma — of the process. It is usually inferred that this "sigma" is an estimate of the "true" variability of the product, but on further examination we see that this "sigma" is really an estimate of the combined variability of the product *and* of the measurement system.

It must be recognized that variability in repeated measurements of the same characteristic is a natural condition, just as is variability in repeated pieces of product. This *random* variability of the measurement system must be managed: It must be understood, quantified, controlled, and used properly by management. An elementary approach with considerable practical appeal is provided in the Western Electric Company *Statistical Process Control Handbook* (1956). It should be noted that the approach given in that reference does not address the question of calibration or bias of the measurement system but only the issue of repeatability. Whatever approach is used to study measurement systems, control chart methods must be used to demonstrate that the measurement process is in a state of statistical control. All such control charts utilize as inputs repeated *independent* measurements of the same characteristics.

When a measurement system has been evaluated and found to be in statistical control, the final step is to determine that the bias and precision of the measurement system are small enough that the measurement system is useful for the purpose intended. These studies are beyond the scope of this textbook.

Appendix A
Table 1

Factors

			With R Chart					With s Chart				$\hat{\sigma} =$		
	3-sigma limits on $\bar{X}$		Limits on R				3-sigma limits on $\bar{X}$	Limits on s				$\dfrac{\bar{R}}{d_2}$ or $\dfrac{\bar{s}}{\bar{c}_4}$		
			3-sigma limits		2-sigma limits			3-sigma limits		2-sigma limits		With R Chart	With s Chart	
n	A_2	$\tilde{A}_2$	D_3	D_4	D_{32}	D_{42}	A_3	B_3	B_4	B_{32}	B_{42}	d_2	c_4	n
2	1.88	1.88	0	3.27	0	2.51	2.66	0	3.27	0	2.51	1.13	0.80	2
3	1.02	1.19	0.	2.58	0	2.05	1.95	0	2.57	0.	2.05	1.69	0.89	3
4	0.73	0.80	0	2.28	0.15	1.85	1.63	0	2.27	0.16	1.84	2.06	0.92	4
5	0.58	0.69	0	2.11	0.26	1.74	1.43	0	2.09	0.27	1.73	2.33	0.94	5
6	0.48	0.55	0	2.00	0.33	1.67	1.29	0.03	1.97	0.35	1.65	2.53	0.95	6
7	0.42	0.51	0.08	1.92	0.38	1.62	1.18	0.12	1.88	0.41	1.59	2.70	0.96	7
8	0.37	0.43	0.14	1.86	0.42	1.58	1.10	0.18	1.82	0.46	1.54	2.85	0.97	8
9	0.34	0.41	0.18	1.82	0.46	1.54	1.03	0.24	1.76	0.49	1.51	2.97	0.97	9
10	0.31	0.36	0.22	1.78	0.48	1.52	.98	0.28	1.72	0.52	1.48	3.08	0.97	10
11	0.29	0.35	0.26	1.74	0.50	1.50	.93	0.32	1.68	0.55	1.45	3.17	0.98	11
12	0.27	0.32	0.28	1.72	0.52	1.48	.87	0.35	1.65	0.57	1.43	3.26	0.98	12
15	N.A.	N.A.	N.A.	N.A.	N.A.	N.A.	.79	0.43	1.57	0.62	1.38	N.A.	0.98	15
20	N.A.	N.A.	N.A.	N.A.	N.A.	N.A.	.68	0.51	1.49	0.67	1.33	N.A.	0.99	20
21 or more	N.A.	N.A.	N.A.	N.A.	N.A.	N.A.	$\dfrac{3}{\sqrt{n}}$	$1-\dfrac{3}{\sqrt{2n-2}}$	$1+\dfrac{3}{\sqrt{2n-2}}$	$1-\dfrac{2}{\sqrt{2n-2}}$	$1+\dfrac{2}{\sqrt{2n-2}}$	N.A.	$\dfrac{4n-4}{4n-3}$	21 or more

N.A. = Not Applicable

Table 2

Limits for
Variables Charts

Chart Type		3-sigma limits		2-sigma limits	
		LCL	UCL	LCL	UCL
mean	$\overline{X}$	$\overline{\overline{X}} - A_2\overline{R}$ or $\overline{\overline{X}} - A_3\overline{s}$	$\overline{\overline{X}} + A_2\overline{R}$ or $\overline{\overline{X}} + A_3\overline{s}$	$\overline{\overline{X}} - (2/3)\,A_2\overline{R}$ or $\overline{\overline{X}} - (2/3)\,A_3\overline{s}$	$\overline{\overline{X}} + (2/3)\,A_2\overline{R}$ or $\overline{\overline{X}} + (2/3)\,A_3\overline{s}$
median	$\widetilde{X}$	$\overline{\overline{X}} - \widetilde{A}_2\overline{R}$	$\overline{\overline{X}} + \widetilde{A}_2\overline{R}$	$\overline{\overline{X}} - (2/3)\,\widetilde{A}_2\overline{R}$	$\overline{\overline{X}} + (2/3)\,\widetilde{A}_2\overline{R}$
range	R	$D_3\overline{R}$	$D_4\overline{R}$	$D_{32}\overline{R}$	$D_{42}\overline{R}$
standard deviation	s	$B_3\overline{s}$	$B_4\overline{s}$	$B_{32}\overline{s}$	$B_{42}\overline{s}$
individuals	X	$\overline{X} - 3\hat{\sigma}$ (LNL) or $\overline{X} - 2.66\,\overline{MR}$	$\overline{X} + 3\hat{\sigma}$ (UNL) or $\overline{X} + 2.66\,\overline{MR}$	$\overline{X} - 2\hat{\sigma}$ or $\overline{X} - 1.77\,\overline{MR}$	$\overline{X} + 2\hat{\sigma}$ or $\overline{X} + 1.77\,\overline{MR}$
moving range	MR	0	$3.27\,\overline{MR}$	0	$2.51\,\overline{MR}$

Table 3

Attribute Charts

Subgroup Size

	may vary	constant
defective (nonconforming pieces)	p chart fraction defective $\sigma_p = \sqrt{\bar{p}(1 - \bar{p})/n}$	np chart number defective in each group of constant size $\sigma_{np} = \sqrt{n\bar{p}(1 - \bar{p})}$
defects (nonconformances)	u chart defects per production unit $\sigma_u = \sqrt{\bar{u}/n}$	c chart defects per subgroup of constant size $\sigma_c = \sqrt{\bar{c}}$

Control chart limits, example:

$$UCL\ (p) = \bar{p} + 3\sigma_p$$
$$LCL\ (p) = \bar{p} - 3\sigma_p$$

Appendix B
Normal Distribution Tail Areas

Assuming the process is in control and can be approximated by a normal distribution, the values in the table give the normal curve tail areas (the proportion of product in the tail) beyond Z standard deviations above or below the process average.

z	x.x0	x.x1	x.x2	x.x3	x.x4	x.x5	x.x6	x.x7	x.x8	x.x9
4.0	.00003									
3.5	.00023									
3.0	.00135									
2.9	.0019	.0018	.0018	.0017	.0016	.0016	.0015	.0015	.0014	.0014
2.8	.0026	.0025	.0024	.0023	.0023	.0022	.0021	.0021	.0020	.0019
2.7	.0035	.0034	.0033	.0032	.0031	.0030	.0029	.0028	.0027	.0026
2.6	.0047	.0045	.0044	.0043	.0041	.0040	.0039	.0038	.0037	.0036
2.5	.0062	.0060	.0059	.0057	.0055	.0054	.0052	.0051	.0049	.0048
2.4	.0082	.0080	.0078	.0075	.0073	.0071	.0069	.0068	.0066	.0064
2.3	.0107	.0104	.0102	.0099	.0096	.0094	.0091	.0089	.0087	.0084
2.2	.0139	.0136	.0132	.0129	.0125	.0122	.0119	.0116	.0113	.0110
2.1	.0179	.0174	.0170	.0166	.0162	.0158	.0154	.0150	.0146	.0143
2.0	.0228	.0222	.0217	.0212	.0207	.0202	.0197	.0192	.0188	.0183
1.9	.0287	.0281	.0274	.0268	.0262	.0256	.0250	.0244	.0239	.0233
1.8	.0359	.0351	.0344	.0336	.0329	.0322	.0314	.0307	.0301	.0294
1.7	.0446	.0436	.0427	.0418	.0409	.0401	.0392	.0384	.0375	.0367
1.6	.0548	.0537	.0526	.0516	.0505	.0495	.0485	.0475	.0465	.0455
1.5	.0668	.0655	.0643	.0630	.0618	.0606	.0594	.0582	.0571	.0559
1.4	.0808	.0793	.0778	.0764	.0749	.0735	.0721	.0708	.0694	.0681
1.3	.0968	.0951	.0934	.0918	.0901	.0885	.0869	.0853	.0838	.0823
1.2	.1151	.1131	.1112	.1093	.1075	.1056	.1038	.1020	.1003	.0985
1.1	.1357	.1335	.1314	.1292	.1271	.1251	.1230	.1210	.1190	.1170
1.0	.1587	.1562	.1539	.1515	.1492	.1469	.1446	.1423	.1401	.1379
0.9	.1841	.1814	.1788	.1762	.1736	.1711	.1685	.1660	.1635	.1611
0.8	.2119	.2090	.2061	.2033	.2005	.1977	.1949	.1922	.1894	.1867
0.7	.2420	.2389	.2358	.2327	.2297	.2266	.2236	.2206	.2177	.2148
0.6	.2743	.2709	.2676	.2643	.2611	.2578	.2546	.2514	.2483	.2451
0.5	.3085	.3050	.3015	.2981	.2946	.2912	.2877	.2843	.2810	.2776
0.4	.3446	.3409	.3372	.3336	.3300	.3264	.3228	.3192	.3156	.3121
0.3	.3821	.3783	.3745	.3707	.3669	.3632	.3594	.3557	.3520	.3483
0.2	.4207	.4168	.4129	.4090	.4052	.4013	.3974	.3936	.3897	.3859
0.1	.4602	.4562	.4522	.4483	.4443	.4404	.4364	.4325	.4286	.4247
0.0	.5000	.4960	.4920	.4880	.4840	.4801	.4761	.4721	.4681	.4641

Appendix C
Table 1

Random Normal Numbers
$\mu = 50 \qquad \sigma = 15$

23	53	40	57	25
51	29	72	32	21
48	42	38	38	43
2	73	61	61	40
41	44	42	61	75
51	29	60	51	37
79	33	49	45	74
53	44	52	74	29
46	58	53	34	73
37	45	65	73	47
34	28	27	52	41
43	65	43	43	67
69	51	52	22	35
60	59	55	43	55
41	70	38	27	56
61	91	39	12	36
41	58	24	42	48
61	22	60	62	53
60	26	49	58	62
36	57	62	78	59
49	43	30	49	36
47	55	57	61	67
53	51	32	62	57
42	39	37	66	70
34	43	61	67	35
29	17	59	65	69
27	83	43	41	60
58	61	62	71	77
23	50	48	42	64
46	58	37	36	68
70	29	59	57	45
36	39	80	41	57
47	41	75	55	56
60	32	69	36	36
37	53	38	53	34
36	16	58	56	27
21	65	65	33	38
43	83	21	44	44
70	51	55	63	34
60	36	46	62	47
39	44	43	47	47
40	59	42	32	44
48	22	73	39	69
76	44	59	57	31
24	33	71	24	55
40	5	50	45	62
59	65	34	51	62
17	35	42	57	60
54	52	34	40	16
41	83	29	47	70
33	32	53	60	31
62	64	46	34	63
37	60	72	61	82
77	66	40	35	40
23	49	44	34	39

Table 2

Random Normal Numbers
$\mu = 20 \qquad \sigma = 5$

22	12	8	14	20
22	22	21	20	19
28	24	26	20	30
16	21	32	23	30
18	19	15	19	21
18	18	21	15	22
15	27	15	20	16
11	29	29	17	25
16	26	9	26	18
17	20	24	12	22
11	23	15	20	21
21	21	17	18	25
26	20	30	19	27
23	17	26	24	20
17	18	20	29	26
16	17	17	15	20
23	17	16	15	29
11	20	25	14	15
21	20	20	26	19
19	23	15	13	19
19	24	19	32	25
14	24	27	14	22
16	21	25	15	22
15	14	19	17	16
32	18	17	15	23
14	24	21	19	21
27	23	23	23	22
20	19	20	15	23
19	18	28	18	17
18	21	27	24	20
23	19	1	26	15
9	27	18	18	22
24	23	20	15	23
17	16	21	15	13
28	18	16	22	24
16	22	15	26	22
14	26	20	21	23
18	30	19	15	21
26	15	19	23	26
28	27	22	18	21
23	23	13	12	15
31	23	11	27	16
19	18	19	20	19
25	30	17	20	20
24	16	21	16	22
23	25	28	12	19
20	22	20	16	25
17	19	20	9	22
20	21	21	26	24
16	18	5	18	23
23	18	17	23	24
21	20	24	27	15
22	17	23	32	17
18	26	27	14	24
13	20	15	23	13

Table 3

Random Normal Numbers
$\mu = 0 \quad \sigma = 1$

.96	1.98	.64	−.08	−.85
−.33	−.17	−1.24	−.04	−.32
−2.54	−.85	.04	−1.38	1.76
.82	−.12	.31	−.24	−.39
1.34	.66	−.61	−.55	−.70
.54	−.37	.40	−.63	−.61
−.36	2.27	.64	.13	−1.05
1.86	−1.38	−1.04	.42	1.25
.16	.37	−.52	.34	−.94
−1.71	.29	−.27	1.22	.24
.88	.74	−.82	.62	−.03
−.42	−.89	−2.02	−.01	.64
−1.32	−.39	−.68	−.06	.44
−.08	1.32	−1.47	.57	−.28
−2.09	−.67	−.06	1.36	1.17
1.21	−.16	.45	.87	−.54
.31	−1.08	1.31	.20	.73
.15	.37	−.44	−.02	.07
−1.55	−.21	−.32	1.53	−.05
−1.21	−1.18	−.24	−.22	1.48
.73	.54	−.39	−.27	.52
.64	−.37	−1.27	1.19	.10
1.66	.30	.66	.28	−.26
.99	.73	−2.75	.87	1.53
−1.24	−2.14	−.22	−.37	−.31
.44	−2.06	.18	3.60	.69
−1.35	−.03	−.01	−1.21	1.36
.77	−.27	−1.34	−.23	−1.08
1.26	.97	1.56	−1.71	.80
−1.08	−1.12	−.01	.93	.52
.52	1.39	−.82	−1.82	−.62
−2.59	−.10	.74	.10	−.63
−.20	−.20	−.04	1.15	.23
.17	−1.38	−1.78	.16	−.31
−.85	2.26	−.72	.80	1.61
1.61	−.32	−1.33	−.52	−.97
.06	−.64	1.59	−1.47	−.32
−2.95	−.86	−.72	−1.26	−.55
−.10	.64	−.66	1.29	−.24
−1.97	.34	.34	.56	1.45
−1.96	−.66	−.77	−.56	.12
−2.16	−1.01	−.24	−.64	.26
−.16	−.37	.48	−.51	.33
−2.02	.19	.59	−.02	−.48
.12	.87	−.94	−.42	2.59
−.57	.24	−2.24	1.10	−1.15
1.37	.67	−.25	.03	−.24
1.25	1.12	−.07	−.23	.47
−.65	−.94	.23	.79	1.48
−.27	.17	−1.94	.10	−.42
.70	.04	.85	1.60	.34
−.68	−1.59	.05	−.14	−.91
.65	1.03	.13	−.16	.34
−.26	.91	.88	1.15	.61
.52	1.24	1.61	2.36	.15

Table 4

Random Uniform Numbers
[0, 99]

21	50	82	13	77
94	46	22	15	12
70	23	33	64	51
39	94	17	97	22
74	97	95	41	41
32	4	58	4	76
93	38	38	0	79
3	73	53	36	63
62	20	93	78	51
94	68	16	49	95
21	38	57	80	25
93	22	67	64	16
10	5	57	26	8
32	90	62	45	4
17	75	8	97	42
82	30	33	28	93
31	87	96	66	99
92	90	38	59	70
80	50	26	43	81
13	34	63	89	18
15	22	47	56	50
45	94	73	49	82
15	3	73	47	77
53	86	11	12	20
72	48	54	45	16
18	73	32	27	18
42	3	33	12	25
82	51	74	50	1
49	58	44	61	17
14	41	96	16	8
47	73	2	88	81
65	70	93	53	23
16	40	88	5	4
8	95	57	65	37
91	55	9	49	33
71	32	12	90	81
19	76	3	3	29
52	5	36	54	17
12	25	39	30	28
35	51	89	33	67
83	41	81	48	21
10	99	52	18	73
74	25	23	67	42
48	1	55	31	87
57	31	8	1	0
5	17	99	34	78
14	9	3	37	34
68	58	17	97	23
65	88	6	40	60
24	69	35	92	16
90	59	29	15	84
16	89	91	66	95
8	59	65	16	19
83	37	94	38	72
82	12	95	88	2

Bibliography

American Society for Testing and Materials. *ASTM Manual on Presentation of Data and Control Charts Analysis — STP15D.* Philadelphia: American Society for Testing and Materials, 1976.

ANSI Standards Z 1.1-1958 (R1975), *Guide for Quality Control*; Z 1.2-1985 (R1975), *Control Chart Method of Analyzing Data*; and Z 1.3-1985 (R1975), *Control Chart Method of Controlling Quality During Production.* New York: American National Standards Institute.

Bicking, C.A. and F.M. Gryna. "Process Control by Statistical Methods." In *Quality Control Handbook*, 3rd ed. Ed. J.M. Juran. New York: McGraw-Hill, 1974.

Burr, I.W. *Engineering Statistics and Quality Control.* New York: McGraw-Hill, 1953.

Burr, I.W. "Specifying the Desired Distribution Rather Than Maximum and Minimum Limits." *Industrial Quality Control* 24, No. 2 (August 1976): 94-101.

Deming, W.E. *Elementary Principles of the Statistical Control of Quality.* Tokyo: Nippon Kagaku Gijutsu Remmei, 1951.

Deming, W.E. "On the Use of Theory." *Industrial Quality Control* 13, No. 1 (July 1956): 12-14.

Deming, W.E. "On Some Statistical Aids Toward Economic Production." *Interfaces* 5, No. 4 (August 1975): 1-15.

Deming, W.E. *Quality, Productivity, and Competitive Position.* Cambridge: Massachusetts Institute of Technology, Center for Advanced Engineering Studies, 1982.

Deming, W.E. *Out of the Crisis.* Cambridge: Massachusetts Institute of Technology, Center for Advanced Engineering Studies, 1986.

Dixon, W.J. and F.J. Massey. *Introduction to Statistical Analysis*, 3rd ed. New York: McGraw-Hill, 1969.

Duncan, A.J. *Quality Control and Industrial Statistics*, 5th ed. Homewood, Ill.: Richard D. Irwin Inc., 1986.

Ford Motor Company. *Process Capability and Continuing Process Control*. Plymouth, Mich.: Ford Motor Company Statistical Methods Publication, 1983.

Grant, E.L. and R.S. Leavenworth. *Statistical Quality Control*, 5th ed. New York: McGraw-Hill, 1980.

Hart, R. and M. Hart. "Quality Control: Changing Mathematical Tools." *Quality* 26 (Special Anniversary Issue, 1987): 96-100.

Hart, R. and M. Hart. "Simpler than X-Bar and R." *Quality* 26, No. 6 (June 1987): 66-67.

Hart, M. "Attribute Control Charts Using Monitor Limits." Ph.D. Thesis, Illinois Institute of Technology, 1987.

Hart, M. "Use of the Run Chart." *Quality* 26, No. 3 (March 1987): 87-88.

Hart, M. "Tools for Quality." *APICS* Conference Proceedings, American Production and Inventory Control Society, Atlanta, February 23-25, 1987, pp. 121-124.

Hart, M. "Overcorrecting." *Quality* 25, No. 10 (October 1986): 77.

Hart, R. and M. Hart. "C_{pk}." *Quality* 25, No. 8 (August 1986): 74.

Hart, R. and M. Hart. "What Target?" *Quality* 24, No. 8 (August 1985): 34.

Hart, R. "Steel by Shewhart." *Quality* 23, No. 26 (June 1984): 66-69.

Jessup, P. "The Value of Continuing Improvement." Proceedings of the International Communications Conference, Institute of Electrical and Electronics Engineers Inc., Chicago, 1985.

Juran, J.M. *Management of Inspection and Quality Control*. New York: Harper and Brothers, 1945.

Juran, J.M. and F.M. Gryna. *Quality Planning and Analysis*, 2nd ed. New York: McGraw-Hill, 1980.

Kackar, R.M. "Off-Line Quality Control, Parameter Design, and the Taguchi Method." *Journal of Quality Technology* 17, No. 4 (October 1985): 176-188.

Kane, V.E. "Process Capability Indices." *Journal of Quality Technology* 18, No. 1 (January 1986): 41-52.

Montgomery, D.C. *Introduction to Statistical Quality Control*. New York: John Wiley and Sons, 1985.

Nelson, L.S. "The Deceptiveness of Moving Averages." *Journal of Quality Technology* 15, No. 2 (April 1983): 99-100.

Ott, E.R. *Process Quality Control*. New York: McGraw-Hill, 1975.

Pearson, E.S. *The Application of Statistical Methods to Industrial Standardization and Quality Control,* British Standard No. 600. London: British Standard Institution, 1935.

Putnam, A.O. "Pre-Control." In *Quality Control Handbook*, 2nd ed. Ed. J.M. Juran. New York: McGraw-Hill, 1962.

Shewhart, W.A. *Economic Control of Quality of Manufactured Product*. Princeton, N.J.: Van Nostrand Reinhold, Co., 1931.

Shewhart, W.A. *Statistical Method from the Viewpoint of Quality Control*. Washington, D.C.: The Graduate School, Department of Agriculture, 1939.

Shewhart, W.A. "Statistical Control in Applied Science." *Transactions of the A.S.M.E. American Society of Mechanical Engineering,* Cleveland, April 1943 pp. 222-225.

StatScan® (Statistical Process Control Software). StatScan, Inc., Milwaukee.

Swenson, H.R. "Economic Models for Design Tolerances." Ph.D. Thesis, University of Chicago, 1963.

Taguchi, G. and Y. Wu. *Introduction to Off-Line Quality Control*. Nagaya, Japan: Central Japan Quality Control Association, 1979.

Taguchi, G. *On Line Quality Control During Production*. Tokyo: Japanese Standards Association, 1981.

Western Electric Company. *Statistical Quality Control Handbook*. Ed. Bonnie Small. Newark, N.J.: Western Electric Company, Inc., 1956.

Short Answers to Selected Odd-Numbered Problems

Part I

1.1) a. 6.05, 5.95, 6.00
      b. 2.706, 2.700, 2.700
      c. 10.283, 10.267,
         10.275
      d. 2.375, 2.367, 2.370

1.3) 2, 0, −5, 1

1.5) 6, 5, 3, 8

1.7) 3.603, 3.599, 3.600,
      3.598

Part II

2.7) B is the best.

2.11) bimodal; 2
      "populations" such as 2
      shifts behaving
      differently

2.15) v, v, a, v, a, a, a

2.17) a. 4, 3
      b. 4.8, 4
      c. 8.67, 9
      d. 38.2, 37
      e. .894, .83
      f. −6, −6
      g. −2, −2

2.19) 10, 3.51

Part III

3.1) a. special causes
      b. common; chance

3.3) a. common
      b. special (assignable)

3.5) common

Part IV

4.1) XDBar = 5.96

RBar = 5.33
UCL (X bar) = 9.85
LCL (X bar) = 2.07
UCL (R) = 12.17

4.3) XDBar = 1.5
      RBar = 10
      UCL (X bar) = 8.79
      LCL (X bar) = −5.79
      UCL (R) = 22.82

4.5) XDBar = 20.69
      RBar = 10.88
      UCL (X bar) = 26.97
      LCL (X bar) = 14.41
      UCL (R) = 23.0

4.7) XTBar = 9.5
      RBar = 2.67
      UCL (tilde) = 12.67
      LCL (tilde) = 6.33
      UCL (R) = 6.86

4.9) XTBar = 20
      RBar = 11.6
      UCL (tilde) = 28.0
      LCL (tilde) = 12.0
      UCL (R) = 24.52

4.11) XTBar = 14.28
      RBar = 5.44
      UCL (tilde) = 20.75
      LCL (tilde) = 7.81
      UCL (R) = 14.0

4.17) XDBar = 5.96
      sBar = 2.33
      UCL (X bar) = 9.76
      LCL (X bar) = 2.16
      UCL (s) = 5.29

4.19) XDBar = 12.81
      sBar = .21
      UCL (X bar) = 12.87

LCL (X bar) = 12.75
UCL (s) = .254
LCL (s) = .166

4.21) UCL (X bar) = 9.99
LCL (X bar) = 2.21

4.23) UCL (X bar) = 45.19
LCL (X bar) = 34.81
UCL (R) = 19.0
subgroup number 1 is
out of control

4.31) 2σ UCL (X bar) = 39.73
2σ LCL (X bar) = 25.43
2σ UCL (s) = 11.28

4.33) 2σ UCL (X bar) = 10.15
2σ LCL (X bar) = 4.35
2σ UCL (R) = 8.7

4.35) 2σ UCL (X bar) = 12.85
2σ LCL (X bar) = 12.77
2σ UCL (s) = .239
2σ LCL (s) = .181

Part V
5.1) a. σ = 2.587
UNL = 13.72
LNL = −1.80
b. σ = 2.515
UNL = 10.79
LNL = −4.29
c. σ = 4.67
UNL = 34.7
LNL = 6.68
d. σ = 4.979
UNL = 34.94
LNL = 5.06

5.3) capable

5.5) C_p = .67

5.7) C_{pk} = 4

5.9) C_p = 2; C_{pk} = 1

5.11) C_p = .8; C_{pk} = .67

5.13) a = 6; b = 6; c = 2;
C_{pk} = .33; C_p = 1

5.15) Z = 2.5; .62%

5.17) Z = 1.2; 11.51%

5.19) σ = 5.38; Z = .89;
18.67%

5.21) a. σ = 10.90
UNL = 40.36
LNL = −25.04
b. σ = 10.952
UNL = 40.52
LNL = −25.20
c. UNL = 42; LNL =
−27

5.25) X bar = 7.8
MR bar = 2.11
UCL (X) = 13.42
LCL (X) = 2.18
UCL (MR) = 6.90

5.27) X bar = 20.1
MR bar = 5.52
UCL (X) = 34.76
LCL (X) = 5.42
UCL (MR) = 18.04

5.29) X bar = 7.8
R bar = 1.6
UCL (X) = 12.06
LCL (X) = 3.54
UCL (R) = 5.23

Part VI
6.1) a. OML = 36, 64
IML = 43, 57
b. no

6.3) a. 15, 25
b. 9, 11
c. 1.75, 5.25
d. 1, 7
e. .5, 5.5

6.5) a. yes
      b. no
      c. no
      d. no

Part VII

7.1) p bar = .04
      shift 1 UCL = .082
      shift 2 UCL = .099
      shift 3 UCL = .099

7.3) p bar = .094
      A UCL = .386
      B UCL = .138
      C UCL = .167

7.5) p bar = .09375
      np bar = 1.5
      UCL = 5.00

7.7) u bar = 1.818
      coil 1 UCL = 4.38
      coil 2 UCL = 3.63
      LCL = .009
      coil 3 UCL = 3.98

7.9) u bar = .00866
      A UCL = .01293
      LCL = .00440
      B UCL = .01239
      LCL = .00494
      C UCL = .01175
      LCL = .00558

7.11) c bar = 22.167
      UCL = 36.291
      LCL = 8.042

Part VIII

8.1) XTBar = −.3
      R bar = 2.1
      UCL (X tilde) = 2.2
      LCL (X tilde) = −2.8
      UCL (R) = 5.4

Index